WILLIAM FAULKNER'S
THE SOUND AND THE FURY

GARLAND FAULKNER CASEBOOKS
(Series Editor: Noel Polk)
VOL. 1

WILLIAM FAULKNER'S
THE SOUND AND THE FURY
A Critical Casebook

André Bleikasten

GARLAND PUBLISHING, INC. • NEW YORK & LONDON
1982

Library of Congress Cataloging in Publication Data
Main entry under title:

William Faulkner's The sound and the fury.

(Garland Faulkner casebooks ; v. 1)
Bibliography: p.
1. Faulkner, William, 1897–1962. The sound
and the fury—Addresses, essays, lectures.
I. Bleikasten, André. II. Series.
PS3511.A86S87   1982   813'.52   81-43365
ISBN 0-8240-9269-4

Printed on acid-free, 250-year-life paper
Manufactured in the United States of America

Contents

Series Editor's Preface   vii

Preface   ix

Introduction   xi

William Faulkner's Commentary
  Letters to Ben Wasson, 1929   3
  Introduction to *The Sound and the Fury*, 1933   7
  Interviews   15
  Discussions at the University of Virginia, 1957–58   21

Essays on *The Sound and the Fury*
  The Composition of *The Sound and the Fury*   33
  Gail M. Morrison
  A Rhetoric for Benjy   65
  L. Moffitt Cecil
  Through the Poet's Eye: A view of Quentin Compson   79
  François L. Pitavy
  The "Loud World" of Quentin Compson   101
  Stephen M. Ross
  The Recollection and the Blood: Jason's Role in
      The Sound and the Fury   115
  Duncan Aswell
  The Rhetoric of Communion: Voice in *The Sound and the Fury*   123
  Margaret Blanchard
  The Comic Structure of *The Sound and the Fury*   135
  Fred Chappell
  Form and Fulfillment in *The Sound and the Fury*   141
  Beverly Gross

Bibliography   155

Series Editor's Preface

Work on the writings of William Faulkner shows no sign of slackening. Articles and books reflecting an ever-widening range of interpretations and critical approaches continue to appear with such frequency that the thickets of Faulkner criticism are in some ways becoming even more tangled and bewildering than those of Yoknapatawpha County itself. In spite of several excellent bibliographical guides, the problem, even for veteran Faulknerians, of keeping up with, sifting through, and evaluating the field, are formidable; for the non-specialist—the student, the professor who simply wants to be a better teacher of Faulkner—these problems are frequently overwhelming.

Garland's Faulkner Casebook Series is designed to come to the aid of both specialist and non-specialist; each volume, devoted to a single Faulkner work, is designed to provide, as it were, a place to start, as well as a place to come back to. Each volume in the series is edited by a scholar who has specialized knowledge of, and, in most cases, who has been a principal contributor to, the scholarship on a particular Faulkner novel. Each editor has been asked to select "the best and most useful" of the available scholarship on that novel for inclusion in the volume, as well as to commission new essays to fill gaps in the scholarship. Writers of previously published essays being anthologized in a volume have been invited to re-write, correct, or simply to update their essays, in light of developments in Faulkner scholarship since the essay's publication.

Each volume will contain (1) an editor's introduction, designed to provide an overview of scholarly study of the novel; (2) an essay, new or old, which brings together all of the available information about the novel's genesis—the inception, the writing, revisions, publication—based upon examination of manuscripts and upon other biographical data; (3) the body of essays described above; and (4) an annotated bibliography of criticism of the novel. The bibliography is *highly* selective for the years prior to 1973, the cut-off date of Thomas L. McHaney's *William Faulkner: A Reference Guide*, in order to provide a key to "the best and most useful" material; an effort has been made to be *complete* for the period since 1973.

Noel Polk
Series Editor

PREFACE

No American novelist of the twentieth century has attracted more critical attention than William Faulkner. On *The Sound and the Fury* alone over two hundred essays have been published during the past four decades. Not surprisingly, many of them now seem obsolete, yet more than can be included in a single volume add permanently to our understanding and appreciation of the novel. The anthologist, then, is faced with an extremely delicate task, and all he can offer is a more or less arbitrary and perforce questionable sampling of the best.

Many fine essays on *The Sound and the Fury* will therefore be missing from the present collection. I have deliberately left out the classical studies of the novel by such prominent Faulkner critics as Olga Vickery, Michael Millgate, and Cleanth Brooks, because they are readily available. I have found it more useful to present heretofore uncollected or, in some cases, previously unpublished essays, which either open new areas of critical investigation or reorient our approach to familiar matters. On the other hand, I have included most of Faulkner's own statements on *The Sound and the Fury*: not that his comments possess more authority than the critics', but they provide information about the book's growth and the writer's intentions and motivations which no serious Faulkner student can afford to neglect.

A selective but fairly substantial bibliography has been appended for further reading. The sheer abundance of commentary on *The Sound and the Fury* is evidence of widespread and unabating interest in the novel; the repetitiveness of so much of it points to the sterilizing effect of academic routine. What is perhaps most needed now in Faulkner studies is critical imagination, the capacity to invent new questions and new answers, and to articulate them in a new language, unencumbered by the clichés of tradition. The essays gathered in this collection are not radical departures from established models of criticism, nor do they supply a comprehensive reappraisal of the novel, yet within the limits of their specific fields of inquiry, they succeed in renewing our perception of the book and alert us to new possibilities of interpretation. At this stage of Faulkner criticism, it would not be sensible to ask for more.

                                                              A.B.

University of Strasbourg

INTRODUCTION

André Bleikasten

Had William Faulkner died after the publication of his first three novels, perhaps he would be remembered today only as a gifted minor writer of the twenties. Had he written only *The Sound and the Fury*, this book alone would have provided sufficient evidence of his genius to ensure him a place among the foremost fiction-makers of the twentieth century.

In writing *Flags in the Dust/Sartoris* Faulkner had discovered "the germ of [his] apocrypha,"[1] but only with *The Sound and the Fury* did he accomplish his breakthrough to mastery. No doubt the latter would not have been possible without the years of intensive reading and writing that preceded it,[2] yet it was an astounding leap, unheralded and unpredictable, an almost miraculous performance that no amount of comment will ever explain away.

For Faulkner himself the writing of *The Sound and the Fury* was a unique adventure, marked by a sudden release of fresh energies, an influx of creative power such as he had not experienced before and would never experience again. According to his own testimony, it gave him an "emotion definite and physical and yet nebulous to describe,"[3] a kind of "ecstasy"[4] that swept him irresistibly away. Of all his novels, however, it was also *The Sound and the Fury* that caused him the deepest anguish: "It was the one I anguished the most over, that I worked the hardest at, that even when I knew I couldn't bring it off, I still worked at it."[5] Small wonder, then, that it remained throughout Faulkner's life the novel for which he felt "the most tenderness."[6]

Faulkner's retrospective comments on his work should be read with caution and discernment, for the truths they convey are seldom literal ones. Yet there can be no doubt that *The Sound and the Fury* (and Caddy, its elusive and ubiquitous heroine) held a privileged place in the author's affections, nor can one discount his insistence on the depth and intensity of his emotional involvement during the process of its composition. No work before it had engaged his imagination

so imperiously and so fully; no story ever held him more last-
ingly in its spell than the sad story of the Compson family.[7]
The reasons for this fascination are perhaps not far to seek:
of Faulkner's fictional families the Compson family is probably the one that bears the closest resemblance to his own--his
own being not at all the Fa(u)lkner family as it actually was,
but rather the family *image* lingering beyond boyhood and youth
in the author's psyche, halfway between remembrance and oblivion, resentment and nostalgia, a dimming yet ineffaceable
configuration preyed on by fantasy, and destined to be dis-
figured and transfigured into the mobile patterns of fiction.

The fictions of literature spring, not from life, but from
the fictions of life; not from reality, but from the gaps in
reality. Faulkner's first writing attempts were indeed little
more than the timid histrionics of a juvenile self, and from
the early poems and prose sketches to the early novels, we
can easily trace the gradual working out of a young romantic's
sense of frustration and loss. *The Sound and the Fury* marked
the culmination and end of this process, bringing Faulkner
back to the earliest loss, the paradigm of all later losses:
that of his childhood.

At this point it is worth recalling the seminal scene,
the central image that was to inform the whole novel:

> ... perhaps the only thing in literature which would
> ever move me very much: Caddy climbing the pear tree
> to look in the window at her grandmother's funeral
> while Quentin and Jason and Benjy and the negroes looked
> up at the muddy seat of her drawers.[8]

Perplexed by their grandmother's death,[9] an event clearly
beyond their powers of understanding, the children here still
seem safely sheltered by their ignorance, yet they are already
perilously poised on the brink of the forbidden knowledge--
sex and death--that will soon cause their fall from innocence.[10]

The Sound and the Fury may be read as the deployment, the
writing out of this primal scene, for the moment expanded and
explored in the novel is precisely that moment of precarious
suspension between a *not-yet* and a *no-longer*: when childhood
is not yet forfeited, but in process of being lost; when
innocence is still somehow preserved, but already clouded by
the ominous intimations of another, vaster and darker world.
In varying degrees, the Compson brothers, as we come to know
them in the novel, appear all three as the helpless hostages
of that ambiguous time of transition. They are no longer
children; they have not yet achieved full manhood and never
will.

Childhood lost and unlost, unlosable, rankling on, endlessly, like an old unhealed wound. Of this paradox Benjy,

the thirty-three-year-old idiot, the defenseless man-child,
with whose chaotic monologue the novel fittingly begins, is
the starkest embodiment. The world is too much for him, and
not enough. There was a time, neither remembered nor forgotten,
when it answered his simple needs. His sister, Caddy, then,
was "the whole world to him,"[11] and the whole world was warm
and friendly. But Caddy went away. Benjy does not know that
she left, yet he keeps waiting at the gate. For him her trace
is forever fresh, and the merest object, the merest sensation
recalls her presence/absence with agonizing immediacy. Nothing
comes between him and raw reality. For pain as well as pleasure
he is at its mercy. As long as things remain in the wonted
order, he drools in imbecile contentment; whenever this order
is in the least disturbed, he howls in blind protest. Benjy's
is indeed the utterly dependent condition of the infant (*in-
fans* = speechless); the more pathetic as his childish mind
is trapped in the body of a grown-up. A degenerate *puer
aeternus*, stripped to naked need, devoid of intelligence and
memory, deprived of language and robbed even of sex and name,
Benjy is nothing but the bleak sum of his bereavements.

    Quentin's world too is one of desolation and mourning,
yet to switch from Benjy's section to his is to leave the
limbo of blank innocence for a private hell of anguish and
guilt. To the hypersensitive and fairly intelligent Quentin,
as to his moronic younger brother, the supreme loss has been
that of the beloved and loving sister, and to both she has
become through her very absence a besetting figure, the tan-
talizing emblem of all that is desirable and forever out of
reach. In the second section, however, sex and death, the
two submerged poles of Benjy's inarticulate brooding, come
to the fore, since from beginning to end Quentin's monologue
reverberates with the twin obsessions of incest and suicide.
In Freudian terms, one might argue that with the second section we move beyond the primal mother-infant relationship to
the oedipal confrontation with the father. Yet the point is
that the confrontation between son and father is evaded and
delayed, that it never actually takes place. To Quentin, Mr.
Compson is not the expected antagonist, but a fraternal double
with nothing to offer but the sour, self-conscious rhetoric
of rationalized impotence. Father and son are secret sharers
in defeat, and the argument between them echoed in the second
section suggests not so much a duel as a doleful duet: their
voices blend so harmoniously that in the end they are all but
one.[12] Mr. Compson never acts as the third party who separates
mother from child, sister from brother; he lamentably fails
in the role of interdictor and lawgiver, and so prevents
Quentin from breaking out of the family circle to venture
into the wider world of human exchange.

From first to last Quentin is trapped in the deceptive, dizzying mirror hall of narcissism, and paradoxically his very self-absorption is what precludes his access to stable selfhood. No true identity can emerge from the vortex of identifications in which he is caught, nor is any relationship based on mutuality conceivable for him. Caddy is the object of his regressive, all-demanding love, but the remembrances of the lost sister are only the echoing of Echo to Narcissus. His father, as we have seen, is little more than a senior *doppelgänger* in crippled sonship, and if the virgin Quentin is unable to avenge Caddy's honor, it is because her seducers are the bold, guiltfree executors of his incestuous wish. For Quentin there is in fact neither self nor other; there are only *other selves*, haunting doubles, demonized or idealized, both within and without.

Similarly, time, in his experience, is endless doubling and repetition. No fresh starts, no real beginnings, are allowed; the present moment always reenacts the past, as though time were bedeviled by memory. Not that the past is ever recovered and repossessed in Proustian bliss. Whenever it returns, it is in the mocking guise of shabby travesty. Episodes of Quentin's last day, such as his bizarre encounter with the little Italian girl, his arrest for allegedly molesting her, or his ludicrous fight with Gerald Bland, are both poignant recapitulations of his absurd predicament and wryly comic footnotes to the story of his wasted life.[13] To the very end Quentin wanders in an uncanny half-world, a spectral space of echoes, shadows, and reflections or, to borrow his own words, in "a long corridor of grey halflight where all stable things [have] become shadowy paradoxical."[14] Time to him is not only bewildering repetition, but a dwindling of reality, a downward spin toward grotesque disaster, the inexorable *reductio ad absurdum* of his desires and hopes and even of his sorrow, and since he can neither accommodate himself to time nor escape it alive, it is hardly surprising that he should eventually seek refuge in death.

Quentin's suicide has often been interpreted as an idealistic gesture of protest against the tyranny of time. His death, however, is no more heroic than his life, and in reading his monologue we are made to feel that the devious course that has taken him from the initial trauma of loss to the self-destructive despair of "melancholy mourning"[15] could not have ended otherwise. No awareness has been gained in the process. As anticipated in the reveries of Quentin's last day, his death by water reveals itself as the ultimate and most successful of his fevered fictions, allowing him in extremis to accomplish the magic reconciliation of his conflicting desires: in drowning himself, Quentin will at once wash off his guilt and rejoin the sister-naiad, the still "unravish'd bride" of his childhood, get rid once and for all of self, time, and flesh, and achieve at long last the radiant transcendence of "apotheosis."

Nothing could be further removed from the plaintive inwardness of the second section than the blustering rhetoric of the third. Another voice is heard now, harsh, petulant, sardonic, a voice far more self-assertive and less cryptically private than Quentin's. Yet Jason, for all his cocky posturings, is unmistakably Benjy's and Quentin's brother, and in his monologue Caddy, though less conspicuous, is hardly less central than in theirs. To him as to his brothers she is a festering memory; for him too she has been the instrument of disaster. Because of her misconduct, he has been deprived of the lucrative position at the bank promised by her husband-- an affront he has neither forgotten nor forgiven, and of which Miss Quentin, Caddy's daughter and debased double, has come to be in his eyes the living "symbol."[16] For Jason too, then, the sister is closely linked to loss, even though his experience of and response to loss are distinctly his own.

Where Quentin dies, Jason survives. With him the pain of loss has not led to suicidal despair, but soured into a chronic sense of insult, a smoldering *ressentiment*,[17] which spares him self-torture and somehow energizes his puny ego. Contrary to Quentin's, Jason's rancors are both private and public. They are not confined to his sister nor even to his kin, but expand into irrepressible animosity against virtually everybody. What is more, they are sustained by the paranoid myth of conspiracy against the "little man" from above (the dreaded "eastern sharks") and below (the scorned "niggers"), and so derive a modicum of respectability from preconceptions widely shared. Jason considers himself the victim of an unfair system which has despoiled him of his rightful due. As might have been expected, his resentment flows quite naturally into the prefabricated ideological molds of common prejudice: xenophobia, anti-Semitism, racism, anti-intellectualism, misogyny--not a single item is missing from the bigot's repertoire.[18] Clinging stubbornly to the flattering images of himself in the roles of hard-working businessman, dutiful son, and meritorious breadwinner of the Compson household, Jason makes desperate efforts to conform to standard patterns in his public life. Yet this brittle surface of conventionality is cracked time and again by the barely controlled violence of anarchic impulses. Jason's is the split attitude of the pseudo-conservative: blind, unthinking adererence to conformity belied by deep-seated dissatisfaction with the

established order, and sporadically betrayed by displaced
gestures of revolt.

As revealed by his words and deeds, Jason's *ressentiment*
turns out to be a poisonous web of pride and shame, fear and
anger, scorn and envy. In social terms, his paranoid suspicions,
status anxieties, and manifold prejudices may be said to reflect feelings and opinions not uncommon among frustrated
Southern whites in the early decades of the twentieth century.
As a social type, however, Jason clearly transcends sectional
and historical boundaries. If, as Faulkner himself pointed
out, "[t]here are too many Jasons in the South who can be
successful,"[19] there has been no shortage of his like outside
the South nor even outside America. The addled petit bourgeois
is a common species in the Western world; he has been with us
for a long time, and as long as our societies produce malcon-
tents and misfits, he is very likely to stay.[20]

Not all petit bourgeois are of course as utterly despicable
as Jason is. Of the Compsons he is beyond doubt the meanest,
the most perversely cruel, and Faulkner himself regarded him
as "the most vicious character"[21] he had ever conceived. Still,
his characterization is so searching and subtle that our
response to Jason is by no means unmitigated contempt and re-
vulsion. For one thing, he is a comic villain, a clamorous
clown fussily presiding over a madhouse world, and because of
his homespun humor and his flashes of wicked wit, the reader
laughs as often *with* him as *at* him. On the other hand, his
life of restless desperation has its own touch of pathos. By
the close of the novel, at the end of his frantic chase for
Miss Quentin and the carnival man, when we see him crushed by
the humiliation of defeat, we almost come to pity the monster.
Jason's villainy cannot be explained away by the pat assumption
that he was born bad and therefore predestined to play the
villain. From the ambiguities of his speech and the eccentricities of his behavior, he finally emerges as neither excusable
nor totally guilty--a bad man, assuredly, all spite and venom,
but also, just like his brothers, a victim of circumstance,
the stunted offspring of a diseased family.

Whether sealed off from normalcy by neurotic obsession or
mental retardation, the first three sections of *The Sound and
the Fury* are fiercely private speeches. In the fourth and final
section there occurs a decisive reversal from within to without, as if after listening to voices in the dark, we were
suddenly allowed to see their owners in broad daylight and to
relate each voice (except Quentin's) to a face and a body.
From interior monologue the novel now moves to a fairly traditional mode of narration. The point of view is at present
that of a perceptive and highly articulate outsider, with

occasional insights into a character's mind, yet none of the godlike privileges of the "omniscient" narrator-interpreter.[22] Distance is the reader's major gain. At last he can stand back and take in the whole scene.

"April Eighth 1928," however, begins inauspiciously with the description of a grey dawn, "bleak and chill,"[23] and in what follows, rare are the moments when that gloom is relieved. In their eagerness to defend the novel against the charge of nihilism, a number of critics have taken great pains to establish Dilsey--admittedly the most admirable character in the book--as the section's focal figure. In fact she is not, for the focus shifts from her to Jason, from Jason to Benjy, and of the section's four narrative sequences, there is only one, the episode of the Easter service, in which she holds a prominent part.[24] It is noteworthy too that this episode and the account of Jason's misadventures are juxtaposed in ironic counterpoint, nor should one miss the ultimate irony of the restoration of Benjy's empty order at the novel's close.

Even great novels often end lamely. If *The Sound and the Fury* ends superbly, it is because it does not end at all: no dramatic resolution, whether tragic or comic, is provided; none of the novel's tensions is eventually eased, nor are any of its ambiguities removed.[25] The ending takes us back full circle to the beginning, to the liminal figure of the speechless idiot and to the "sound and fury" which the writer has sought all along to translate into words; it also recapitulates the necessary failure of his endeavor, a failure the more significant as the fourth section stands for the final, "authorial" attempt to get the story told.[26]

An author now attempts to seize authority. A richer, denser, more ceremonious language unfolds, infusing the text with new energies, and projecting a different light upon the actors of the drama. While Dilsey, the old black servant, is given an aura of ravaged nobility,[27] Benjy, the slobbering idiot, becomes in the solemn, myth-laden context of the Easter service a paradigm of crucified innocence.[28] Yet Benjy, in this section, is also a constant reminder of what lies outside language. In their haunting repetition his cries--his whinings, wailings, whimperings, howlings, bellowings[29]--are the raucous eloquence of unspeakable suffering. Failing to say what Benjy failed to preserve, they are the wordless language of lack and loss--nothing, "just sound."[30] In this nothing, though, there is everything: "all time and injustice and sorrow," "all voiceless misery under the sun."[31]

Voicing the voiceless, naming the nameless: such is also the writer's dream, and in none of his other novels did

Faulkner try so hard to convey the "eyeless" and "tongueless"[32] agony of utter dispossession. It was of course an impossible wager. For in the pregnant silence of the printed page the cry is no longer a cry, and all that literature can accomplish is to turn Benjy's whimperings and bellowings into the mute symbols of its own impotence.

For Faulkner as for all innovative practitioners of fiction since Flaubert, Conrad, and James, the determination to explore and exploit language to its utmost possibilities was matched by a sharp awareness of its limitations and inadequacies-- hence, in *The Sound and the Fury*, his desperate efforts to do justice to the inarticulate, to get as close as possible, in language, to the ragged intensities and inchoate meanings (Benjy's "trying to say") out of which language arises, but hence, too, the symmetrical urge to reach out beyond words for the plenitude of the mythic Word, an urge best exempli- fied by the black preacher's inspired sermon during the Easter Sunday service.

Much has been written about this memorable episode, and Reverend Shegog's sermon has been used time and again to legitimize orthodox Christian interpretations of the novel. Yet critics have gone astray whenever they have sought to reduce the intricacies, obliquities, and ambiguities of Faulkner's fiction to unequivocal ideological statements. The Easter sermon is no doubt one of the novel's pivotal scenes, but it is also part of an ingeniously crafted text, so that before settling for final comments on its significance, we would do well to attend to the hidden logic of its composi- tion. One of the salient features of the narrative here is that it proceeds through a fast succession of inversions,[33] ultimately leading to the climactic moment of the Easter service when the cold, controlled brilliance of the "white" sermon blazes into the sacred fire of "black" eloquence: con- suming the preacher's, another voice then takes over, enig- matically self-generated and irresistibly powerful; another language is heard and shared by the gathered congregation, eventually resolving itself into "chanting measures beyond the need for words."[34] While Benjy's animal cries kept us below words, the mythic discourse relayed by the mysterious "voice" carries us beyond them to a point where they are no longer needed: in the peaceful chant of Easter celebration, true communion has been achieved at last.

This rare experience of at(-)onement, however, has been induced by the magic of words, and Reverend Shegog's sermon strikes us first of all as a triumph of Faulkner's verbal virtuosity. A tour de force it certainly is, yet at the same time it is also a remarkable gesture of humility and self-

effacement on the novelist's part, for he scrupulously refrained
from improving on the well-established tradition of the oral
sermon as he found it in Afro-American culture.[35] This means
that in a sense we are *truly* listening to the anonymous voice
of an unwritten tradition, grown out of ancient roots and
periodically replenished by the rites of popular piety, a
voice through whose agency a mythic heritage has been transmitted from generation to generation and kept alive within
the community. Yet through a further paradox the spoken here
enfolds the written, as the oral tradition embodied in the
sermon also points back to what in Western culture has long
been read and venerated as *the* Book and therefore held for
the supreme model of all great writing ambitions: the Bible.[36]

Voice and myth, living speech and holy scripture: these
mirages of presence and plenitude have fascinated our writers
and thinkers for many centuries; that they also fascinated
Faulkner is hardly a surprise. To come back to *The Sound and
the Fury*, one might argue that myth is to the novel's last
section what individual fantasy was to the two previous ones.
Myth and fantasy alike are creations of desire, stratagems
conceived to outwit time and death. Contrary to fantasy, however, myth, inasmuch as it lives on as an object of collective
belief, serves an integrative purpose and attests to the
permanence of a cultural order. This is precisely what it
does in the paschal episode: for the black congregation, the
remote events of Christ's story, as retold by the preacher,
come alive once more, and to Dilsey, the fervent believer,
Reverend Shegog's words offer once again the comforts of
eternity, the mystical and prophetic vision of "the beginning
and the ending." Whether Faulkner himself believed in the
transcendental value of Christian revelation is a matter for
speculation, but his work suggests belief in the necessity
of belief and in the necessity of myth to sustain belief.
That *The Sound and the Fury* is shot through with biblical
references, that its present action is framed by the events
of Holy Week (or, to put it in theological terms, that *chronos*,
the "passing time" of the doomed Compsons, is encompassed and
transcended by *kairos*, God's season), and that the last section climaxes in the communal commemoration of the resurrected
God[37] is surely not enough to warrant a religious interpretation. What should not be denied, however, is that in many of
Faulkner's novels, from *The Sound and the Fury* to *A Fable*,
Christianity seems to beckon us like a receding horizon of
truth.

Or should we rather say that Faulkner had to work through
the myths of Christianity to produce his own? For he obviously
wanted to become a myth-maker in his own right or, better

still, to become in turn the medium of immemorial truths. One may be tempted, then, to see Reverend Shegog, the frail vessel of the sovereign Word, as an analogue of the novelist himself, reaching the moment of (dis)possession when his individuality as author gives way to the nameless authority of the "voice." And the vision granted to the preacher might likewise be said to be a metaphor for the secret object of the writer's quest. What these analogies seem to point to is the promise of an ultimate reversal: that which would restore the absolute presence of language to itself, and thus convert its emptiness into plenitude, its fragmentation into wholeness. It cannot be done, of course. The quest is never completed, the reversal forever postponed. Yet in its very failure the novel succeeds. Even though the gap between text and meaning is always there, the writing process has generated an order of its own. It is an order, or rather an ordering, out of the very vacuum of language, and one waiting for the reader to bring it to provisional completion. Not that he can succeed where the writer failed. But reading and rereading the book, he will write it again.

There are many ways of reading *The Sound and the Fury*. One can read it in Sartre's wake as a metaphysical novel about time;[38] it can also be interpreted in socio-historical terms, as a novel on the decline of a Southern family and the collapse of the Southern tradition, or from a psychological perspective, as a study in frustration and failure, a spectral analysis of wounded narcissism, or again, if one chooses to stress its moral implications, as a searching inquiry into the ambiguities and ravages of "innocence." These thematic approaches do not exclude one another, and all of them are valid and rewarding if used with proper discrimination. Yet if close attention to referent and meaning hardly needs justification in a text so desperately concerned with the "sound and fury" of the real world, one should not overlook that it is first and foremost a work of language and a piece of fiction: a *novel*.

What kind of novel? In one sense, as several critics have noted, *The Sound and the Fury* carries on the realistic tradition of nineteenth-century fiction. There is a "story," and that story—the dissolution of a family—had been told many times before, perhaps most superbly in Thomas Mann's *Buddenbrooks*. There are "characters," too, with identifiable traits, and once we have accommodated ourselves to the conventions of "stream of consciousness," their monologues come to acquire their own kind of plausibility. Though little is left of the mimetic solidity of the realistic novel (at least in the early sections), psychological verisimilitude still obtains: even the wildest divagations can be "recuperated" if one postulates a narrator who is idiotic or psychotic.

These traditional elements, however, hardly detract from the novel's modernity. In the last resort modern and even postmodern fictions are but the decompositions and recompositions of earlier narrative forms. They may tell no story, but they cannot do without a story to tell, nor can they dispense entirely with characters, however ectoplasmic the latter may have become in our "age of suspicion." The point, in *The Sound and the Fury*, is that the story is both told and not told, that while by the novel's ending we are in possession of all the facts we need to reconstruct the Compson chronicle, the final truth of the matter is as conspicuously elusive as ever. What engages us is not so much the tale as the hazardous, re-iterative, never completed business of its tellings. It is not fortuitous that the novel begins with Faulkner's most radical experiment in achronological "memory monologue."[39] The first section confronts us with a seemingly random display of remembered (?) scenes; strictly speaking, it is no narra-tive at all, for it lacks even the minimal guarantee of a point of view. Jolted out of our reading habits, we are thus made aware from the outset not only of the severe limitations imposed on an idiot's mind, but also of the arbitrariness of all verbal and rhetorical constructs, and although the novel gradually moves back to more conventional procedures, one is not likely to forget the initial caveat.

Pointing toward a world beyond itself which language fails to encompass and articulate, *The Sound and the Fury* summons us time and again to measure the gap between what is said and what is meant, between what is meant and what simply *is*: opaque, unaccountable, inexpressible reality, as innocent of significance as "a tale told by an idiot." Failure, it should be noted, informs the very pattern of the book, since its four sections, according to Faulkner himself, represent as many futile attempts to get the story told: "... I was still trying to tell one story which moved me very much and each time I failed."[40] Like all modernist writers, that is, like all self-conscious heirs to the Romantic dream, Faulkner strove for the wholeness of the "well-wrought urn." And like the greatest among them, he grandly failed in the attempt. His most fascinating novels are his most reckless, those in which he courted defeat, those he barely managed to snatch from disaster. They are the furious records of his lost gambles, of his lost battles, coming to us all sooty and tattered, with none of the pomp and polish we are used to associating with certified masterpieces.

Trained to equate aesthetic achievement with unity of form and meaning, critics are seldom willing to acknowledge this raggedness in Faulkner's fiction.[41] Fragments, for them, should not be left alone; they must be gathered into wholes again, and then shown to have been wholes from the start. Yet *The Sound and the Fury* does consist of separate sections (from *secare* = to cut), and each of them is a planet in its own orbit. Not that their order in the novel is left to chance, nor that the author has omitted to supply the expected cross-references and interconnections. Far from it. Ever since *The Sound and the Fury* fell prey to critical exegesis, new structural patterns, new mythic designs, new webs of imagery and symbolism have kept turning up year after year, and it would be unfair to ascribe them all to the perverse ingenuity of overzealous commentators. All this is not enough, however, to fill in the gaps, to totalize the parts, the less so as the fragmentariness of Faulkner's text is not a matter only of broken surfaces, of dismantled narrative and fractured point of view, but also of something related to the disruptive force, to the secret violence at work in the very writing process. Language itself seems to be under the constant threat of dis-integration. Nowhere is this menace more heavily felt than in the first two monologues--in the erratic sequence of Benjy's memories and the eerie labyrinth of Quentin's mental associations. Consider, for example, the following passage from the final pages of the second section:

> I had forgotten the glass, but I could *hands can see cooling fingers invisible swan-throat where less than Moses rod the glass touch tentative not to drumming lean cool throat drumming cooling the metal the glass full overfull cooling the glass the fingers flushing sleep leaving the taste of dampened sleep in the long silence of the throat....*[42]

Here the collapse of syntax is complete. All that is left is a perplexing cluster of words, with subjects and predicates all adrift. Interpretation, then, becomes a very aleatory enterprise. What shall we make, for instance, of the cryptic allusion to Moses' rod? The scriptural reference can be given relevance in terms of the section's water motif; we can also speculate about the Freudian implications of the magic rod, construe Moses as a lawgiving father figure, and read the whole sequence as a dream text about castration. With astute metalanguages like psychoanalysis, there will always be a way out of confusion. Yet by itself this passage has no ascertainable significance: it throbs with meanings; it does not deliver them. Language breaks asunder into random particles, and even the speaking subject subsides in "the long silence of the throat."

At this point the text slips off from the readable to the unreadable or to what Roland Barthes terms the "writable" (*le scriptible*).[43] To Barthes such extreme disruptions of established models of intelligibility are the tokens of radical modernity. In Faulkner, however, they occur only sporadically, and even in his most experimental novels they are seldom sustained. Whatever his audacities with language and his irreverence for inherited codes of fiction, Faulkner still wrote novels about people and their world. His forays into the inarticulate were not intended as departures from mimesis, but rather as maneuvers to expand its field of possibilities. Far from being unmotivated, the lapses into verbal chaos in the second section of *The Sound and the Fury* serve their specific purpose as indices to the increasing disorder in Quentin's neurotic mind; like anything else in the book, they are "in their ordered place."

This is not to say that on closer inspection Faulkner turns out to be less modern than he was assumed to be. What needs to be stressed, however, is that he was no more intimidated by the purist claims of the avant-garde than he was hampered by the dead weight of tradition. True, his novels cannot be dissociated from their cultural moment and one can easily see how they relate to the works of other modernist authors like Joyce or Viginia Woolf; yet they are above all the unique *bricolages* of a fiercely independent writer, texts written under the pressure of private need and assembled, patiently and impatiently, with whatever tools were at hand. Hence they produce a feeling of urgency and precariousness, a sense of energies as yet in motion, of turbulences not yet stilled.

Yet the more we read a novel like *The Sound and the Fury*, the more we are dazzled by the impeccable craftsmanship of its author. And if compared to the exuberance of some of his later novels (*Absalom, Absalom!*, the apotheosis of his baroque manner, at once comes to mind), his first masterpiece strikes us by its tautness and spareness, the economy of its composition and the concentration of its effects. To many early readers, ill prepared for its newness, it must have seemed a mushy novel; to us, more than fifty years later, it has acquired the luminous hardness of a rare gem.

Not all of Faulkner's novels age well, and some of them have already begun to gather fat and wrinkles. Not so *The Sound and the Fury*, as electrically alive today as on the day of its publication--a classic, assuredly, of what we still call our modernity.

NOTES

1. *Faulkner in the University: Class Conferences at the University of Virginia, 1957-1958*, ed. Frederick L. Gwynn and Joseph L. Blotner (Charlottesville: University of Virginia Press, 1959), p. 285. See also *Lion in the Garden: Interviews with William Faulkner, 1926-1962*, ed. James B. Meriwether and Michael Millgate (New York: Random House, 1968), p. 255.

2. When H. Edward Richardson asked Phil Stone, the writer's early mentor, what happened to Faulkner between *Mosquitoes* and *The Sound and the Fury*, Stone's laconic answer was, "He was writing all the time." See H. Edward Richardson, *William Faulkner: The Journey to Self-Discovery* (Columbia: University of Missouri Press, 1969), p. 167.

3. "An Introduction for *The Sound and the Fury*," *The Southern Review*, N.S. 8 (Autumn 1972), 709. The text of Faulkner's introduction has been included in this collection.

4. "An Introduction for *The Sound and the Fury*," p. 709.

5. *Faulkner in the University*, p. 61. See also *Lion in the Garden*, p. 146.

6. *Lion in the Garden*, p. 147.

7. Faulkner's abiding interest in the Compsons is evidenced by the "Appendix" he wrote in the Fall of 1945, which was first published in the Viking *Portable Faulkner* edited by Malcolm Cowley in 1946.

8. "An Introduction for *The Sound and the Fury*," p. 710.

9. Leila Dean Swift, the maternal grandmother whom the first three Faulkner boys called Damuddy, died June 1, 1907, when William was nine years old.

10. For further comments on this scene, see my study, *The Most Splendid Failure: Faulkner's The Sound and the Fury* (Bloomington and London: Indiana University Press, 1976), pp. 53-55.

11. *Faulkner in the University*, p. 64.

12. For a more detailed analysis of the father-son relationship in *The Sound and the Fury*, see my article, "Noces noires, noces blanches: le jeu du désir et de la mort dans le monologue de Quentin Compson," *Recherches Anglaises et Nord-Américaines*, no. 6 (1973), 142-69; rev. and trans. in *The Most Splendid Failure*, pp. 90-120. For a general discussion of fatherhood in Faulkner's fiction, see my essay "Fathers in Faulkner," in Robert C. Davis, ed., *The Fictional Father:*

Lacanian Readings of the Text (Amherst: University of Massachusetts Press, 1981). See also John T. Irwin's brilliant contribution to the subject in *Doubling and Incest, Repetition and Revenge: A Speculative Reading of Faulkner* (Baltimore and London: The Johns Hopkins University Press, 1976). In his reading of *The Sound and the Fury*, Irwin introduces the extremely useful notions of "brother seducer" and "brother avenger," yet he tends to overemphasize the hostility between father and son, and one wonders why someone so familiar with recent developments in French psychoanalysis does not take advantage of Lacan's concept of "the Name-of-the-Father," i.e., of the Father as the symbolic agency of the Law.

13. On the comic aspects of *The Sound and the Fury*, see Fred Chappell's refreshing essay included in this collection.

14. *The Sound and the Fury* (New York: Jonathan Cape and Harrison Smith, 1929), p. 211. The first printing, first edition text has been reproduced by photo-offset in the 1966 Random House issue, the 1967 Modern Library issue, and the Vintage paperback issue.

15. On this point, see Sigmund Freud, "Mourning and Melancholia" (1917), *Standard Edition*, XIV, 243-58.

16. See *The Sound and the Fury*, pp. 383-84.

17. I am using this concept with all the moral and social connotations it has taken since Nietzsche. *Ressentiment* in Faulkner's fiction has gone largely unnoticed by the critics, yet it is a feature shared in various shades by many of his male characters from Jason Compson to Mink Snopes. Further exploration of its significance would probably reveal its close relationship to the Faulknerian problematic of memory (*ressentiment* as resensing) as well as to the Faulknerian sense of outrage. It might also yield new insights into the ambiguous idealism of Faulkner's quixotic intellectuals, from Horace Benbow through Quentin Compson, Gail Hightower, and Ike McCaslin to Gavin Stevens, whose behavior often seems to confirm Nietzsche's suspicion that in the last analysis idealism is little more than *ressentiment*'s sickly flower.

18. See *The Sound and the Fury*, pp. 223, 237-38, 239, 270, 313-14, 315.

19. *Faulkner in the University*, p. 17.

20. All too often Jason has been mistaken for a representative of Snopesism. Apart from greed and dishonesty, he has in fact very little in common with the rising Snopeses, and as can be seen in *The Mansion*, the last volume of the

trilogy, he is obviously no match for the wily Flem. The last
male survivor of an impoverished, status-losing middle-class
family, Jason has no doubt abandoned all allegiance to its
traditions, yet he has not given up all social pretensions and
does his best to keep up appearances. The paradoxical plight
of the petit bourgeois is precisely that, while resenting his
exclusion from the ruling class, he cannot help identifying
with the values of its ideology.

21. *Lion in the Garden*, p. 149.

22. On the narrative stance in the fourth section, see
Margaret Blanchard's judicious discussion included in this
collection.

23. *The Sound and the Fury*, p. 330.

24. On the narrative structure of the final section, see
John V. Hagopian, "Nihilism in Faulkner's *The Sound and the
Fury*," *Modern Fiction Studies*, 13 (Spring 1967), 45-55.

25. On the ending, see Beverly Gross's essay included in
this collection.

26. See Faulkner's comments in *Lion in the Garden*, pp.
147 and 245.

27. See *The Sound and the Fury*, pp. 330-31.

28. See *The Sound and the Fury*, p. 370.

29. See *The Sound and the Fury*, pp. 359, 395, 400.

30. *The Sound and the Fury*, p. 400.

31. *The Sound and the Fury*, pp. 359 and 395.

32. *The Sound and the Fury*, p. 400.

33. See Victor Strandberg, "Faulkner's Poor Parson and
the Technique of Inversion," *Sewanee Review*, 73 (Spring 1965),
181-90.

34. *The Sound and the Fury*, p. 367.

35. On this point, see Bruce A. Rosenberg's useful study
"The Oral Quality of Reverend Shegog's Sermon in William
Faulkner's *The Sound and the Fury*," *Literatur in Wissenschaft
und Unterricht*, 2 (1969), 73-88.

36. "La Bible détient tous les livres, fussent-ils les
plus étrangers à la révélation, au savoir, à la poésie, à la
proverbialité bibliques, parce qu'elle détient l'esprit du
livre." Maurice Blanchot, *L'Entretien infini* (Paris: Gallimard
1969), p. 627.

37. One might note here that Christ's redemptive self-sacrifice and glorious resurrection are implicitly contrasted with Quentin's pointless "passion" and absurd death.

38. "A propos de 'Le Bruit et la Fureur': la temporalité chez Faulkner," *La Nouvelle Revue Française*, 52 (June 1939), 1057-61.

39. See Dorrit Cohn, *Transparent Minds: Narrative Modes for Presenting Consciousness in Fiction* (Princeton, N.J.: Princeton University Press, 1978), pp. 183-85, 248-55. As Dorrit Cohn rightly notes, such established critical phrases as "first-person narrative" or "interior monologue" are too vague to be useful in a discussion of Faulkner's narrative technique.

40. *Lion in the Garden*, p. 244.

41. Donald M. Kartiganer's book *The Fragile Thread: The Meaning of Form in Faulkner's Novels* (Amherst: University of Massachusetts Press, 1979), is a meritorious move in the right direction (i.e., away from organicist models), but its critical performance does not follow up its premises.

42. *The Sound and the Fury*, p. 216.

43. See *S/Z* (Paris: Seuil, 1970), pp. 10-12.

WILLIAM FAULKNER'S COMMENTARY

LETTERS TO BEN WASSON, 1929

Faulkner wrote the following letters after receiving the proofs of *The Sound and the Fury*, which Ben Wasson, his friend and literary agent, had partially edited.

To Ben Wasson
[early summer, 1929]

MS. FCVA
c/o F.H. Lewis
Pascagoula, Miss.

Dear Ben--
    Thank you for the letter.
    I received the proof. It seemed pretty tough to me, so I corrected it as written, adding a few more italics where the original seemed obscure on second reading. Your reason for the change, i.e., that with italics only 2 different dates were indicated I do not think sound for 2 reasons. First, I do not see that the use of breaks clarifies it any more; second, there are more than 4 dates involved. The ones I recall off-hand are: Damuddy dies. Benjy is 3. (2) His name is changed. He is 5. (3) Caddy's wedding. He is 14. (4) He tries to rape a young girl and is castrated. 15. (5) Quentin's death. (6) His father's death. (7) A visit to the cemetery at 18. (7) [*sic*] The day of the anecdote, he is 33. These are just a few I recall. So your reason explodes itself.
    But the main reason is, a break indicates an objective change in tempo, while the objective picture here should be a continuous whole, since the thought transference is subjective, i.e., in Ben's mind and not in the reader's eye. I think italics are necessary to establish for the reader Benjy's confusion; that unbroken-surfaced confusion of an idiot which is outwardly a dynamic and logical coherence. To gain this, by using breaks it will be necessary to write an induction for each transference. I wish publishing was advanced enough

From Selected Letters of William Faulkner, *ed. Joseph Blotner (New York: Random House, 1977), pp. 44-46. Reprinted by permission of Random House, Inc.*

to use colored ink for such, as I argued with you and Hal in
the speak-easy that day. But the form in which you now have it
is pretty tough. It presents a most dull and poorly articulated
picture to my eye. If something must be done, it were better
to re-write this whole section objectively, like the 4th section. I think it is rotten, as is. But if you wont have it so,
I'll just have to save the idea until publishing grows up to
it. Anyway, change all the italics. You overlooked one of them.
Also, the parts written in italics will all have to be punctuated again. You'd better see to that, since you're all for
coherence. And dont make any more additions to the script, bud.
I know you mean well, but so do I. I effaced the 2 or 3 you
made.

We have a very pleasant place on the beach here. I swim and
fish and row a little. Estelle sends love.

I hope you will think better of this. Your reason above dis-
proves itself. I purposely used italics for both actual scenes
and remembered scenes for the reason, not to indicate the different dates of happenings, but merely to permit the reader
to anticipate a thought-transference, letting the recollection
postulate its own date. Surely you see this.

                                                         Bill

To Ben Wasson   MS. [?] SHELBY FOOTE
[early summer, 1929]   [Oxford]

    Italics here indicate a speech by one person within a speech
by another, so as not to use quotes within quotes, my use of
italics has been too without definite plan, I suppose i.e.,
they do not always indicate a thought transference as in this
case, but the only other manner of doing this paragraph seems
clumsy still to me, since it breaks the questions interminably
of Mrs Compson's drivelling talk if set like the below:
    '... You must think, Mother said.
    'Hold still now, Versh said. He put etc.
    'Some day I'll be gone etc., Mother said.
    'Now stop, Versh said.
    'Come here and kiss ... Mother said.
    ....
    Galley 6
    Set first three lines of new scene in italics. Transference
indicated then. I should have done this, but missed it. Sorry.
    ....
    Excuse recent letter. Didnt mean to be stubborn and inconsid-
erate. Believe I am right, tho. And I was not blaming you with
it. I just went to you with it because I think you are more

interested in the book than anyone there, and I know that us both think alike about it, as we already argued this very point last fall. Excuse it anyway. Estelle sends regards.

Love to all.
Bill

INTRODUCTION TO *THE SOUND AND THE FURY*, 1933

For a new limited edition of *The Sound and the Fury*, announced by Random House in 1933 (but never published), Faulkner wrote during the summer of that year an introduction which survives in several drafts. One of them was edited by James B. Meriwether and published in the *Southern Review*, N.S. 8 (Autumn 1972), 705-10. Another, longer--later or earlier?-- version, also edited by Meriwether, appeared in the *Mississippi Quarterly*, 26 (Summer 1973), 410-15.

In a letter to Ben Wasson, Faulkner wrote that he had "worked on it a good deal, like a poem almost" (*Selected Letters*, p. 74), yet in 1946, when Robert Liscott, an editor at Random House, requested permission to include it in the new Modern Library volume, Faulkner, who had always been reluctant to write introductions, dismissed the piece as "smug false sentimental windy shit" (*Selected Letters*, p. 235), refused its publication, and was even willing to pay for its destruction. The reason for this violent reaction is probably to be sought in Faulkner's strong sense of privacy. His introduction to *The Sound and the Fury* is one of the rare texts in which he reveals something about the hidden springs of his creation, and this is precisely what makes it so valuable to us.

Each of its two versions deserves publication in its own right; we therefore reproduce both.

I wrote this book and learned to read. I had learned a little about writing from Soldiers' Pay--how to approach language, words: not with seriousness so much, as an essayist does, but with a kind of alert respect, as you approach dynamite; even with joy, as you approach women: perhaps with the same secretly unscrupulous intentions. But when I finished

From the William Faulkner Collections, University of Virginia Library. Reprinted by permission of Mrs. Paul D. Summers, Jr., Executrix, The Estate of William Faulkner.

The Sound and The Fury I discovered that there is actually something to which the shabby term Art not only can, but must, be
applied. I discovered then that I had gone through all that I
had ever read, from Henry James through Henty to newspaper
murders, without making any distinction or digesting any of
it, as a moth or a goat might. After The Sound and The Fury
and without heeding to open another book and in a series of
delayed repercussions like summer thunder, I discovered the
Flauberts and Dostoievskys and Conrads whose books I had read
ten years ago. With The Sound and The Fury I learned to read
and quit reading, since I have read nothing since.

     Nor do I seem to have learned anything since. While writing
Sanctuary, the next novel to The Sound and The Fury, that part
of me which learned as I wrote, which perhaps is the very
force which drives a writer to the travail of invention and
the drudgery of putting seventy-five or a hundred thousand
words on paper, was absent because I was still reading by
repercussion the books which I had swallowed whole ten years
and more ago. I learned only from the writing of Sanctuary
that there was something missing; something which The Sound
and The Fury gave me and Sanctuary did not. When I began As
I Lay Dying I had discovered what it was and knew that it
would be also missing in this case because this would be a
deliberate book. I set out deliberately to write a tour-de-
force. Before I ever put pen to paper and set down the first
word, I knew what the last word would be and almost where the
last period would fall. Before I began I said, I am going to
write a book by which, at a pinch, I can stand or fall if I
never touch ink again. So when I finished it the cold satis-
faction was there, as I had expected, but as I had also expected that other quality which The Sound and The Fury had
given me was absent: that emotion definite and physical and
yet nebulous to describe: that ecstasy, that eager and joyous
faith and anticipation of surprise which the yet unmarred
sheet beneath my hand held inviolate and unfailing, waiting
for release. It was not there in As I Lay Dying. I said, It
is because I knew too much about this book before I began to
write it. I said, More than likely I shall never again have
to know this much about a book before I begin to write it,
and next time it will return. I waited almost two years, then
I began Light in August, knowing no more about it than a
young woman, pregnant, walking along a strange country road.
I thought, I will recapture it now, since I know no more about
this book than I did about The Sound and The Fury when I sat
down before the first blank page.

     It did not return. The written pages grew in number. The
story was going pretty well: I would sit down to it each

morning without reluctance yet still without that anticipation
and that joy which alone ever made writing pleasure to me. The
book was almost finished before I acquiesced to the fact that
it would not recur, since I was now aware before each word
was written down just what the people would do, since now I
was deliberately choosing among possibilities and probabilities
of behavior and weighing and measuring each choice by the
scale of the Jameses and Conrads and Balzacs. I knew that I
had read too much, that I had reached that stage which all
young writers must pass through, in which he believes that
he has learned too much about his trade. I received a copy
of the printed book and I found that I didn't even want to
see what kind of jacket Smith had put on it. I seemed to have
a vision of it and the other ones subsequent to The Sound and
The Fury ranked in order upon a shelf while I looked at the
titled backs of them with a flagging attention which was
almost distaste, and upon which each succeeding title registered
less and less, until at last Attention itself seemed to say,
Thank God I shall never need to open any one of them again.
I believed that I knew then why I had not recaptured that
first ecstasy, and that I should never again recapture it;
that whatever novels I should write in the future would be
written without reluctance, but also without anticipation
or joy: that in the Sound and The Fury I had already put
perhaps the only thing in literature which would ever move
me very much: Caddy climbing the pear tree to look in the
window at her grandmother's funeral while Quentin and Jason
and Benjy and the negroes looked up at the muddy seat of her
drawers.

This is the only one of the seven novels which I wrote
without any accompanying feeling of drive or effort, or any
following feeling of exhaustion or relief or distaste. When
I began it I had no plan at all. I wasn't even writing a book.
I was thinking of books, publication, only in the reverse, in
saying to myself, I wont have to worry about publishers liking
or not liking this at all. Four years before I had written
Soldiers' Pay. It didn't take long to write and it got published quickly and made me about five hundred dollars. I
said, Writing novels is easy. You dont make much doing it,
but it is easy. I wrote Mosquitoes. It wasn't quite so easy
to write and it didn't get published quite as quickly and
it made me about four hundred dollars. I said, Apparently
there is more to writing novels, being a novelist, than I
thought. I wrote Sartoris. It took much longer, and the
publisher refused it at once. But I continued to shop it
about for three years with a stubborn and fading hope, perhaps to justify the time which I had spent writing it. This

hope died slowly, though it didn't hurt at all. One day I
seemed to shut a door between me and all publishers' addresses
and book lists. I said to myself, Now I can write. Now I can
make myself a vase like that which the old Roman kept at his
bedside and wore the rim slowly away with kissing it. So I,
who had never had a sister and was fated to lose my daughter
in infancy, set out to make myself a beautiful and tragic
little girl.

. . .

Art is no part of southern life. In the North it seems
to be different. It is the hardest minor stone in Manhattan's
foundation. It is a part of the glitter or shabbiness of the
streets. The arrowing buildings rise out of it and because
of it, to be torn down and arrow again. There will be people
leading small bourgeois lives (those countless and almost invisible bones of its articulation, lacking any one of which
the whole skeleton might collapse) whose bread will derive
from it--polyglot boys and girls progressing from tenement
schools to editorial rooms and art galleries; men with grey
hair and paunches who run linotype machines and take up
tickets at concerts and then go sedately home to Brooklyn
and suburban stations where children and grandchildren await
them--long after the descendents of Irish politicians and
Neapolitan racketeers are as forgotten as the wild Indians
and the pigeon.

And of Chicago too: of that rythm not always with harmony
or tune; lusty, loudvoiced, always changing and always young;
drawing from a river basin which is almost a continent young
men and women into its living unrest and then spewing them
forth again to write Chicago in New England and Virginia and
Europe. But in the South art, to become visible at all, must
become a ceremony, a spectacle; something between a gypsy
encampment and a church bazaar given by a handful of alien
mummers who must waste themselves in protest and active self-
defense until there is nothing left with which to speak--a
single week, say, of furious endeavor for a show to be held
on Friday night and then struck and vanished, leaving only
a paint-stiffened smock or a worn out typewriter ribbon in
the corner and perhaps a small bill for cheesecloth or bunt-
ing in the hands of an astonished and bewildered tradesman.

Perhaps this is because the South (I speak in the sense
of the indigenous dream of any given collection of men having
something in common, be it only geography and climate, which
shape their economic and spiritual aspirations into cities,
into a pattern of houses or behavior) is old since dead. New

York, whatever it may believe of itself, is young since alive;
it is still a logical and unbroken progression from the Dutch.
And Chicago even boasts of being young. But the South, as
Chicago is the Middlewest and New York the East, is dead, killed
by the Civil War. There is a thing known whimsically as the
New South to be sure, but it is not the south. It is a land
of Immigrants who are rebuilding the towns and cities into
replicas of towns and cities in Kansas and Iowa and Illinois,
with skyscrapers and striped canvas awnings instead of wooden
balconies, and teaching the young men who sell the gasoline
and the waitresses in the restaurants to say O yeah? and to
speak with hard r's, and hanging over the intersections of
quiet and shaded streets where no one save Northern tourists
in Cadillacs and Lincolns ever pass at a gait faster than a
horse trots, changing red-and-green lights and savage and
peremptory bells.

Yet this art, which has no place in southern life, is
almost the sum total of the Southern artist. It is his breath,
blood, flesh, all. Not so much that it is forced back upon
him or that he is forced bodily into it by the circumstance;
forced to choose, lady and tiger fashion, between being an
artist and being a man. He does it deliberately; he wishes
it so. This has always been true of him and of him alone. Only
Southerners have taken horsewhips and pistols to editors about
the treatment or maltreatment of their manuscript. This--the
actual pistols--was in the old days, of course, we no longer
succumb to the impulse. But it is still there, still within
us.

Because it is himself that the Southerner is writing about,
not about his environment: who has, figuratively speaking,
taken the artist in him in one hand and his milieu in the
other and thrust the one into the other like a clawing and
spitting cat into a croker sack. And he writes. We have never
got and probably will never get, anywhere with music or the
plastic forms. We need to talk, to tell, since oratory is our
heritage. We seem to try in the simple furious breathing (or
writing) span of the individual to draw a savage indictment
of the contemporary scene or to escape from it into a make-
believe region of swords and magnolias and mockingbirds which
perhaps never existed anywhere. Both of the courses are rooted
in sentiment; perhaps the ones who write savagely and bitterly
of the incest in clayfloored cabins are the most sentimental.
Anyway, each course is a matter of violent partizanship, in
which the writer unconsciously writes into every line and
phrase his violent despairs and rages and frustrations or
his violent prophesies of still more violent hopes. That cold
intellect which can write with calm and complete detachment

and gusto of its contemporary scene is not among us; I do not
believe there lives the Southern writer who can say without
lying that writing is any fun to him. Perhaps we do not want
it to be.

I seem to have tried both of the courses. I have tried to
escape and I have tried to indict. After five years I look
back at *The Sound and the Fury* and see that that was the turning point; in this book I did both at one time. When I began
the book, I had no plan at all. I wasn't even writing a book.
Previous to it I had written three novels, with progressively
decreasing ease and pleasure, and reward or emolument. The
third one was shopped about for three years during which I
sent it from publisher to publisher with a kind of stubborn
and fading hope of at least justifying the paper I had used
and the time I had spent writing it. This hope must have died
at last, because one day it suddenly seemed as if a door had
clapped silently and forever to between me and all publishers'
addresses and booklists and I said to myself, Now I can write.
Now I can just write. Whereupon I, who had three brothers
and no sisters and was destined to lose my first daughter in
infancy, began to write about a little girl.

I did not realise then that I was trying to manufacture
the sister which I did not have and the daughter which I was to
lose, though the former might have been apparent from the fact
that Caddy had three brothers almost before I wrote her name
on paper. I just began to write about a brother and a sister
splashing one another in the brook and the sister fell and
wet her clothing and the smallest brother cried, thinking
that the sister was conquered or perhaps hurt. Or perhaps
he knew that he was the baby and that she would quit whatever
water battles to comfort him. When she did so, when she quit
the water fight and stooped in her wet garments above him,
the entire story, which is all told by that same little brother
in the first section, seemed to explode on the paper before
me.

I saw that peaceful glinting of that branch was to become
the dark, harsh flowing of time sweeping her to where she
could not return to comfort him, but that just separation,
division, would not be enough, not far enough. It must sweep
her into dishonor and shame too. And that Benjy must never
grow beyond this moment; that for him all knowing must begin
and end with that fierce, panting, paused and stooping wet
figure which smelled like trees. That he must never grow up
to where the grief of bereavement could be leavened with
understanding and hence the alleviation of rage as in the
case of Jason, and of oblivion as in the case of Quentin.

I saw that they had been sent to the pasture to spend the afternoon to get them away from the house during the grandmother's funeral in order that the three brothers and the nigger children could look up at the muddy seat of Caddy's drawers as she climbed the tree to look in the window at the funeral, without then realising the symbology of the soiled drawers, for here again hers was the courage which was to face later with honor the shame which she was to engender, which Quentin and Jason could not face: the one taking refuge in suicide, the other in vindictive rage which drove him to rob his bastard niece of the meagre sums which Caddy could send her. For I had already gone on to night and the bedroom and Dilsey with the mudstained drawers scrubbing the naked backside of that doomed little girl--trying to cleanse with the sorry byblow of its soiling that body, flesh, whose shame they symbolised and prophesied, as though she already saw the dark future and the part she was to play in it trying to hold that crumbling household together.

Then the story was complete, finished. There was Dilsey to be the future, to stand above the fallen ruins of the family like a ruined chimney, gaunt, patient and indomitable; and Benjy to be the past. He had to be an idiot so that, like Dilsey, he could be impervious to the future, though unlike her by refusing to accept it at all. Without thought or comprehension; shapeless, neuter, like something eyelesss and voiceless which might have lived, existed merely because of its ability to suffer, in the beginning of life; half fluid, groping: a pallid and helpless mass of all mindless agony under sun, in time yet not of it save that he could nightly carry with him that fierce, courageous being who was to him but a touch and a sound that may be heard on any golf links and a smell like trees, into the slow bright shapes of sleep.

The story is all there, in the first section as Benjy told it. I did not try deliberately to make it obscure; when I realised that the story might be printed, I took three more sections, all longer than Benjy's, to try to clarify it. But when I wrote Benjy's section, I was not writing it to be printed. If I were to do it over now I would do it differently, because the writing of it as it now stands taught me both how to write and how to read, and even more: It taught me what I had already read, because on completing it I discovered, in a series of repercussions like summer thunder, the Flauberts and Conrads and Turgenievs which as much as ten years before I had consumed whole and without assimilating at all, as a moth or a goat might. I have read nothing since; I have not had to. And I have learned but one thing since about writing. That is, that the emotion definite and physical and yet nebulous to describe which the writing of Benjy's section of *The Sound and The Fury* gave me--that ecstasy, that eager and joyous faith and anticipation of surprise which the yet un-marred sheets beneath my hand held inviolate and unfailing--will not return. The unreluctance to begin, the cold satis-faction in work well and arduously done, is there and will continue to be there as long as I can do it well. But that other will not return. I shall never know it again.

So I wrote Quentin's and Jason's sections, trying to clarify Benjy's. But I saw that I was merely temporising; That I should have to get completely out of the book. I realised that there would be compensations, that in a sense I could then give a final turn to the screw and extract some ultimate distillation. Yet it took me better than a month to take pen and write *The day dawned bleak and chill* before I did so. There is a story somewhere about an old Roman who kept at his bedside a Tyrrhenian vase which he loved and the rim of which he wore slowly away with kissing it. I had made myself a vase, but I suppose I knew all the time that I could not live forever inside of it, that perhaps to have it so that I too could lie in bed and look at it would be better; surely so when that day should come when not only the ecstasy of writing would be gone, but the unreluctance and the some-thing worth saying too. It's fine to think that you will leave something behind you when you die, but it's better to have made something you can die with. Much better the muddy bottom of a little doomed girl climbing a blooming pear tree in April to look in the window at the funeral.

Oxford.
    19 August, 1933.

INTERVIEWS

Interview in Japan, 1955

Q: Could you tell me your best story in your own estimation?

Faulkner: In my own estimation, none of them are good
enough, that's why I have spent thirty years writing another
one, hoping that one would be good enough. And so my personal
feeling would be a tenderness for the one which caused me
the most anguish, just as the mother might feel for the child,
and the one that caused me the most anguish and is to me the
finest failure is *The Sound and the Fury*. That's the one that
I feel most tender toward.

Q: Going back to the notes, did you make any when you
wrote the first section of *The Sound and the Fury*?

Faulkner: No.

Q: Would you tell us something about the time you wrote
the first section, it seems to be so complicated, and I wonder
if you wrote it just as you did *The Wild Palms*.

Faulkner: That began as a short story, it was a story
without plot, of some children being sent away from the house
during the grandmother's funeral. They were too young to be
told what was going on and they saw things only incidentally
to the childish games they were playing, which was the lugu-
brious matter of removing the corpse from the house, etc.,
and then the idea struck me to see how much more I could have
got out of the idea of the blind, self-centeredness of innocence, typified by children, if one of those children had
been truly innocent, that is, an idiot. So the idiot was born
and then I became interested in the relationship of the idiot
to the world that he was in but would never be able to cope
with and just where could he get the tenderness, the help,

From Lion in the Garden: Interviews with William Faulkner,
1926-1962, *ed. James B. Meriwether and Michael Millgate (New
York: Random House, 1968). Reprinted by permission of Michael
Millgate.*

to shield him in his innocence. I mean "innocence" in the
sense that God had stricken him blind at birth, that is, mindless at birth, there was nothing he could ever do about it.
And so the character of his sister began to emerge, then the
brother, who, that Jason (who to me represented complete evil.
He's the most vicious character in my opinion I ever thought
of), then he appeared. Then it needs the protagonist, someone
to tell the story, so Quentin appeared. By that time I found
out I couldn't possibly tell that in a short story. And so I
told the idiot's experience of that day, and that was incomprehensible, even I could not have told what was going on then,
so I had to write another chapter. Then I decided to let
Quentin tell his version of that same day, or that same occasion, so he told it. Then there had to be the counterpoint,
which was the other brother, Jason. By that time it was completely confusing. I knew that it was not anywhere near
finished and then I had to write another section from the outside with an outsider, which was the writer, to tell what had
happened on that particular day. And that's how that book
grew. That is, I wrote that same story four times. None of
them were right, but I had anguished so much that I could not
throw any of it away and start over, so I printed it in the
four sections. That was not a deliberate *tour de force* at all,
the book just grew that way. That I was still trying to tell
one story which moved me very much and each time I failed,
but I had put so much anguish into it that I couldn't throw
it away, like the mother that had four bad children, that she
would have been better off if they all had been eliminated,
but she couldn't relinquish any of them. And that's the reason
I have the most tenderness for that book, because it failed
four times.

   Q: I made a thorough study of the first section and I
felt that it was humanly impossible to write it down from the
very beginning without any notes, but you did that?

   Faulkner: One time I thought of printing that first section in different colors, but that would have been too expen-
sive. That was about 1930, I think, and at that time they had
not advanced the printing of different, separate colors as
they have now, and that would have been almost prohibitive
in color. But if it could have been printed in different colors
so that anyone reading it could keep up with who was talking
and who was thinking this and what time, what moment in time,
it was. To that idiot, time was not a continuation, it was
an instant, there was no yesterday and no tomorrow, it all is
this moment, it all is [now] to him. He will be tomorrow, he
doesn't know whether he dreamed it, or saw it.

   Q: You mean to say you wanted to print one whole first
chapter in different colors?

Faulkner: Yes.

Q: In modern editions we have some italic letters.

Faulkner: Yes, that was the next recourse because italics were easy to be cut into the plates but color would have been prohibitive.

Q: Which work do you like best, all your life?

Faulkner: I just answered that, none of them are good enough. So, I like the one which caused me the most trouble. That is *The Sound and the Fury*. But none of them are good enough, as good as I am convinced I could do if I had my life to live over and could write them again. But that is impossible, so all I can do is use the rest of my time to write one that will be good enough, which I'm sure I won't do, but I'll probably try.

Interview with Cynthia Grenier, 1955

Faulkner: ... The book which took the most agony was *The Sound and the Fury*. Took me five years of re-working and re-writing. Never did finish it.

Q: How did you come to write *The Sound and the Fury*?

Faulkner: It started out as a short story about two children being sent out to play in the yard during their grandmother's funeral. Only one of the little girls was big enough to climb a tree to look in the window to see what was going on. It was going to be a story of blood gone bad. The story told wasn't all. The idiot child had started out as a simple prop at first as a bid for extra sympathy. Then I thought what would the story be told like as he saw it. So I had him look at it. When I'd finished I had a quarter of the book written, but it still wasn't all. It still wasn't enough. So then Quentin told the story as he saw it and it still wasn't enough. Then I tried to tell the story and it still was not enough, and so I wrote the appendix and it wasn't enough. It's the book I feel tenderest towards. I couldn't leave it alone, and I never could tell it right, though I tried hard and would like to try again though I'd probably fail again. It's the tragedy of two lost women: Caddy and her daughter.

Interview with
Jean Stein vanden Heuvel, 1956

Faulkner: ... The quality an artist must have is objectivity in judging his work, plus the honesty and courage not to kid himself about it. Since none of my work has met my own stan-

dards, I must judge it on the basis of that one which caused
me the most grief and anguish, as the mother loves the child
who became the thief or murderer more than the one who became
the priest.

Q: What work is that?

Faulkner: *The Sound and the Fury.* I wrote it five separate
times trying to tell the story, to rid myself of the dream
which would continue to anguish me until I did. It's a tragedy
of two lost women: Caddy and her daugher. Dilsey is one of my
own favorite characters because she is brave, courageous,
generous, gentle and honest. She's much more brave and honest
and generous than me.

Q: How did *The Sound and the Fury* begin?

Faulkner: It began with a mental picture. I didn't realize
at the time it was symbolical. The picture was of the muddy
seat of a little girl's drawers in a pear tree where she could
see through a window where her grandmother's funeral was taking
place and report what was happening to her brothers on the
ground below. By the time I explained who they were and what
they were doing and how her pants got muddy, I realized it
would be impossible to get all of it into a short story and
that it would have to be a book. And then I realized the
symbolism of the soiled pants, and that image was replaced by
the one of the fatherless and motherless girl climbing down
the rainpipe to escape from the only home she had, where she
had never been offered love or affection or understanding. I
had already begun to tell it through the eyes of the idiot
child since I felt that it would be more effective as told
by someone capable only of knowing what happened, but not why.
I saw that I had not told the story that time. I tried to tell
it again, the same story through the eyes of another brother.
That was still not it. I told it for the third time through
the eyes of the third brother. That was still not it. I tried
to gather the pieces together and fill in the gaps by making
myself the spokesman. It was still not complete, not until
15 years after the book was published when I wrote as an appendix to another book the final effort to get the story told
and off my mind, so that I myself could have some peace from
it. It's the book I feel tenderest towards. I couldn't leave
it alone, and I never could tell it right, though I tried hard
and would like to try again, though I'd probably fail again.

Q: What emotion does Benjy arouse in you?

Faulkner: The only emotion I can have for Benjy is grief
and pity for all mankind. You can't feel anything for Benjy
because he doesn't fell anything. The only thing I can feel
about him personally is concern as to whether he is believable
as I created him. He was a prologue like the gravedigger

in the Elizabethan dramas. He serves his purpose and is gone.
Benjy is incapable of good and evil because he had no knowledge of good and evil.

Q: Could Benjy feel love?

Faulkner: Benjy wasn't rational enough even to be selfish.
He was an animal. He recognized tenderness and love though
he could not have named them, and it was the threat to tenderness and love that caused him to bellow when he felt the change
in Caddy. He no longer had Caddy; being an idiot he was not
even aware that Caddy was missing. He knew only that something
was wrong, which left a vacuum in which he grieved. He tried
to fill that vacuum. The only thing was he had one of Caddy's
discarded slippers. The slipper was his tenderness and love
which he could not have named, but he knew only that it was
missing. He was dirty because he couldn't coordinate and because dirt meant nothing to him. He could no more distinguish
between dirt and cleanliness than between good and evil. The
slipper gave him comfort even though he no longer remembered
the person to whom it had once belonged, any more than he could
remember why he grieved. If Caddy had reappeared he probably
would not have known her.

Q: Does the narcissus given to Benjy have some significance?

Faulkner: The narcissus was given to Benjy to distract
his attention. It was simply a flower which happened to be
handy that 5th of April. It was not deliberate.

DISCUSSIONS AT THE
UNIVERSITY OF VIRGINIA, 1957-58

Q. Mr. Faulkner, in *The Sound and the Fury* the first
three sections of that book are narrated by one of the four
Compson children, and in view of the fact that Caddy figures
so prominently, is there any particular reason why you didn't
have a section with--giving her views or impressions of what
went on?

A. That's a good question. That--the explanation of that
whole book is in that. It began with the picture of the little
girl's muddy drawers, climbing that tree to look in the parlor
window with her brothers that didn't have the courage to climb
the tree waiting to see what she saw. And I tried first to
tell it with one brother, and that wasn't enough. That was
Section One. I tried with another brother, and that wasn't
enough. That was Section Two. I tried the third brother, because Caddy was still to me too beautiful and too moving to
reduce her to telling what was going on, that it would be
more passionate to see her through somebody else's eyes, I
thought. And that failed and I tried myself--the fourth sec-
tion--to tell what happened, and I still failed.

. . .

Q. Speaking of Caddy, is there any way of getting her
back from the clutches of the Nazis, where she ends up in
the Appendix?

A. I think that that would be a betrayal of Caddy, that
it is best to leave her where she is. If she were resurrected
there'd be something a little shabby, a little anti-climactic

From Faulkner in the University: Class Conferences at the
University of Virginia 1957-1958, *ed. Frederick L. Gwynn and
Joseph L. Blotner (Charlottesville: The University of Virginia
Press, 1959), pp. 1-2, 2-3, 6, 17-18, 31-32, 61-62, 63-64,
68, 76-77, 84, 85, 87, 94-95, 147-48, 262-63. Reprinted by
permission.*

about it, about this. Her tragedy to me is the best I could
do with it--unless, as I said, I could start over and write
the book again and that can't be.

. . .

Q. Mr. Faulkner, I am interested in the symbolism in *The
Sound and the Fury*, and I wasn't able to figure exactly the
significance of the shadow symbol in Quentin. It's referred
to over and over again: he steps in the shadow, shadow is
before him, the shadow is often after him. Well then, what is
the significance of this shadow?

A. That wasn't a deliberate symbolism. I would say that
that shadow that stayed on his mind so much was foreknowledge
of his own death, that he was--Death is here, shall I step
into it, or shall I step away from it a little longer? I won't
escape it, but shall I accept it now or shall I put it off
until next Friday? I think that if it had any reason that must
have been it.

. . .

Q. Mr. Faulkner, I'd like to ask you about Quentin and
his relationship with his father. I think many readers get
the impression that Quentin is the way he is to a large extent
because of his father's lack of values, or the fact that he
doesn't seem to pass down to his son many values that will
sustain him. Do you think that Quentin winds up the way he
does primarily because of that, or are we meant to see, would
you say, that the action that comes primarily from what he
is, abetted by what he gets from his father?

A. The action as portrayed by Quentin was transmitted to
him through his father. There was a basic failure before that.
The grandfather had been a failed brigadier twice in the
Civil War. It was the--the basic failure Quentin inherited
through his father, or beyond his father. It was a--something
had happened somewhere between the first Compson and Quentin.
The first Compson was a bold ruthless man who came into
Mississippi as a free forester to grasp where and when he
could and wanted to, and established what should have been
a princely line, and that princely line decayed.

. . .

Q. Mr. Faulkner, I've been very much interested in what
it seems to me you did--maybe you didn't--in *The Sound and
the Fury*, in the character of Caddy. To me she is a very

sympathetic character, perhaps the most sympathetic white
woman in the book, and yet we get pictures of her only through
someone else's comments and most of these comments are quite
[?] and wouldn't lead you to admire her on the surface, and
yet I do. Did you mean for us to have this feeling for Caddy,
and if so, how did you go about reducing her to the negative
picture we get of her?

A. To me she was the beautiful one, she was my heart's
darling. That's what I wrote the book about and I used the
tools which seemed to me the proper tools to try to tell, try
to draw the picture of Caddy.

. . .

[... Q. In connection with the character of Christ, did
you make any conscious attempts in *The Sound and the Fury* to
use Christian references, as a number of critics have suggested?

A. No. I was just trying to tell a story of Caddy, the
little girl who had muddied her drawers and was climbing up
to look in the window where her grandmother lay dead.

Q. But Benjy, for example, is thirty-three years old,
the traditional age of Christ at death.

A. Yes. That was a ready-made axe to use, but it was just
one of several tools.

. . .

Q. Your work has sometimes been compared with that of
Hawthorne's tales with hard-hearted people like Jason. Do
you think that one of the things that's wrong with the South
is that there are too many characters like this, like Jason
Compson, in it?

A. Yes, there are too many Jasons in the South who can
be successful, just as there are too many Quentins in the
South who are too sensitive to face its reality.

. . .

Q. In *The Sound and the Fury*, where Quentin sees the
boys fishing, does his remark about the big fish have any
symbolism? He says to them, I hope you don't catch that big
fish, he deserves to be let alone.

A. Well, it doesn't have any meaning by itself, but
Quentin knows he is going to die and he sees things much more
clearly than he would otherwise. He sees things that are more
important to him since he doesn't have to worry about them
now, and when he wants the old fish to live, it may represent
his unconscious desire for endurance, both for himself and

for his people. It is just like when some people know they are
going to die, and the dross is burned away and they know they
can say things because in a while they won't be around to have
to defend them.

Q. In the last part of Quentin's section, why do you
begin to omit capitals on the names and on "I"?

A. Because Quentin is a dying man, he is already out of
life, and those things that were important in life don't mean
anything to him any more.

· · ·

Q. What is the trouble with the Compsons?

A. They are still living in the attitudes of 1859 or '60.

Q. Why is it that Mrs. Compson refers to Benjy as having
been sold into Egypt? Wasn't that Joseph in the Bible? Is the
mistake yours or hers?

A. Is there anybody who knows the Bible here?

Q. I looked it up and Benjamin was held hostage for Joseph.

A. Yes, that's why I used them interchangeably....]

· · ·

Q. You had said previously that *The Sound and the Fury*
came from the impression of a little girl up in a tree, and I
wondered how you built it from that, and whether you just, as
you said, let the story develop itself?

A. Well, impression is the wrong word. It's more an image,
a very moving image to me was of the children. 'Course, we
didn't know at that time that one was an idiot, but they were
three boys, one was a girl and the girl was the only one that
was brave enough to climb that tree to look in the forbidden
window to see what was going on. And that's what the book--
and it took the rest of the four hundred pages to explain why
she was brave enough to climb the tree to look in the window.
It was an image, a picture to me, a very moving one, which
was symbolized by the muddy bottom of her drawers as her
brothers looked up into the apple tree that she had climbed
to look in the window. And the symbolism of the muddy bottom
of the drawers became the lost Caddy, which had caused one
brother to commit suicide and the other brother had misused
her money that she'd send back to the child, the daughter.
It was, I thought, a short story, something that could be done
in about two pages, a thousand words, I found out it couldn't.
I finished it the first time, and it wasn't right, so I wrote
it again, and that was Quentin, that wasn't right. I wrote
it again, that was Jason, that wasn't right, then I tried to
let Faulkner do it, that still was wrong.

• • •

Q. Sir, why do you regard *The Sound and the Fury* as your best work?

A. It was the best failure. It was the one that I anguished the most over, that I worked the hardest at, that even when I knew I couldn't bring it off, I still worked at it. It's like the parent feels toward the unfortunate child, maybe. The others that have been easier to write than that, and in ways are better books than that, but I don't have the feeling toward any of them that I do toward that one, because that was the most gallant, the most magnificent failure.

Q. Mr. Faulkner, you said that even though you did not bring it off, you worked hardest at it. How do you feel that you failed to bring *The Sound and the Fury* off?

A. It don't make me feel good enough, to use Hemingway's phrase. That's a condition that probably I can't put into words, but if I ever do strike it, I will know it. I think that that's true of any writer.

Q. Well, aren't there parts of it that make you feel good enough?

A. Well, that's not enough—parts of it are not enough, it must be all, you see. You can't compromise, you know, it's either good or it ain't, there's no degrees of goodness. It's either all right or it's not all right.

• • •

Q. What is your purpose in writing into the first section of *The Sound and the Fury* passages that seem disjointed in themselves if the idea is not connected with one another?

A. That was part of the failure. It seemed to me that the book approached nearer the dream if the groundwork of it was laid by the idiot, who was incapable of relevancy. That's—I agree with you too, that's a bad method, but to me it seemed the best way to do it, that I shifted those sections back and forth to see where they went best, but my final decision was that though that was not right, that was the best to do it, that was simply the groundwork of that story, as that idiot child saw it. He himself didn't know what he was seeing. That the only thing that held him into any sort of reality, into the world at all, was the trust that he had for his sister, that he knew that she loved him and would defend him, and so she was the whole world to him, and these things were flashes that were reflected on her as in a mirror. He didn't know what they meant.

. . .

Q. What symbolic meaning did you give to the dates of *The Sound and the Fury*?

A. Now there's a matter of hunting around in the carpenter' shop to find a tool that will make a better chicken-house. And probably--I'm sure it was quite instinctive that I picked out Easter, that I wasn't writing any symbolism of the Passion Week at all. I just--that was a tool that was good for the particular corner I was going to turn in my chicken-house and so I used it.

. . .

Q. Mr. Faulkner, what do you consider your best book?

A. The one that failed the most tragically and the most splendidly. That was *The Sound and the Fury*--the one that I worked at the longest, the hardest, that was to me the most passionate and moving idea, and made the most splendid failure. That's the one that's my--I consider the best, not--well, best is the wrong word--that's the one that I love the most.

. . .

Q. Well, this is more or less a question of fact. In *The Sound and the Fury* was Jason Compson, was he a bastard?

A. No. Not an actual one--only in behavior.

. . .

Q. In that connection, did you write it in the order in which it was published?

A. Yes.... I wrote the Benjy part first. That wasn't good enough so I wrote the Quentin part. That still wasn't good enough. I let Jason try it. That still wasn't enough. I let Faulkner try it and that still wasn't enough, and so about twenty years afterward I wrote an appendix still trying to make that book what--match the dream.

. . .

Q. Then may I ask if all of these characters in *The Sound and the Fury*--that you would call them "good people"?

A. I would call them tragic people. The good people, Dilsey, the Negro woman, she was a good human being. That she held that family together for not the hope of reward but just because it was the decent and proper thing to do.

. . .

Q. Mr. Faulkner, in reference to *The Sound and the Fury*
again is the "tale told by an idiot, full of sound and fury,
signifying nothing" applicable to Benjy as is generally thought,
or perhaps to Jason?
A. The title, of course, came from the first section, which
was Benjy. I thought the story was told in Benjy's section,
and the title came there. So it--in that sense it does apply
to Benjy rather than to anybody else, though the more I had to
work on the book, the more elastic the title became, until it
covered the whole family.

. . .

Q. Mr. Faulkner, in *The Sound and the Fury*, can you tell
me exactly why some of that is written in italics? What does
that denote?
A. I had to use some method to indicate to the reader that
this idiot had no sense of time. That what happened to him ten
years ago was just yesterday. The way I wanted to do it was to
use different colored inks, but that would have cost so much,
the publisher couldn't undertake it.
Q. Doesn't that go on with Quentin, too?
A. Yes, because he was about half way between madness and
sanity. It wasn't as much as in Benjy's part, because Quentin
was only half way between Benjy and Jason. Jason didn't need
italics because he was quite sane.
Q. And another thing I noticed; you don't advise that
people have to have a subject and predicate for verbs and all
those things.
A. Well, that--I think that's really not a fair question.
I was trying to tell this story as it seemed to me that idiot
child saw it. And that idiot child to me didn't know what a
question, what an interrogation was. He didn't know too much
about grammar, he spoke only through his senses.
Q. I'm referring mostly to Quentin and he certainly--he
attended Harvard, he should have known.
A. Well, Quentin was an educated half-madman and so he
dispensed with grammar. Because it was all clear to his half-
mad brain and it seemed to him it would be clear to anybody
else's brain, that what he saw was quite logical, quite clear.

. . .

... Q. Mr. Faulkner, I saw something not long ago that
took *The Sound and the Fury* in four sections and tried to draw

a parallel between the id, the ego and super-ego and the author's person. Now don't you think that is indicative of what a lot of critics and scholars are doing today with the views of contemporary writers, making psychological inferences and finding symbols which the author never intended?

A. Well, I would say that the author didn't deliberately intend but I think that in the same culture the background of the critic and of the writer are so similar that a part of each one's history is the seed which can be translated into the symbols which are standardized within that culture. That is, the writer don't have to know Freud to have written things which anyone who does know Freud can divine and reduce into symbols. And so when the critic finds those symbols, they are of course there. But they were there as inevitably as the critic should stumble on his own knowledge of Freud to discern symbol [sic]. But I think the writer is primarily concerned in telling about people, in the only terms he knows, which is out of his experience, his observation, and his imagination. And the experience and the imagination and the observation of a culture are--all the people in that culture partake of the same three things more or less. The critic has a valid part in any culture. I think that it's--it might be a good thing if most writers were like me and didn't bother to read them. That is, the writer knows what is in his book and he knows whether it failed or didn't fail. It--and so it's possible that reading the criticisms could do a young writer harm because it could confuse him. It could get him to think in terms of the symbolism which the critic, who is usually a good deal more erudite than the writer, can find in his work.

. . .

Q. Does it give the author as much pain as it does the reader to produce scenes such as when Caddy wanted to see her baby and Jason just drove by?

A. Yes, it does, but that's--the writer is not simply dragging that in to pull a few tears, he is--he puts that down as an instance of man's injustice to man. That man will always be unjust to man, yet there must always be people, men and women who are capable of the compassion toward that injustice and the hatred of that injustice, and the will to risk public opprobrium, to stand up and say, This is rotten, this stinks, I won't have it.

. . .

Q. Speaking of symbolism, on the dust jacket of the first edition of *The Sound and the Fury*, two figures seem to be wrestling. A black one is pinning down a whiter one. Do you recall who the artist was, and whether anything in particular was intended?

A. No, I don't, I don't know who did that. Of course the symbolism was simply the powers of darkness and of light wrestling, struggling. I don't know whose idea that jacket was nor who did it.

. . .

Q. Did Quentin before actually have that conversation with his father about sleeping with his sister, or was that part of his--?

A. He never did. He said, If I were brave, I would--I might say this to my father, whether it was a lie or not, or if I were--if I would say this to my father, maybe he would answer me back the magic word which would relieve me of this anguish and agony which I live with. No, they were imaginary. He just said, Suppose I say this to my father, would it help me, would it clarify, would I see clearer what it is that I anguish over?

Q. The feeling between him and his sister is pretty strong though, isn't it?

A. Yes, yes. But in Caddy's opinion he was such a weakling that even if they had been no kin, she would never have chosen him for her sweetheart. She would have chosen one like the ex-soldier she did. But never anybody like Quentin.

Q. Is Candace a common name in Mississippi, or--?

A. No. No, Caddy seemed a nice name for her and I had to think of something to justify it.

. . .

Q. Mr. Faulkner, I'm curious about Jason.... That Negro boy tells him to keep his hands out of his pockets, because he's falling on his face all the time, he stumbles. Why, was he fat and clumsy...?

A. Probably. That was a mannerism, keeping his hands in his pockets, to me that presaged his future, something of greediness and grasping, selfishness. That he may have kept his hands in his pocket to guard whatever colored rock that he had found that was to him, represented the million dollars he would like to have some day.

ESSAYS ON
THE SOUND AND THE FURY

THE COMPOSITION OF *THE SOUND AND THE FURY*

Gail M. Morrison

Faulkner's early--and succinct--judgment on *The Sound and the Fury* was that his fourth novel was "a real sonofabitch."[1] Although its sales would turn out to be as disappointing as those of his first three novels and do little to alleviate his financial distress, the reviews were generally favorable and more than justified Faulkner's remark. Since that time this brilliant, difficult work has continued to attract more critical attention than any other single Faulkner work, and its popularity seems unlikely to fade. Faulkner's initial sense of exhilaration would become tempered in his maturity by his sense of having attempted something other than what he had achieved--of having written a book that was "the most gallant, the most magnificent failure."[2] But that reservation notwithstanding, Faulkner's moving and frequently quoted remarks about the novel uniformly testify to the very special place, to the highly personal significance, he accorded the work that was a long awaited and, from the artist's point of view, a timely critical if not financial breakthrough.

His first two novels, *Soldier's Pay* and *Mosquitoes*, had failed to sell. When his publisher, Horace Liveright, rejected *Flags in the Dust*, Faulkner wrote him in wry dismay in February 1928:

> I want to submit the mss. which you refused, to another publisher.
> Will you agree to this with the understanding that I either pay you the what-ever-it-is I owe you, or that I submit to you the next mss. I complete? I do not know just when I'll have another ready, but if I can place the one I have on hand and get an advance, I can pay you the money. I have just sent some short stories to an agent; perhaps I shall derive something from them with which to pay you. Otherwise I dont know what we'll do about it, as I have a belly full of writing, now, since you folks in the publishing business claim that a book like that last one I sent you is blah. I think

33

now that I'll sell my typewriter and go to work--though
God knows, it's sacrilege to waste that talent for idle-
ness which I possess.[3]

Although for Faulkner *Flags in the Dust* was "THE book, of which
those other things were but foals" and "the damdest best book
you'll look at this year,"[4] Liveright remained unencouraging.
Even after considerable revision the novel spent almost
a year making the rounds at various publishers under the aus-
pices of Faulkner's friend and literary agent Ben Wasson.[5]
Ultimately, Wasson's friend Harrison Smith at Harcourt, Brace
agreed to publish an abbreviated form of the novel as *Sartoris*.
Faulkner was in New York when the contract was issued on
September 20, 1928. There he finished the typescript of *The
Sound and the Fury*, inscribing the date "October 1928" on its
last page.

A remarkable thing had occurred during the interval between
the rejection of *Flags* in February 1928 and the completion of
the *Sound and the Fury* typescript that October. As Faulkner
expressed it a few years afterwards, "one day it suddenly seemed
as if a door had clapped silently and forever to between me
and all publishers' addresses and booklists and I said to myself, Now I can write. Now I can just write."[6] That door closed,
apparently, because, as Faulkner commented in 1932, "I believed
then that I would never be published again. I had stopped
thinking of myself in publishing terms."[7] *The Sound and the
Fury* would be written "for fun"[8] and would evoke, Faulkner recalled in 1933, an "emotion definite and physical and yet
nebulous to describe ... that ecstasy, that eager and joyous
faith and anticipation of surprise which the yet unmarred sheets
beneath my hand held inviolate and unfailing...."[9] The rejection of *The Sound and the Fury* by Harcourt, Brace would not
elicit the despair produced by Liveright's refusal of *Flags*,
in part, Faulkner wrote, because "I did not believe that anyone would publish it; I had no definite plan to submit it to
anyone. I told Hal [Harrison Smith] about it once and he dared
me to bring it to him. And so it really was to him that I
submitted it, more as a curiosity than aught else."[10]

When Faulkner closed the door between himself and his
publishers after his initial failure to place *Flags in the
Dust*, the conjunction was evidently a happy one of his sense
of freedom from the strictures imposed on an author attempting
to write a marketable book and whatever compelling personal
problems he referred to years later as besetting him at that
time.[11] Certainly the technical virtuosity of *The Sound and
the Fury* is the most striking manifestation of this freedom.
Another is the display of what he called in later years the
responsibility of the artist to be "completely amoral" and

"completely ruthless" in his need to "rob, borrow, beg or
steal from anybody and everybody to get the work done."[12] And
"rob, borrow, beg, or steal" he did, consciously or uncon-
sciously--and not just from Shakespeare and Milton, Keats and
Shelley, Flaubert and Dostoevski, Lawrence and Joyce, Conrad
and Hardy, Swinburne, Eliot, Housman, Wilde, Yeats, Hemingway,
Anderson, and Fitzgerald, but from Freud and Jung, Frazer,
Nietzsche, Kierkegaard, Bergson, and others--drawing not only
on specific literary masters but on the rich social and
cultural milieu of the 1920s and indeed of all Western
civilization, to make clear that what he called his carpenter's
workshop was not centered in a cultural vacuum in those bleak
and barren Mississippi hills.[13] Or, as he wrote in the summer
of 1933 in an introduction for a projected new edition of the
novel by Random House:

> I wrote this book and learned to read. I had learned a
> little about writing from Soldiers' Pay--how to approach
> language, words: not with seriousness so much, as an
> essayist does, but with a kind of alert respect, as you
> approach dynamite; even with joy, as you approach women:
> perhaps with the same secretly unscrupulous intentions.
> But when I finished The Sound and The Fury I discovered
> that there is actually something to which the shabby term
> Art not only can, but must, be applied. I discovered
> then that I had gone through all that I had ever read,
> from Henry James through Henty to newspaper murders,
> without making any distinction or digesting any of it,
> as a moth or a goat might. After The Sound and The Fury
> and without heeding to open another book and in a series
> of delayed repercussions like summer thunder, I dis-
> covered the Flauberts and Dostoievskys and Conrads whose
> books I had read ten years ago. With The Sound and The
> Fury I learned to read and quit reading, since I have
> read nothing since.[14]

I

      This is not to imply in the least that *The Sound and the
Fury* is a derivative book, although its literary borrowings
are perhaps not as assimilated in this early work as they are
in the later fiction. If, in some ways, it seems to grow
logically out of the three novels which preceded it, it is
nevertheless safe to say that *Soldiers' Pay*, *Mosquitoes*, and
Flags in the Dust simply do not prepare us for the achievements of *The Sound and the Fury*. Its complexity of character
and theme, its emotional intensity, and its technical vir-

tuosity far surpass those of the earlier works.[15] However,
neither our own sense of the uniqueness of Faulkner's fourth
novel nor Faulkner's comments about it should delude us into
believing that the novel sprang into being, like the mythical
phoenix, full grown in all its resplendent plumage. While the
published and unpublished earlier works cannot entirely explain
the flowering of genius, the sudden achievement of tremendous
artistic control, they do show that Faulkner's phoenix did
not step totally unassisted out of the flames. A rich and
fertile ten-year apprenticeship as a writer lay behind Faulkner, and if in closing the publishers' doors he learned to
read, he also drew again on materials, both published and unpublished, prose and poetry, that lay strewn around his carpenter's workshop.[16]

Adumbrations of *The Sound and the Fury*, for instance, have
frequently been pointed out in the prose sketches written in
the twenties, especially those written for the New Orleans
Times-Picayune and the *Double Dealer*:[17] the idiot who grasps
a narcissus, bellows inarticulately, and has eyes that are
intensely blue in "The Kingdom of God"; the appearance of a
Little Sister Death figure in "The Kid Learns"; a Mr. Compson-
like philosophy that "living is not only not passionate or
joyous, but is not even especially sorrowful" in "Out of
Nazareth";[18] the use in "The Priest" of twilight, lilacs,
hyacinths, and the famous passage from *Macbeth* that gave
Faulkner's novel its title.[19] To these might be added the
experimentation with Negro dialect in "The Longshoreman" and
other pre-Jason vernacular expressions in sketches such as
"Frankie and Johnny."

Perhaps even more interesting are several prose sketches
that Faulkner did not publish, which display close affinities
with *The Sound and the Fury*. Juliet Bunden, the protagonist
of "Adolescence," for example, reminds us particularly of
Caddy Compson: Juliet is a tomboy, climbs better than a boy,
possesses a "fierce sensitive pride"[20] and spends long hours
in the creek. Like Caddy's family, Juliet's is composed of
three brothers, the youngest of whom is her favorite. Juliet's
attitude toward the male members of her family, including
her weak, ineffectual father, mirrors something of Caddy's
affection for Mr. Compson, Quentin, and Benjy. Even some of
the imagery of the sketch looks forward to that of the novel,
not only in its several references to twilight, but also in
Juliet's feeling that she is "like one who has cast the dice
and must wait an eternity for them to stop" and that "the
attainment of happiness was thwarted by blind circumstance."[21]
These recall Jason's sense of helpless entrapment as he chases
his niece about the countryside "where the rear guards of

Circumstance peeped fleetingly back at him" and "the opposed
forces of his destiny and his will [drew] swiftly together."[22]
   To turn from this awkward yet curiously moving sketch of
a lost and almost tragic young girl to "The Devil Beats His
Wife" is to come to what amounts to a fragment--three unnumbered manuscript pages without much merit--rather than a fully
developed sketch.[23] One of the unnumbered pages begins with
a description of the black maid Della returning to her cabin.
Here in embryonic form is the opening of the fourth section
of the novel, although Dilsey will not "waddle" across the
yard like Della. Nevertheless, Della's dominant characteristic,
her "placid implacability" as reflected on her "placid in-
scrutable face," foreshadows Dilsey's more fully realized
character. Both women wear a "stiff black straw hat" (p. 330)
over a turban, and this phrase occurs in both opening paragraphs.
   Equally noteworthy is Della's interaction with a young
white girl named Doris, who is unhappily married, and who in
her briefly delineated, whining immaturity somewhat foreshadows the young girl Quentin. In one scene, Della and Harry,
Doris's husband, knock at the door of her bedroom in much the
same way that Jason, Mrs. Compson, and Dilsey knock at Quentin's
on the morning they discover her theft and flight. The description of Doris's room anticipates the fine passage in the novel
in which Quentin's empty room is described.
   A much more ambitious prose sketch, and one with considerably more artistic merit, is "Nympholepsy," probably
written early in 1925 shortly after Faulkner's arrival in
New Orleans.[24] An expansion of an earlier sketch, "The Hill,"
published in the *Mississippian*, "Nympholepsy" displays close
affinities to the imagery of the novel. Even more striking,
however, is the use of the quest as a controlling structural
device. Carefully complicated as it is by flashbacks, Quentin's
monologue depicts his spending the last day of his life
wandering through the countryside evoking the past and his
memory of Caddy. In the earlier sketch, the laborer pursues
an equally unattainable woman across hill and field and
eventually falls into a pool of water, at which point the
woman is revealed as yet another of the early associations
of a beautiful woman with death, an image which culminates
in the association of Caddy with Little Sister Death.
   Another early, unpublished work that has tangential relationship to *The Sound and the Fury* is an unfinished novel
entitled "Elmer," which was begun in Paris in 1925. The
characters and ideas apparently retained some degree of fascination for Faulkner since he returned to the material in
the early 1930s and attempted to salvage portions of it in

the short story "Portrait of Elmer."[25] Despite Faulkner's
unsuccessful treatment of an artist as a comic figure in
this work, he returns to the problem of the artist in *The
Sound and the Fury* with Quentin's monologue, which has often
been viewed as Faulkner's version of *A Portrait of the Artist
as a Young Man*.[26] Most striking is Faulkner's depiction of
another pre-Caddy figure who looks backward not only to Juliet
Bunden but also forward to Addie Bundren and the young protagonist of "Barn Burning."

While much of the Elmer material is clearly related to
the Snopes material which Faulkner would explore in the
unfinished novel "Father Abraham" (out of which at least
tangentially grew *As I Lay Dying* [1930]), Elmer's sister,
Jo-Addie, foreshadows several crucial details of the portrait
of Caddy as conveyed particularly in Benjy's monologue. In
the corrected 123-page typescript of "Elmer," while the early
description of Elmer's family sounds more like Snopeses than
Compsons, Elmer's relationship with his sister shares something of both Benjy's and Quentin's obsessive concern with
Caddy. Elmer, like Benjy, is identified as the baby in his
family; and like Benjy, Elmer sleeps in the same bed with
his sister. However, that he quite unabashedly sleeps naked
with her suggests something more of Quentin's sexual preoccupations than of Benjy's fulfilling in Caddy his need for
maternal affection. In one scene, Elmer asks Jo-Addie to
sleep with him after the family has moved again. In the later
novel this scene is paralleled by Caddy's lying down beside
Benjy to comfort him when he is thirteen and has trouble
falling asleep by himself. Despite their physical differences,
Caddy and Jo-Addie are both associated with the masculine
virtues of daring and strength which Quentin so admires in
his sister. Further, both girls are associated with fire,
Jo-Addie as her home burns, Caddy through Benjy's associations of love and tenderness with the flames in the fireplace
and the reflection of light in the mirror. In the eyes of
the young Elmer, Jo-Addie "stood fiercely erect as ever,
watching the fire in a dark proud defiance, ridiculing her
sorrowing brothers by her very sharp and arrogant ugliness";
Elmer sees her as "a young ugly tree" and as "a fierce young
mare."[27] Jo-Addie, too, disappears from her family forever,
although, as McHaney notes, we are given a brief glimpse
of her as a New Orleans prostitute. This is perhaps echoed
in the later novel, which clearly implies that such is Caddy's
fate; the later Compson Appendix seems to confirm those
suspicions.

In contrast to these awkward and unfinished pieces are
two more ambitious, polished accomplishments: *Marionettes*,

written in 1920 and prepared by its author in several hand-
lettered and hand-illustrated copies, and *Mayday*, another
hand-lettered, illustrated booklet dated January 27, 1926,
which Faulkner gave to Helen Baird. Like *Mayday*,[28] *Marionettes*
reveals a number of Faulkner's early literary sources as well
as his experiments with crucial structural devices, including the frame, shifting point of view, and counterpointed
plot, that recur in the later novel. And, as the character of
Galwyn in *Mayday* anticipates Quentin in so many respects, so
the figure of Marietta adumbrates Caddy as well as her brother
Quentin. Through Marietta's seduction and abandonment by
Pierrot, the themes of change, time, sexuality, and death are
explored, issues which lie at the very heart of *The Sound and
the Fury* and are mirrored in Caddy's seduction and abandonment by Dalton Ames. However, although Marietta is associated
with trees, like Caddy Compson and so many of the young women
in Faulkner's early prose and poetry, including Cecily Saunders
and Patricia Robyn, she reminds us rather more of the elder
Quentin than of Caddy. Like Marietta, who is troubled by
"strange desires" so that her "garden is like a dark room
when the candles are extinguished," Quentin refuses, or at
least lacks the capacity, to adknowledge that both his and
Caddy's entries into the world of sexuality are part of the
natural order of things, part of the natural flux of time.[29]
Caddy has nothing in her of Marietta's cold reluctance to
acknowledge that change, symbolized specifically in both works
through sexual initiation, is as necessary as the inevitable
passage of the seasons. And while Caddy, like Marietta, im-
merses herself in water, Caddy's stream signifies her fer-
tility, her capacity for love, rather than her narcissism.
The scene at the pool, where Marietta admires her reflection
is more accurately a precursor of Quentin's staring down into
the Charles River, bent on stasis and self-destruction, in-
sisting on a denial of life rather than acceptance of change.

A final piece of Faulkner's apprenticeship must be mentioned as a significant precursor to *The Sound and the Fury*.
Originally composed for Margaret Brown, Faulkner later made
a copy of a little fable he entitled *The Wishing Tree* for his
future wife's daughter by her first marriage.[30] Several commentators have cited a number of details emphasized in *The
Wishing Tree*, including the wisteria-scented breezes, grey
mists, the use of a flat-iron, a clock, a rolling pin, and
a shoe, as parallels to *The Sound and the Fury*.[31] But it is
with Dulcie's descent down a ladder from her bedroom window
that we move closer to the double image at the heart of the
later novel. In the novel, Caddy climbs up a tree to peer
into Damuddy's window and thus begins metaphorically her

journey toward knowledge and experience. Her ascent is later
reflected in the descent of her daughter Quentin down a pear
tree. The image of Caddy climbing up the tree was frequently
cited by Faulkner as the inception of the short story which
grew into the novel.

Caddy's three brothers peer up at her from the ground
below and are soon joined by Dilsey; in *The Wishing Tree* Dulcie
climbs down the ladder assisted by the boy magician Maurice
while her neighbor, George, and her little brother, Dicky,
accompanied by their black nurse, Alice, watch from below.
In the fable, Faulkner not only explores the possibilities
of perception from a child's point of view but plays variations on a theme by differentiating among the children as to
their levels of sensitivity and awareness. Maurice, the leader
of Dulcie's expedition, appears to be the most knowledgeable;
it is he, after all, who controls their magical adventures.
Like Maurice, who shares with Quentin a name with romantic,
chivalric connotations, Quentin is clearly differentiated
from the other children by virtue of his more sophisticated
understanding of the situations in which they are involved,
in both the novel and the closely related short story "That
Evening Sun." Like George, Jason remains oblivious to everything but the gratification of his own desires. His glut-
tony as a child is mirrored in George's wish for a bowl of
strawberries and a chocolate cake, which he eats until he
feels sick. George's stubborn contrariness may also remind
us of the young Jason's bratty behavior. Both wish themselves
home, and in *The Wishing Tree*, at least, Maurice's magical
powers are obliging and whisk George directly out of the
tale. Dulcie's little brother, Dicky, is a baby like Benjy.
His limited vocabulary, pronunciation, and syntactical difficulties suggest that he is around three, approximately the
same age as Benjy.

Still other characters in *The Wishing Tree* foreshadow
their more masterful and extended counterparts in *The Sound
and the Fury*. Alice, for instance, has something in her of
Dilsey without Dilsey's complexity and maturity. Despite her
child-like amazement and strained relationship with her husband, which ally her with Nancy in "That Evening Sun," Alice
is as protective of the children, particularly of Dicky, as
Dilsey is of Benjy. Dilsey will, as a matter of fact, echo
two of Alice's lines: "'You hush yo mouf'" (p. 355)/"'Hush
your mouf'" (TS 33) and "'You vilyun'" (p. 395)/"'You triflin'
vilyun'" (TS 35). The jaybirds of the fourth section of the
novel that "came up from nowhere, whirled up on the blast
like gaudy scraps of cloth or paper" (p. 331) cannot but recall that huge jaybird which "whirled about them" (TS 53) in

The Wishing Tree, although the image also appears in Faulkner's
poetry. Alice even protests Maurice's giving a whip to Dicky
to use on the pony that pulls their cart. Dilsey's response
to Luster's whip, as he prepares to take Benjy for a ride in
the carriage in the closing pages of the novel, is similar,
although, unlike Alice, she does not relent.

Other details suggest the close relationship of the two
works, including the importance of ponies and the birthday motif
which look forward to the Benjy section of the novel where
both come to figure so prominently by the typescript stage.[32]
Suffice it to say that *The Wishing Tree* seems very close indeed to what Faulkner described as the kernel of *The Sound
and the Fury*, minus that one ingredient which perhaps gave
Faulkner the tremendous creative spurt with which to begin it:

> [*The Sound and the Fury*] began as a short story, it was
> a story without plot, of some children being sent away
> from the house during the grandmother's funeral. They
> were too young to be told what was going on and they
> saw things only incidentally to the childish games they
> were playing ... then the idea struck me to see how much
> more I could have got out of the idea of the blind, self-
> centeredness of innocence, typified by children, if one
> of those children had been truly innocent, that is, an
> idiot. So the idiot was born....[33]

The carpenter would find other scraps of material scattered
around his workshop. The poetry would contribute many images,
even specific lines, such as "Nazarene and Roman and Virginian"
from Poem XLII of *A Green Bough*, although this line would
be deleted from the typescript of the novel. Faulkner would
turn to "Father Abraham" and reuse passages describing the
pain from Armstid's broken leg to depict Quentin's in similar
circumstances as well as to characterize Louis Hatcher's
voice.[34] For the opening description of Quentin's room at
Harvard Faulkner would turn to a three-page untitled manuscript fragment about two characters named Brad and Jack,
which is now located with the *Soldiers' Pay* typescript and
other related materials pertaining to that novel.[35] But whatever materials from his apprenticeship he may have drawn on,
Faulkner's later remarks about the novel make clear--in retro-
spect, at least--that the novel's creative impetus began with
"perhaps the only thing in literature which would ever move
me very much: Caddy climbing the pear tree to look in the
window at her grandmother's funeral while Quentin and Jason
and Benjy and the negroes looked up at the muddy seat of her
drawers."[36] Echoing Heathcliff's reference to Catherine Earn-
shaw in *Wuthering Heights*, Caddy was for Faulkner "the beauti-

ful one, she was my heart's darling. That's what I wrote the
book about and I used the tools which seemed to me the proper
tools to try to tell, try to draw the picture of Caddy."[37]
Thus, *The Sound and the Fury* is the bringing to life of an
image that had, in various forms--from the young tree-like
girls of the poetry to Marietta to Juliet Bunden, to Jo-Addie
to Doris to Dulcie--intrigued Faulkner almost from the beginning of his career as a writer.

    This is not to say that the path to *The Sound and the
Fury* is an orderly, logical sequence of development, for such
is clearly not the case. Nothing by Faulkner, published or
unpublished, before this novel equals it in sheer creative
brilliance nor foretells the arrival of this work. Rather,
the ten years preceding its writing saw tentative explorations
made by the maturing writer--explorations of character,
imagery, structure, theme, and tone--strikings out in different directions with varying degrees of success but with no
lesson lost on the struggling craftsman. Then, finally, when
he was ready, Faulkner closed that door between himself and
the world and wrote the first of his great novels.

                                II

    Given the frequency and consistency of statements made
later in his career, it seems virtually certain that the
novel did originate as a short story: it "began as a short
story, it was a story without plot, of some children being
sent away from the house during the grandmother's funeral."[38]
Possibly that story was originally conceived in connection
with "a collection of short stories of my townspeople" about
which Faulkner wrote Horace Liveright on February 18, 1927.[39]
However, Carvel Collins has argued for an even earlier composition date on the strength of testimony from a "friend"
of Faulkner's who in Paris in 1925 read a work in progress
that dealt with a girl and her brothers. Although he vigorously defends the accuracy and reliability of this friend's
memory, Collins does not identify him. While it is possible
that what Collins alludes to is "Elmer," or a fragment, or
a short story later incorporated into the novel, or even an
early version of "That Evening Sun," Faulkner's own comments
do not seem to support such an early date for the beginning
composition of the novel proper.[40]

    For example, in the 1932 introduction for the Modern
Library reissue of *Sanctuary*, Faulkner wrote that "with one
novel completed [*Flags in the Dust*] and consistently refused
for two years, I had just written my guts into *The Sound and*

the Fury though I was not aware until the book was published that I had done so, because I had done it for pleasure."[41] In interviews Faulkner's statements regarding the time it took him to write the novel, though they vary somewhat, most frequently cite six months: "I wrote *As I Lay Dying* in six weeks, *The Sound and the Fury* in six months...."[42] In a letter to Horace Liveright written in mid- or late February 1928, Faulkner states that he had "gotten no further forward with another novel as yet, having put aside the one I had in mind to do some short stories."[43] He is presumably referring to the "Father Abraham" novel about the Snopes family which he worked on sporadically beginning in late 1926 or early 1927. But by early March 1928, Faulkner was able to write Liveright that he had "got going on a novel, which, if I continue as I am going now, I will finish within eight weeks."[44] While he was in New York City in the fall of 1928, Faulkner wrote Alabama McLean that Harcourt, Brace was bringing out a book (*Sartoris*, the cut version of *Flags in the Dust*) in February and "Also another one, the damndest book I ever read. I dont believe anyone will publish it for 10 years."[45]

Commentators have occasionally suggested that the manuscript of the novel's first section, entitled "Twilight," may have been the seminal short story to which Faulkner referred. However, given its complexity and length, this claim seems highly unlikely; but an earlier version of it may well have been completed as a story, and may even have been intended for the collection of stories about Faulkner's townspeople projected in 1927. Another possible precursor to the novel is the closely related story "Never Done No Weeping When You Wanted to Laugh," an unpublished manuscript that later became "That Evening Sun Go Down" and finally "That Evening Sun."[46] Although this story focuses on the Compson children, it does not contain the image of the little girl climbing up a tree to peer into the window of her grandmother's funeral which Faulkner originally envisioned as requiring a ten-page treatment and which he cited as constituting the starting point of the novel--an image which does figure prominently in "Twilight."[47] We can only speculate which story, "Twilight" or "Never Done No Weeping When You Wanted to Laugh," came first.

The general point, then, is that we must be extremely cautious in assuming that "Twilight" and "Never Done No Weeping" were composed sequentially or that the latter story necessarily precedes the novel, for available evidence is simply not conclusive as to order or date of composition. However, an examination of the paper used for both works is suggestive. The handwriting in both is similar, and the

onionskin paper on which "Never Done No Weeping" is written
is similar to the paper used--not in the Benjy section of the
manuscript of the novel which is entitled "Twilight" and in
the rejected and repositioned manuscript opening of Quentin's
monologue, which are on heavier paper--in the new opening and
the remainder of Quentin's section, excluding the repositioned
pages.

     In light of both Faulkner's later, well-established method
of building novels out of short stories (*The Hamlet* [1940]
and *Go Down, Moses* [1942], for instance) and his ability to
extract a story out of a novel in progress for the more lucrative short story market ("The Bear" out of *Go Down, Moses*,
for example), it is certainly possible that Faulkner turned
to characters brought to life in "Twilight," perhaps after
recognizing the novelistic potential of that material, and
used them in a far less ambitious, more narrowly circumscribed
work in hopes of alleviating increasing financial burdens and
buying time in which to write the novel. Further, the revision
of "Never Done No Weeping" into "That Evening Sun Go Down"
is intriguing in suggesting that it may have played a crucial
role in leading Faulkner to the novel's second narrator,
particularly if the story was composed after "Twilight" and
before Faulkner began over again on the novel's second section
after rejecting its original opening.

     The rejected opening (ultimately positioned as pages 70-
76 in the manuscript; Vintage text 185.20-200.18) consists
of the dramatic confrontation of Quentin and Caddy at the
branch after Caddy loses her virginity to Dalton Ames. It is
dramatic in form, whereas the final opening of the novel's
second section is characterized by an immediate sense of the
presence of the first-person narrator, Quentin. In "Never
Done No Weeping" the events involving Nancy and Jesus are
recounted by Quentin as first-person narrator, but as in the
rejected opening for the novel's second section, his personality
is entirely submerged in the events of the narrative. In "That
Evening Sun Go Down," however, the addition of a narrative
frame, which introduces Quentin as a narrator recounting from
a point in time fifteen years later when he is twenty-four
years old events that took place when he was nine, places
the story in an entirely different context and shifts the
focus of events from Nancy and Jesus to Quentin's perceptions
and reminiscences in which, like the narrator of Sherwood
Anderson's "Death in the Woods," he is attempting to come
to terms with an important childhood incident by assessing
his father's handling of Mrs. Compson and his behavior in
regard to Nancy. It is, then, an intriguing possibility that
the revisions of the short story moved Faulkner away from the

neutral, dramatic presentation of events with which Quentin's monologue began originally and closer to the shift in focus to the sensitive, reflective, brooding personality of Quentin which is so striking in the opening pages of the final version of the manuscript. But this must remain only speculative unless further external evidence turns up to assist in dating these writings more precisely.

In any event, by early March 1928 Faulkner's new novel was well under way. He completed typing the manuscript in New York in October and submitted it to Harrison Smith at Harcourt, Brace, the publisher that accepted *Flags in the Dust* in its condensed form, *Sartoris*. In a letter dated February 15, 1929, Harcourt rejected it, and when Harrison Smith left Harcourt to form a partnership with Jonathan Cape, he took the typescript with him.[48] Faulkner made some extensive revisions in the novel's second section, withdrawing forty-one pages of the typescript and substituting forty-one rewritten pages in their place, presumably before copy editing was begun on the typescript. A contract was executed on February 18, 1929. Ben Wasson copy edited the typescript, perhaps with the assistance of another editor at Cape & Smith.[49] Robert Ballou designed the book, and it was set in type.[50] When Faulkner read galley proofs in Pascagoula, Mississippi, in July 1929, he rejected a number of changes made by Wasson and made a number of additional changes himself. Published on October 7, 1929, a small printing of only 1,789 copies was sufficient until the notoriety of *Sanctuary* led to a second printing of 518 copies in February 1931; a third printing of 1,000 copies from a copy of the second impression was made by offset lithography the following November.[51]

On completion of the novel, the "belly full of writing" that Faulkner had experienced as a result of his failure to place *Flags in the Dust* yielded to quite different emotions. He would variously refer to the process of writing *The Sound and the Fury* with such favorable nouns as "pleasure," "joy," "anticipation," "ecstasy," "surprise." Such exuberance would be displayed for no other novel. Yet, paradoxically, Faulkner would affirm later that this novel "was the one that I anguished the most over, that I worked the hardest at, that even when I knew I couldn't bring it off, I still worked at it."[52] Perhaps because he began the novel with no "plan"[53] other than the image of a tragic little girl climbing a tree, the first and second sections of the manuscript especially show the author hard at work. As James B. Meriwether has noted, "[o]ne or more complete drafts, or none; extensive working notes or none, may have preceded the extant manuscript but have not been preserved. For this particular novel, we might

well suppose such measures a necessity; for this particular
novelist, we may well assume that they were not."[54] Given the
complexity of the novel, the manuscript is remarkably close
to the published novel. However, its first two sections display
considerable revision, above and beyond the expected verbal
polishing that occurs between manuscript and typescript and
again between typescript and the first edition, including
frequent cancellations and marginal additions.

Of the considerable number of manuscript revisions, certainly the most interesting involves the rejected opening of
Quentin's monologue. In fact, how to open Quentin's monologue
presented Faulkner with perhaps the most difficult organizational task wrestled with in the course of this enormously complex novel. In the original manuscript, the second section
opened with a six-page confrontation between Quentin and Caddy
at the branch concerning Dalton Ames, Caddy's first lover. At
the top of the first of these pages, this episode bears the
heading "June 2, 1910." According to deleted page numbers this
episode occupied three different positions (MS 34-40; 43-49;
44-50) before coming to rest toward the end of the monologue
(MS 70-76; Vintage text 185.20-200.18) where it was placed with
drastic alterations in punctuation but very little substantive
revision. However, almost three additional pages (Vintage text
200.19-203.11) were added to the original version.

That these pages originally opened Quentin's monologue
is evinced not only by their heading but because the paper
matches that of Benjy's section and is far heavier than the
rest of the paper used for Quentin's monologue. This suggests
that the particular scene was probably composed about the
same time as the novel's first section, or very soon after,
with Faulkner moving forward at high creative speed to reveal
the actual events of the evening that upset Benjy so dread-
fully in the closing pages of his monologue. After completing
the Dalton Ames-Caddy-Quentin confrontation scene, Faulkner
may have set aside the novel and then returned to it, perhaps
after rereading the first section. Resuming work on the novel's
second section on different paper, Faulkner evidently revised
his plan as to how to proceed since the scene was relocated
several times before coming to rest toward the end of the
monologue.

The rejected opening grew directly out of Benjy's monologue and suggests that it was composed in the same burst
of creative energy, with the same emotional fervor, that led
to the composition of the novel's first section. Toward the
end of his monologue, in two separate flashbacks, Benjy remembers Caddy's coming in to supper from outside (pp. 84,
85). When he sees her, Benjy pulls at her dress, remembering

that "we went to the bathroom" (p. 85). With these events
Quentin's monologue originally opened:

> one minute she was standing there the next he was
> yelling and pulling at her dress they went into the hall
> and up the stairs yelling and shoving at her up the
> stairs to the bathroom door and stopped her back against
> the door and her arm across her face yelling and trying
> to shove her into the bathroom when she came in to
> supper (p. 185)

Within the context of Benjy's monologue alone, the two flashbacks Benjy makes to these events are, at best, cryptic. Yet
they are placed strategically toward the end of the novel's
first section, unexplained, mysterious, provocative, and the
monologue winds down with an intermingling from past and
present of the activities of eating supper and being put to
bed. Thus it seems clear that Faulkner originally intended
to begin Quentin's monologue by clarifying those two incomplete,
brief fragments by Benjy which provoke such an outburst from
him, thereby expanding our understanding of events by eluci-
dating immediately Caddy's behavior on that evening through
Quentin and his more detailed knowledge and more sophisticated
inferences about his sister's activities.

However, the events in this scene gave Faulkner pause.
In this episode Quentin attempts to kill Caddy and then himself. Unsuccessful, he goes so far as to hold a knife to her
throat before—pitifully, helplessly—dropping the knife.
This desperate effort and Quentin's anguished failure have
great dramatic impact, but by opening his monologue with these
tortured and tormented actions, Faulkner must actually back-
track to offer much more detailed explanation for such extraordinary behavior. Only Quentin's two references to the
evening of Damuddy's funeral during his confrontation with
Caddy ("do you remember the day damuddy died when you sat
down in the water in your drawers" [p. 188] and "Caddy do
you remember how Dilsey fussed at you because your drawers
were muddy" [p. 189]) seem to provide some meagre insight
into Quentin's state of mind by recalling his childhood
slapping of his sister when she attempted to remove her dress
as well as the image of her muddied undergarments. That Caddy
has violated Quentin's early-developed sense of maidenly
virtue and modesty seems clear, but this oversimplification
of Quentin's complex character undoubtedly was one of the
reasons that Faulkner postponed the scene until considerably
more amplification of Quentin's character could occur. Thus
Faulkner could also preserve the climactic drama of the confrontation by revealing it late in the monologue; by position-
ing it early he must have been aware that the rest of the
monologue could not help seeming anticlimactic.

Structurally, additional elements seem likely to have prompted the postponement of this key scene. Along the lines of Joyce's *Ulysses*, Benjy's monologue had traced a character's behavior and thought from morning to evening during the course of one apparently but not in actuality typical day in his life. The repetition of a similar pattern could not only greatly expand characterization possibilities for Quentin but could also provide a series of reflections and refractions of the events narrated by Benjy, thereby enhancing the work's novelistic unity in spite of its apparently so disparate narrators and narrative voices. Further, by withholding information about Quentin's first, unsuccessful suicide attempt until the reader can learn that June 2, 1910, is Quentin's last day and that the activities he pursues on that day are linked to the suicide which he commits later that evening, Faulkner creates a dramatic convergence of the past and present which Quentin finds increasingly difficult to separate.

Thus Faulkner recreated the structural pattern observed in Benjy's monologue. That is, Quentin's narrative no longer begins in medias res, but, like Benjy's and Jason's, it begins at the beginning, in the morning of a special day whose particular events will be presented in chronological sequence. Appropriately, Quentin will recall in flashback the twilight confrontation with Caddy and Ames on the evening of his last day on earth. Possibly after he wrestled with organizational strategy and decided finally to imitate the morning-afternoon-evening pattern of the novel's first section, the novel's last two sections presented Faulkner with fewer structural problems as well as with already established characters, themes, and conflict. With their increasingly lucid styles, in manuscript these two sections are even closer to the published text than are Benjy's and Quentin's monologues and display no major recasting or repositioning of material.

Nevertheless, after the completion of Jason's monologue, work on the novel may have been interrupted for approximately a month before Faulkner began the final section:

> So I wrote Quentin's and Jason's sections, trying to clarify Benjy's. But I saw that I was merely temporising; That I should have to get completely out of the book. I realised that there would be compensations, that in a sense I could then give a final turn to the screw and extract some ultimate distillation. Yet it took me better than a month to take pen and write *The day dawned bleak and chill* before I did so.[55]

Ironically, this distancing produces an emotional decrescendo, and while the novel's fourth section contains some of the most

effective, most mature, and most tightly controlled writing
in the entire novel, it has received far less than its critical
due.

Similar accounts of the novel's having taken shape in
"quarters" were often repeated in interviews late in Faulkner's
career:

> When I'd finished [with Benjy's monologue] I had a
> quarter of the book written, but it still wasn't all.
> It still wasn't enough. So then Quentin told the story
> as he saw it and it still wasn't enough. Then Jason
> told the story and it still wasn't enough. Then I tried
> to tell the story and it still was not enough.[56]

There is considerable charm to Faulkner's description of his
wish to tell the same story four different times and his sense
of having failed each time to achieve the desired end. But
this litany must be regarded with a certain amount of skepticism. For one thing, none of the "quarters" is an exact
recapitulation of the same story, although that may have been
what Faulkner originally intended. (Might this have been the
source of his sense of having failed to tell "enough"?) While
there are a number of intersecting events that link each of
the various "quarters" with the others, the narrative thrust
forward is a strong one that moves through Caddy's childhood,
depicted largely in Benjy's monologue; her adolescence,
emphasized in Quentin's section; and various events of her
adulthood, especially as they concern her daughter, as depicted
in the novel's third and fourth sections, which simultaneously increase their focus on Jason and his reenactment with his
niece of his brother Quentin's conflict with Caddy. But as
Michael Millgate has pointed out, Faulkner's account is
extremely important in that it suggests that the novel was
"evolved under creative pressure, not conceived beforehand."[57]
Nowhere is it more evident than in the novel's final section
that Faulkner did *not* attempt to tell the *same* "story" four
times albeit from four different vantage points. The brilliant
technical achievements in the first three sections of the
novel, as well as their very diversity, help to obscure the
very traditional, chronologically based, horizontal plot line
which emerges with greatest clarity in the fourth section.

III

Faulkner surely must have realized well before completing
what came to be the novel's first section that the restrictions of Benjy's idiocy and his resultant limited knowledge

of events would ultimately render him inadequate to tell this
particular tale of sound and fury. Nevertheless, when confronted
with the difficulties of Quentin's monologue, those of Benjy's
seem at second glance far less rigorous. Ultimately, the unconventionality of narrative technique in Benjy's monologue
is neither chaotic nor absurd. Quite the contrary, it is
governed by rigid, although terribly literal, rules of logic.
Often beyond his control and understanding, a word, a phrase,
or an object triggers Benjy's memory, but these associational
devices are always readily visible. For the unwary, there are
a few quagmires along the way: confusion of names (two Quentins,
two Jasons, two Maurys), or the inadvertent omission of italics
to signal a time transference to a different scene, for example.
Yet despite the apparent fragmentation of Benjy's consciousness, he persistently returns to three major episodes: Damuddy's
funeral when he is around three; the evening his name is
changed from "Maury" to "Benjy" when he is five; the traumatic
evening of Caddy's wedding. Although his memory returns to
each of these scenes at different times throughout his monologue, it is important that the events involved in each of
these major episodes are nevertheless presented sequentially,
albeit in fragmented form.

 Because of his literalness, his very inability to understand and therefore reason and draw conclusions, Benjy is a
remarkably reliable narrator. He reports only what he sees,
not what he thinks: action, not abstraction; fact, not probability; dialogue itself rather than the meaning behind it.
The amount of detail and word-for-word dialogue that Benjy
remembers is astounding, although narrowly restricted to
episodes in which Caddy plays a particularly important role
or in which there is some heightened emotional content. If any
conclusions are to be drawn from Benjy's reports, the reader
must infer them, and although a number of significant gaps
are not filled in until later in the novel, the reader can
predict accurately a remarkable number of occurrences.

 In actuality, however, Quentin's monologue is far more
complex than Benjy's. In style it differs markedly from Benjy's
faithful journalistic recording of every detail. Instead,
Quentin's narrative is more properly a stream-of-consciousness
monologue, much like Eliot's "The Love Song of J. Alfred Prufrock," in which factual details of the present are mingled
with memories of the past and speculations about events and
their significance by a protagonist who is torn and divided
against himself.

 Those very attributes lacking in Benjy which ideally ought
to make Quentin superior as narrator--including his articu-
lateness, his sensitivity, and his intelligence--compound the

complexity of his tautly strung, frenzied stream of consciousness. Despite Quentin's facility with words, his narrative is
as fragmented between past and present as Benjy's, but unlike
Benjy's monologue, the associational devices in Quentin's are
not always clear. Because his intelligence is far more sophisticated than his retarded brother's, Quentin's transitions
and leaps are frequently more subtle and far-ranging than
Benjy's, and hence considerably more difficult to follow.
Unlike Benjy, Quentin is obsessed with emotion rather than
action; he is a subjective interpreter rather than an objective, detached reporter. He draws conclusions freely and as
freely draws on his extensive reading for phrase and allusion
in which to couch these conclusions. The style of his monologue, unlike Benjy's, varies extensively from tightly controlled, dispassionate narrative and descriptive passages
which focus on events in the present to unpunctuated, uncapi-
talized fragments of inner consciousness.

Given the unusual demands of Benjy and Quentin as the
novel's first two narrators, then, it is not surprising to
find that Faulkner revised the manuscript rather extensively
as he typed it, particularly its first two sections. Although
it is not possible within the confines of this essay to do
more than cast a cursory glance at the major revisions,
Faulkner was working toward what Michael Millgate has so
aptly termed "an elaboration and a simplification of his
technique in the opening section of the book."[58] Millgate
was among the first commentators who pointed out the major
substantive changes made in Benjy's monologue: the addition
of the material concerning Benjy's birthday, the cake Dilsey
has made for him, Luster's search for his lost quarter, and
his obsession with visiting the show.[59] All of this material
occurs in the narrative present of the novel and thereby
serves, Millgate notes, "as a kind of motif or signal of
present time in the section and [can] thus assist the reader
in keeping his bearings among the shifting and merging time-
planes."[60] The only other passage of some length added in
typescript in the novel's first section is the discussion
between Mrs. Compson and T.P. about turning the carriage
around (Vintage text 11.06-11.25). This dialogue is evidently
intended to expand the portrait of Mrs. Compson's exaggerated
fearfulness and her pitiable indecisiveness, which are such
potent eroding forces of affection, warmth, and stability in
the family. She is afraid to continue forward; she is afraid
to turn around; she is afraid to hurry.

Millgate has also noted that among the even more extensive
revisions in Quentin's monologue are those which emphasize
the importance of time as a thematic motif and heighten our

sense of Mr. Compson's presence and the weight of his voice
throughout the monologue.[61] This is achieved through the frequent addition of the phrase "Father said." There are substantially more expansions and additions in Quentin's monologue as
well as more shifting of material and extensive rewriting than
in Benjy's. Particularly noteworthy are the stream-of-consciousness passages that are added in typescript and retained
in substantially the same form in the published text.[62] For
instance:

> *Roses. Roses. Mr and Mrs Jason Richmond Compson announce*
> *the marriage of.* Roses. Not virgins like dogwood, milk-
> weed. I said I have committed incest, Father I said.
> Roses. Cunning and serene. If you attend Harvard one
> year, but dont see the boat-race, there should be a re-
> fund. Let Jason have it. Give Jason a year at Harvard.
> (p. 95)

> Like all the bells that ever rang still ringing in the
> long dying light-rays and Jesus and Saint Francis talk-
> ing about his sister. Because if it were just to hell;
> if that were all of it. Finished. If things just finished
> themselves. Nobody else there but her and me. If we
> could just have done something so dreadful that they
> would have fled hell except us. *I have committed incest*
> *I said Father it was I it was not Dalton Ames* And when
> he put Dalton Ames. Dalton Ames. Dalton Ames. When he
> put the pistol in my hand I didn't. That's why I didn't.
> He would be there and she would and I would. Dalton
> Ames. Dalton Ames. Dalton Ames. If we could have just
> done something so dreadful and Father said That's sad
> too, people cannot do anything that dreadful they cannot
> do anything very dreadful at all.... (pp. 97-98)

> Dalton Ames. Dalton Ames. Dalton Shirts. I thought all
> the time they were khaki, army issue khaki, until I saw
> they were of heavy Chinese silk or finest flannel because
> they made his face so brown his eyes so blue. (p. 113)

A number of such passages were evidently added in light of
Faulkner's decision to reject his original opening for Quentin's
monologue, which focused on the Ames-Caddy-Quentin confrontation. With their disjointed, fragmented styles, many of these
passages heighten our sense of Quentin's inner torments and
the conflicts that will result in his decision to commit suicide.

     Another group of passages added after the manuscript was
completed pertain to Quentin's purchase of and subsequent
thoughts about the two flat-irons. Faulkner apparently decided

that stronger signals concerning Quentin's intention to kill
himself at the end of his monologue were necessary to intensify the dramatic tension between the past and present throughout Quentin's stream of consciousness. Typical of such passages
are:

> I saw the hardware store from across the street. I
> didn't know you bought flat-irons by the pound.
>   The clerk said, "These weigh ten pounds." Only they
> were bigger than I thought. So I got two six-pound little
> ones, because they would look like a pair of shoes
> wrapped up. They felt heavy enough together, but I
> thought again how Father had said about the reducto
> absurdum of human experience, thinking how the only
> opportunity I seemed to have for the application of
> Harvard. Maybe by next year; thinking maybe it takes
> two years in school to learn to do that properly. (p.
> 105)

> ... the shadow of the package like two shoes wrapped
> up lying on the water. Niggers say a drowned man's
> shadow was watching for him in the water all the time.
> It twinkled and glinted, like breathing, the float
> slow like breathing too, and debris half submerged,
> healing out to the sea and the caverns and the grottoes
> of the sea. The displacement of water is equal to the
> something of something. Reducto absurdum of all human
> experience, and two six-pound flat-irons weigh more
> than one tailor's goose. What a sinful waste Dilsey
> would say.... (p. 111)

> In three years I can not wear a hat. I could not. Was.
> Will there be hats then since I was not and not Harvard
> then. Where the best of thought Father said clings like
> dead ivy vines upon old dead brick. Not Harvard then.
> Not to me, anyway. Again. Sadder than was. Again.
> Saddest of all. Again. (pp. 117-18)

Yet another group of passages is added to intensify the
portrait of Quentin's paradoxical fascination with and ab-
horrence of sexuality, which clarifies not only his conflict
with Ames and Caddy but elucidates the reasons for his suicide:

> Ah let him alone, Shreve said, if he's got better sense
> than to chase after the little dirty sluts, whose
> business. In the South you are ashamed of being a
> virgin. Boys. Men. They lie about it. Because it means
> less to women, Father said. He said it was men invented
> virginity not women. Father said it's like death: only

a state in which the others are left and I said, But
to believe it doesn't matter and he said, That's what's
so sad about anything: not only virginity, and I said,
Why couldn't it have been me and not her who is unvirgin
and he said, That's why that's sad too; nothing is even
worth the changing of it, and Shreve said if he's got
better sense than to chase after the little dirty sluts
and I said Did you ever have a sister? Did you? Did
you? (p. 96)

It's not not having them. It's never to have had them
then I could say O That That's Chinese I dont know
Chinese. And Father said it's because you are a virgin:
dont you see? Women are never virgins. Purity is a
negative state and therefore contrary to nature. It's
nature is hurting you not Caddy and I said That's just
words and he said So is virginity and I said you dont
know. You cant know and he said Yes. On the instant when
we come to realise that tragedy is second-hand. (p.
143)

Other changes exist, including the drastically rewritten closing paragraphs of the monologue. However, the preponderance
of the major alterations occurs in the first half of Quentin's
section.

By contrast, and not surprisingly, given its less rigorous narrative structure, Jason's monologue exhibits comparatively little revision from manuscript to typescript to published text. Only two major additions exist. The first is
the scene with Jason and Mrs. Compson where she burns the
phony support check she believes is from Caddy (Vintage
text 272.10-273.26). The second is the marvelous little exchange between Jason and Mac (Vintage text 314.01-314.27)
where Jason stubbornly disparages the great Yankees team of
1928 and its star, Babe Ruth. The novel's fourth and closing
section is even closer to the manuscript.

Paradoxically, the typescript is striking in two different
ways. On one hand, this extremely complex novel is remarkably
close to the manuscript, i.e., the bulk of the novel is
present in the manuscript and, collectively, revisions made
in the typescript and in later stages of the production of
the novel are remarkably few given the complicated design
of the novel. On the other hand, there is sufficient rewriting, reorganizing, and adding of material to support Faulkner's claim that he worked carefully with the novel--anguished
over it--as he sorted out various problems in designating
time, revealing character, clarifying plot, heightening
images and themes.

   Important as such concerns are, they were not the only
points that absorbed Faulkner's attention. Perhaps more than
any other of his novels, *The Sound and the Fury* shows Faulkner
grappling with the crucial minutiae of spacing, punctuation,
paragraph indentation, and italicization as he worked toward
the unconventionality of Benjy's and Quentin's monologues.
Again, however, as with the substantive revisions, the third
and fourth sections presented virtually no problems in comparison to the novel's first two monologues. Despite his
efforts, despite his tinkering with these details virtually
until the actual printing of the book, considerable inconsistency and a minor number of demonstrable errors are displayed.
Hence, again, we can speculate that Faulkner's comments about
anguishing over the novel and his sense of having failed to
achieve a desired end--"the most gallant, the most magnificent
failure"[63]--reflect in part his dissatisfaction with the details of its presentation. Meriwether notes that Faulkner's
concern about printing the novel was expressed in a proposal
to Ben Wasson and Harrison Smith that parts of the sections
be printed in inks of different colors.[64] In the absence of
such a possibility, Faulkner used other tools more readily
at his disposal and experimented with them.
   For instance, Faulkner experimented with punctuation
almost to the actual printing of the book.[65] Although the
manuscript is consistent in its use of traditional punctuation except in Quentin's section, where some experimentation
occurs, the typescript is inconsistent in its use of non-
traditional punctuation and contains many passages that are
punctuated conventionally. However, a number of unusual changes
appear (although again not with complete consistency) in the
published book, thus suggesting that perhaps as late as
galleys or page proofs Faulkner was still experimenting,
especially with the intricacies of Benjy's section and the
complexities of utilizing such a character as first-person
narrator, with the end punctuation of direct address and the
punctuation of speaker identification tags when they inter-
rupt direct address. Faulkner eventually evolved a system of
punctuating all spoken discourse in Benjy's monologue with
periods, rather than other kinds of end punctuation, including commas, exclamation points, or question marks, as a technique for establishing the limits of Benjy's comprehension.
Benjy records all spoken discourse literally, without understanding its meaning or differentiating among vocal inflections
and interrogatory, declarative, and imperative sentences.
However, since Faulkner evolved this method of punctuating
unconventionally with periods terminating all spoken discourse
only after completing the typescript, it seems likely that

implementation would have been left to editorial hands, and
thus we may perhaps account for its considerable inconsistency
in the published text.[66] In addition, the typesetter(s), already challenged by a difficult text, and confronted with
others of Faulkner's unusual but generally consistent practices
(omitting apostrophes in words like "dont" and "cant" or
periods after "Mr" and "Mrs") may have followed setting copy
inconsistently and further complicated matters.

Ben Wasson's tampering with the text (presumably copy editing Faulkner's ribbon typescript before it went to the printer)
has been well established.[67] Wasson questioned Faulkner's use
of italics, and although Faulkner vigorously defended it, a
comparison of the manuscript, typescript, and published book
makes clear that he changed italicized passages extensively
and added italics heavily when he read proof. Italics were
used initially to signal what Faulkner called a "transference"
from one point in time to another.[68] They may signal the beginning of a flashback, or they may signal a return from the
past to a different time level, which is frequently but not
always the novel's narrative present (April 1928). On other
occasions, italics are used to indicate "a speech by one person within a speech by another," which led Faulkner to speculate that his "use of italics has been too without definite
plan" but was adopted to perform this last function to avoid
clumsy paragraphs.[69] Wasson suggested that Faulkner use new
breaks--extra spaces--between paragraphs instead of italics,
a suggestion which Faulkner emphatically rejected, although
a printer's sample octavo gathering, including the first
fourteen pages of *The Sound and the Fury*, was printed adopting
Wasson's rather than Faulkner's method.[70] The romanization of
italicized passages, the italicization of roman passages, and
the general addition of new italicized passages are extensive.
Therefore, it is not surprising that in Benjy's monologue in
four instances italics were inadvertently omitted.[71]

Critics have long been aware that additional revision
occurred between the extant carbon typescript and the published
book. The ribbon typescript, which presumably served as setting
copy, the galleys, and the page proofs have apparently not
survived. However, some new light is shed on those revisions
by a forty-one-page ribbon typescript and two leaves of Faulkner's requests for revisions on pages not contained within the
first forty-one. This typescript of irregularly numbered pages
from Quentin's monologue has only recently surfaced, purchased
in November 1975 from J. Periam Danton by the University of
Virginia Library.[72]

We can only speculate as to the timetable of Faulkner's
revision of these forty-one pages. The typescript contains no

printer's marks; thus Faulkner must have decided to make the
revisions after copy editing but before type was set for the
novel's second section. Arriving in New York in late September
1928, Faulkner completed typing the manuscript in Greenwich
Village in October 1928 according to the date on the final
page of the typescript. He returned to Mississippi in December
without having had a definite acceptance from Harcourt, Brace.
In a letter dated February 15, 1929, however, Alfred Harcourt
rejected the novel, which Harrison Smith subsequently took
with him when he entered into partnership with Jonathan Cape.
Copies of the contract for publication were executed on February 18, 1929, and it is unlikely although not impossible that
the typescript was copy-edited much before this date. Galley
proofs were sent to Faulkner in early July 1929, in Pascagoula,
Mississippi, where he was honeymooning. Thus it is probable
that sometime in that four-and-a-half-month period Faulkner
must have revised the Quentin section and substituted forty-
one retyped pages for the pages already at Cape & Smith. These
revisions were probably made before Faulkner's wedding on
June 20, 1929, but it is possible that they were made as early
as December 1928 or January 1929, when Faulkner would presumably have had a good idea that Cape & Smith was going to
publish *The Sound and the Fury* but before February 1929, by
which time he was writing *Sanctuary*.[73] However, whether Faulkner wrote Cape & Smith from Mississippi requesting that the
pages be substituted or whether he made the revisions while
he was in New York in November and December 1928 (although
in light of the above chronology the former seems far more
likely)[74] as well as *when* he made these revisions is impossible
to say with absolute certainty in the absence of further evidence.

Apparently, Faulkner remained dissatisfied with Quentin's
monologue and decided at a relatively late date that it required additional revision. The underlying motivation for
these revisions seems to have been Faulkner's determination
that his use of double or triple spaces to designate shifts
in the narrative time level was not sufficient to guide his
readers through the complexities of Quentin's monologue. Most,
although not all, of the rejected pages employ this spacing
device. In the rewritten pages (whose ribbon copies evidently
were reunited with the original ribbon typescript that served
as setting copy and whose carbons were included in the bound
carbon typescript Faulkner preserved for himself), Faulkner
substituted paragraph indentations and added more italicized
phrases as the vehicle by which greater clarity in designating
the time shifts could be achieved. Considerable stylistic
polishing occurs: tightening for clarity and precision; ex-

panding passages slightly for accuracy; deleting overblown,
overwritten phrases or passages; revising punctuation to make
it more traditional, especially insofar as designating word
groups to facilitate the reader's following Quentin's stream
of consciousness; and intensifying Mr. Compson's presence. The
two pages of additional corrections contain requests for changes
that occur largely at beginnings of pages immediately following rewritten ones where changes became necessary in light
of the revisions. By far the second largest area of concern
in these two sheets is the request to italicize twelve passages
and to delete italics in two others.

IV

The novel was published October 7, 1929. The generally
favorable reviews[75] must have been some compensation for the
anguish of Faulkner's labors as well as confirmation of his
exuberant sense that he had not only learned to read but to
write. If Faulkner would emerge from behind his closed door
as master rather than as apprentice, however, the Compson
story was not yet exhausted. Throughout the remainder of
Faulkner's long career it would remain firmly linked with
demanding, innovative works in which Faulkner continued to
experiment with point of view, from *Absalom, Absalom!* (1936)
to *Go Down, Moses* (1942), where in a typescript of "The Old
People" Quentin Compson is the character who later becomes
Ike McCaslin.

Perhaps the most experimental work of all is the 1946
Compson Appendix which reveals the imaginative fascination
the Compson material continued to hold for Faulkner. In retelling the Compson story, he cast it in yet another narrative
form, provided the family with a rich, sweeping historical
context, and amplified, modified, reassessed, and reinter-
preted the characters, recreating them in the process. The
Appendix became a separate work of fiction rather than the
simple recapitulation of a work written seventeen years
earlier which Faulkner had intended to provide for Malcolm
Cowley's 1946 Viking *Portable Faulkner*.

Thus, it is little wonder that in later years Faulkner
looked backward to *The Sound and the Fury* and called it his
"heart's darling."

NOTES

1. James B. Meriwether, "The Textual History of *The Sound and the Fury*" in *The Merrill Studies in The Sound and the Fury*, comp. James B. Meriwether (Columbus, Ohio: Charles E. Merrill, 1970), p. 5. This important article first brought together much of the information about the publication of the novel and I have drawn on it throughout this essay.

2. *Faulkner in the University: Class Conferences at the University of Virginia 1957-1958*, ed. Frederick L. Gwynn and Joseph L. Blotner (New York: Vintage, 1965), p. 61.

3. *Selected Letters of William Faulkner*, ed. Joseph Blotner (New York: Random House, 1977), p. 39.

4. *Selected Letters*, p. 38. For additional information pertaining to the publication of *Flags in the Dust* see George F. Hayhoe, "William Faulkner's *Flags in the Dust*," *Mississippi Quarterly*, 28 (Summer 1975), 370-86.

5. Hayhoe, "William Faulkner's *Flags in the Dust*," pp. 370-74.

6. James B. Meriwether, ed., "An Introduction to *The Sound and the Fury*," *Mississippi Quarterly*, 26 (Summer 1973), 412-13.

7. "Introduction" to the Modern Library issue of *Sanctuary* (1932), in *Essays, Speeches and Public Letters*, ed. James B. Meriwether (New York: Random House, 1965), p. 177.

8. *Selected Letters*, p. 236.

9. "An Introduction to *The Sound and the Fury*," p. 414.

10. *Selected Letters*, p. 43.

11. See "The Preface to *The Sound and the Fury*" by Maurice Coindreau in *The Time of William Faulkner: A French View of Modern American Fiction*, ed. and trans. George M. Reeves (Columbia: University of South Carolina Press, 1971), p. 49.

12. Interview with Jean Stein vanden Heuvel in 1956 in *Lion in the Garden: Interviews with William Faulkner, 1926-1962*, ed. James B. Meriwether and Michael Millgate (New York: Random House, 1968), p. 239.

13. In *Faulkner in the University*, p. 103, Faulkner commented that "the writer has three sources, imagination, observation, and experience ... he uses his material from the three sources as the carpenter reaches into his lumber room and finds a board that fits that particular corner he's building."

14. James B. Meriwether, ed., "An Introduction for *The Sound and the Fury*," *Southern Review*, N.S. 8 (Autumn 1972), 708. For a fuller discussion of the significance of this statement see André Bleikasten, *The Most Splendid Failure: Faulkner's The Sound and the Fury* (Bloomington: Indiana University Press, 1976), pp. 44-47.

15. The best treatment to date of the relationships of Faulkner's first three novels to his fourth is in Bleikasten, *The Most Splendid Failure*, pp. 3-42.

16. For an expanded discussion of the significance of key works from Faulkner's apprenticeship to the novel, see Gail M. Morrison, "William Faulkner's *The Sound and the Fury*: A Critical and Textual Study," Diss. University of South Carolina, 1980, pp. 1-64.

17. These sketches have until recently been most readily available in Carvel Collins, *New Orleans Sketches* (New York: Random House, 1968). However, a soon-to-be-published University of South Carolina dissertation by Leland H. Cox, Jr., "Sinbad in New Orleans: Early Short Fiction by William Faulkner--An Annotated Edition" (1976), should be consulted for its detailed introduction as well as for its annotations. Both Collins and Cox point out similarities among the works under discussion here.

18. Collins, *New Orleans Sketches*, p. 47.

19. "The Priest," ed. James B. Meriwether, *Mississippi Quarterly*, 30 (Summer 1976), 445-50.

20. William Faulkner, "Adolescence" in *Uncollected Stories*, ed. Joseph Blotner (New York: Random House, 1979), p. 460. In his biography, *Faulkner: A Biography*, 2 vols. (New York: Random House, 1974), Joseph Blotner provides a plot summary of this sketch and states that it "may have been written" around 1922 (pp. 333-34). Michael Millgate in *The Achievement of William Faulkner* (New York: Vintage, 1971) discusses briefly the relationship of "Adolescence" to "Elmer" and *As I Lay Dying* (pp. 11 and 12).

21. "Adolescence," p. 472.

22. William Faulkner, *The Sound and the Fury* (New York: Vintage, 1963), pp. 382, 384. Subsequent quotations from the novel will be indicated parenthetically in the text.

23. Blotner states that Faulkner remembered writing "The Devil Beats His Wife" shortly after his return from Europe in December 1925 (I, 491). Although Faulkner's memory for dates was not always accurate, he did remember sequences of

events accurately. It is interesting to note that the first
page is in the form of dialogue in a play and thus indicates
Faulkner's early interest in a form later used in *Requiem for
a Nun* (New York: Random House, 1951). This fragment is located
in the William Faulkner Foundation Collection of the University
of Virginia Library.

24. "Nympholepsy," ed. James B. Meriwether, *Mississippi
Quarterly*, 26 (Summer 1973), 403-9.

25. This story was submitted for publication to Bennett
Cerf at Random House. For a thorough discussion of the Elmer
materials, see Thomas McHaney, "The Elmer Papers: Faulkner's
Comic Portraits of the Artist," *Mississippi Quarterly*, 26
(Summer 1973), 281-311.

26. See, for instance, Lewis P. Simpson, "Faulkner and
the Legend of the Artist" in *Faulkner: Fifty Years After the
Marble Faun*, ed. George H. Wolfe (University: University of
Alabama Press, 1976), and Jackson J. Benson, "Quentin Compson:
Self Portrait of a Young Artist's Emotions," *Twentieth Century
Literature*, 17 (July 1971), 143-59.

27. "Elmer," p. 5. This typescript is in the William
Faulkner Foundation Collection of the Alderman Library of the
University of Virginia.

28. For a more detailed discussion of the relationship
of *Mayday* to *The Sound and the Fury*, see Gail M. Morrison,
"'Time, Tide, and Twilight': *Mayday* and Faulkner's Quest
Toward *The Sound and the Fury*," *Mississippi Quarterly*, 31
(Summer 1978), 337-57.

29. William Faulkner, *The Marionettes: A Play in One Act*
([Charlottesville:] The Bibliographical Society of the University of Virginia and the University Press of Virginia,
1975), pp. 11 and 12. See also Noel Polk, "Introduction" to
The Marionettes. Charlottesville: The Bibliographical Society
of the University of Virginia and The University Press of
Virginia, 1977 for discussion of the structural devices experimented with in this work.

30. Although this work has been published (New York: Random House, 1967), I have quoted from the seventy-one-page
bound manuscript in the Alderman Library at the University
of Virginia since the published text contains a number of
silent emendations. These will be indicated parenthetically
in the text. Blotner incorrectly states that Faulkner initially composed *The Wishing Tree* for Victoria (I, 1718-19);
however, he cites a letter from Faulkner to Harold Ober
(February 4, 1959) in which Faulkner stated that he "invented
this story for Mrs Brown's daughter, about ten at the time,

who was dying of cancer" (II, 1718-19; *Selected Letters*, p. 421). Although actual dates of the gift giving may have been such that Victoria received her copy before Margaret did, references in the typescript inscribed to Margaret to Sir Galwyn and *Mayday* (which do not appear in Victoria's copy) suggest that Margaret's is the earlier of the two typescripts.

31. See Boyd Davis, "Caddy Compson's Eden," *Mississippi Quarterly*, 30 (Summer 1977), 381-94.

32. See Morrison, "William Faulkner's *The Sound and the Fury*: A Critical and Textual Study," pp. 47-56, for a more extended discussion of the parallels between the novel and the fable.

33. *Lion in the Garden*, p. 146.

34. The "Father Abraham" manuscript is in the Arents Collection of the New York Public Library.

35. This fragment is in the Berg Collection of the New York Public Library.

36. "An Introduction for *The Sound and the Fury*," p. 710.

37. *Faulkner in the University*, p. 6. Heathcliff calls Cathy his "heart's darling" in Brontë, *Wuthering Heights* (1847; rpt. New York: Modern Library, 1926), p. 33.

38. *Lion in the Garden*, p. 146.

39. *Selected Letters*, p. 34.

40. The claims for a 1925 date are advanced in Carvel Collins, "Faulkner's *Mayday*" in *Mayday* ([South Bend, Ind.:] University of Notre Dame Press, 1977), p. 19. This afterword has become the "Introduction" (and is slightly expanded) in the trade edition (South Bend, Ind.: University of Notre Dame Press, 1980), pp. 23-26.

41. "Introduction" to the Modern Library issue of *Sanctuary* (1932), in *Essays, Speeches and Public Letters*, pp. 176-77.

42. *Lion in the Garden*, p. 55.

43. *Selected Letters*, p. 39.

44. *Selected Letters*, p. 40.

45. *Selected Letters*, p. 41.

46. The manuscript is located in the Beinecke Library at Yale University. "That Evening Sun Go Down" was published in *American Mercury*, 22 (March 1931), and revised for inclu-

sion in *Collected Stories* (New York: Random House, 1950) as "That Evening Sun."

47. Blotner, I, 566-67. Blotner equates this image with the funeral of Faulkner's grandmother, also called Damuddy, on June 2, 1907.

48. *Selected Letters*, p. 43; Blotner, I, 602-3; Meriwether, "The Textual History of *The Sound and the Fury*," pp. 8-9.

49. See Meriwether, "The Textual History of *The Sound and the Fury*," pp. 9-15 for details pertaining to Wasson's copy editing.

50. *The Making of William Faulkner's Books 1929-1937: An Interview with Evelyn Harter Glick*, ed. James B. Meriwether (Columbia: Southern Studies Program, University of South Carolina, 1979), p. 4. Mrs. Glick was in charge of production and design at Cape & Smith and notes that "I came in when *The Sound and the Fury* was already in the works. Bob Ballou had planned it, and I carried through on it. Then I went on to the others. *As I Lay Dying* was my first. But Bob had done the whole job on *The Sound and the Fury*."

51. Meriwether, "The Textual History of *The Sound and the Fury*," p. 13.

52. *Faulkner in the University*, p. 61.

53. "An Introduction for *The Sound and the Fury*," p. 710.

54. Meriwether, "The Textual History of *The Sound and the Fury*," p. 6. The only "notes" that have been preserved are a sheet entitled "Twilight" which lists birth, death, and marriage dates for many of the novel's characters, some of which do not conform to internal evidence provided within the novel. Blotner (I, 572) has reproduced these notes.

55. "An Introduction to *The Sound and the Fury*," p. 415.

56. *Lion in the Garden*, p. 222. See also pp. 147 and 245.

57. Millgate, *The Achievement of William Faulkner*, p. 90.

58. Millgate, *The Achievement of William Faulkner*, p. 92.

59. Passages from the published text such as 17.19-17.24; 18.27-19.15; 23.12-23.13; 60.02-61.08; 73.08-73.13 are among the many added in typescript.

60. Millgate, *The Achievement of William Faulkner*, p. 93.

61. Millgate, *The Achievement of William Faulkner*, p. 95.

62. I am quoting from the published text here, but obviously these passages do not occur verbatim in the typescript, although they are very close indeed.

63. *Faulkner in the University*, p. 61.

64. Meriwether, "The Textual History of *The Sound and the Fury*," pp. 9-10.

65. See Morrison, "William Faulkner's *The Sound and the Fury*: A Critical and Textual Study" for more detailed discussion of the textual collation between typescript and first edition.

66. See Morrison, "William Faulkner's *The Sound and the Fury*: A Critical and Textual Study," pp. 706-43, for my recommendations to emend the first edition.

67. See Meriwether, "The Textual History of *The Sound and the Fury*," pp. 8-9; Blotner, I, 626-67; *Selected Letters*, pp. 44-46.

68. *Selected Letters*, p. 44.

69. *Selected Letters*, p. 45.

70. See Meriwether, "The Textual History of *The Sound and the Fury*," p. 14, for a reprinting of one of these sample pages.

71. See *The Sound and the Fury*, published text, 40.13-40.15; 46.14-46.15; 52.03-52.05; 53.16-53.17, and Morrison, "William Faulkner's *The Sound and the Fury*: A Critical and Textual Study," pp. 736-37.

72. I am grateful to Joan St. C. Crane, Curator of American Literature Collections at the University of Virginia Library, for first drawing it to my attention. Mr. Danton began collecting Faulkner materials in 1930-33 and believes that it was during this time that he acquired the typescript pages from a book dealer. In a telephone interview on June 23, 1980, Ben Wasson expressed considerable surprise at my explanation of these pages, and was quite emphatic that he had not been involved. He suggested that Faulkner may have worked with Lenore Marshall, and stated that he had not known Mr. Danton.

73. Blotner, I, 598, 602-4, 626.

74. Also, Faulkner was evidently going through the carbon typescript in his possession and making corrections.

75. For a summary of the reviews, see O.B. Emerson, "William Faulkner's Literary Reputation," Diss. Vanderbilt University, 1962, pp. 15-38, and Blotner, I, 632-33.

A RHETORIC FOR BENJY

L. Moffitt Cecil

When William Faulkner decided to filter Section I of *The Sound and the Fury* through the consciousness of Benjy Compson, he took upon himself as author the extraordinary task of improvising a language suitable to a mute, an idiot. The shape and size of his assignment in this regard are brought into focus when one considers the problem of language which confronts any author who undertakes a first person narrative. Mark Twain's *The Adventures of Huckleberry Finn* offers a brilliant example. Twain's task, one can see, was to put into Huck's mouth words, speech patterns, images, and ideas which would be consistently appropriate to a pre-adolescent boy like Huck, who lived in a Missouri river-town during the late 1840's. Huck's vernacular language would have to be simple, natural, predominantly concrete. Besides, it would have to be literary enough, that is, flexible and subtle enough, to convey the complex meanings of the novel. How well Mark Twain fulfilled these diverse demands is not of moment here. What is important is the fact that the dimensions of his language problems are characteristic and clear. The resources upon which he could draw to help him solve them are obvious, too. As a pre-adolescent boy Sam Clemens had lived in a Missouri river-town in the late 1840's. He could depend confidently upon memories of his own boyhood, not only to supply suitable incidents for his narrative, but also to validate the vernacular language in which his story would be told.

By comparison, Faulkner's problems with Benjy were formidable. Whereas Huck is intelligent, trustful, charmingly loquacious, Benjy, the idiot, is mute. Thus the traditional first person point of view was closed to Faulkner, who had to resort to the more modern, more highly specialized perspective of the interior monologue. In theory it is all one to the omniscient author whether he monitor the stream of

From Southern Literary Journal, *3 (Fall 1970), 32-46. Reprinted by permission.*

consciousness of an idiot or a genius, a mute or a spellbinder.
So there is at least a technical plausibility in making Benjy
a center of revelation in the novel.

But the problem of language remains. Though it is understood that an interior monologue is not actually spoken, but
instead is thought or experienced by a persona; and though
it is conceded that the omniscient author, as monitor, reports
to the reader the flux of images and ideas which transpire;
still, dramatic integrity demands that both the content of
the monologue and the language in which it is recorded be
peculiarly and consistently appropriate to that persona whose
consciousness is being exposed. The author is merely the
medium, the transcriber, who assists in the communicative
process; and the freely ruminating persona becomes in fact
a first person narrator, though once removed. Thus we may
properly speak of Benjy, Quentin, and Jason as narrators in
The Sound and the Fury. Faulkner was notably successful in
distinguishing these three Compson brothers by attributing
to each an appropriate manner of speaking or manner of thinking. In fashioning Quentin's and Jason's "language" his task
was essentially the same as Mark Twain's had been in fashioning Huck's. But dealing with Benjy was something special.

Had thirty-three-year-old Benjy, though mute, possessed
an average mentality, it would have required but a minor
authorial miracle on Faulkner's part to discover a voice for
him. The device of the interior monologue, which by-passes
the spoken word and purports to set up communication directly
with the uncharted and mysterious consciousness, opens the
necessary channel. The characteristics of the "speech" of
such a Benjy would have been assured. It is plausible to
assume that the consciousnesses of intelligent persons operate
in comparable ways. This hypothetically intelligent Benjy's
"speech," then, would not have differed radically from that
of his two brothers.

It is the fact of Benjy's idiocy which compounded Faulkner's problems and demanded that he effect the major authorial
miracle of causing not only a mute to "speak," but a blither-
ing idiot to narrate the first section of *The Sound and the
Fury*. To accomplish these ends, Faulkner had to invent a
language which would both sustain the illusion of Benjy's
mental deficiencies and serve as a dependable verbal medium
for the transmission of good sense. He could not, as Mark
Twain had done in the case of Huck Finn, depend upon his own
memory of personal experience to guide him in this undertak-
ing. He had to rely finally upon his own creative imagination,
his inventive faculty. "I was trying," he explained later,
"to tell this story as it seemed to me that idiot child saw
it."[1]

Ironically, it can be said of Benjy Compson, perhaps more
truthfully than of other characters in fiction, that he will
be known by his "speech." For Benjy's appearance and his characteristic idiotic behavior are effective barriers to a knowledge of his true personality. Having become acquainted with
him through his monologue in Section I, having become convinced of his innocence, his helplessness, his pitifulness, a
reader becomes justly indignant at Jason's contemptuous reference to Benjy as the "Great American Gelding." And one is
hardly prepared for the grossness of Faulkner's thumbnail
portrait in Section IV, the first objective view a reader gets
of Benjy:

> ... and Luster entered, followed by a big man who appeared
> to have been shaped of some substance whose particles
> would not or did not cohere to one another or to the
> frame which supported it. His skin was dead looking and
> hairless; dropsical too, he moved with a shambling gait
> like a trained bear. His hair was pale and fine. It had
> been brushed smoothly down upon his brow like that of
> children in daguerrotypes. His eyes were clear, of the
> pale sweet blue of cornflowers, his thick mouth hung
> open, drooling a little.[2]

Only the clear eyes "of the pale sweet blue of cornflowers"
give a hint of the hopelessly encumbered sensibility and the
guileless conscience which languish within.

This paper is a study of the language of the Benjy section
in *The Sound and the Fury*. Benjy's "speech" affords the surest
evidence we have of the kind of person he is. Not only does
it allow us to know something of his otherwise hopelessly
hidden inner life, but it reveals, through its eccentricities
as language, the attributes, sensory, mental, and moral, with
which Faulkner as author endowed his creature. Benjy's "speech"
tells us a great deal about Faulkner, too; it testifies to his
remarkable virtuosity as a writer of fiction.

In reading Benjy's monologue one soon discovers the fact
that not one but two distinct levels of language are employed
side by side throughout. One of these levels is made up of
Benjy's own impressions of events which flow willy-nilly'
through his consciousness. On this level he serves in his
fashion as narrator, in which capacity he makes use of the
rudimentary language Faulkner devised for him. This is the
level which may properly be called Benjy's language; its verbal
limitations continuously reflect his mental disabilities.

Interspersed throughout, making up in volume more than
half of his monologue, are pertinent bits of dialogue that
Benjy remembers as having been spoken by one or another of

the principal characters in the novel. This element constitutes
a second and considerably more sophisticated language level
in the section. The verbal precision with which Benjy recalls,
reexperiences, the comparatively complex speech patterns of
his more intelligent companions astounds one, especially since
it must be conceded that he can understand little if any of
the conversations he recalls so exactly. His phenomenally acute
memory, a surprising attribute for an idiot to possess, represents a calculated departure from verisimilitude which it was
necessary for Faulkner to make in order to allow Benjy to
tell his own story.

Though extraordinary, Benjy's memory, too, is flawed. By
casting the quoted conversations into stereotyped patterns,
by frequently using a period instead of the usual comma after
directive expressions like "Father said" or "he said," and by
consistently omitting question marks and exclamation points,
Faulkner keeps the reader constantly aware of Benjy as narrator. The following excerpt illustrates the form most frequently employed to distinguish direct quotations within
Benjy's monologue:[3]

> "Maury says he's going to shoot the scoundrel."
> Father said. "I told him he'd better not mention it to
> Patterson beforehand." He drank.
> "Jason." Mother said.
> "Shoot who, Father." Quentin said. "What's Uncle
> Maury going to shoot him for."
> "Because he couldn't take a little joke." Father
> said.
> "Jason." Mother said, "How can you. You'd sit right
> there and see Maury shot down in ambush, and laugh."
> "Then Maury'd better stay out of ambush." Father
> said.
> "Shoot who, Father." Quentin said, "Who's Uncle
> Maury going to shoot."
> "Nobody." Father said. "I don't own a pistol."
> (p. 52)

Except for the clauses identifying speakers and the simple
observation "He drank," none of this excerpt is actually
Benjy's language. A pattern, a formula, is discernible:
first a statement is made by an undesignated speaker; then
Benjy, parrot-like, interjects the identifying clause; then
the speaker resumes or another undesignated speaker begins.
The omission of question marks indicates that the subtleties
of voice inflection are lost upon Benjy. His indiscriminate
use of the verb *said* to designate all modes and forms of
human speech reveals that most of the talk which swirls around
him is, to him, merely sound.

These two levels of language--Benjy's given rudimentary
"speech" and the more sophisticated dialogue which miraculous-
ly he recalls but cannot fully understand--work effectively
together to accomplish the purpose which Faulkner had set for
himself. The crudeness and obvious inadequacy of the lines
assigned to Benjy help to preserve the impression of his de-
rangement. And when, in the telling, his own few words are
quickly exhausted, the remembered speech of others filters
conveniently through his consciousness, carrying the burden
of his narrative. Thus his role as narrator is an inverted
one. Instead of mastering, ordering, interpreting events so
as to make their meanings clear to a reader, Benjy is made
to give a garbled and necessarily confused account of his
experiences and to rely upon the recollected speech of others,
speech which he does not understand, to give meaning to his
own earnest but often obfuscating reports.

The authorial stratagem of clearly distinguishing between
these two levels of language in Benjy's monologue, of keeping
them parallel and for the most part separate throughout, was
essential to the achievement of Faulkner's purposes. To have
endowed Benjy with the verbal ingenuity necessary to transform
direct to indirect discourse would have been to deny the major
premise of his idiocy, which somehow, despite the phenomenal
memory, Faulkner has managed to sustain. But in this, as in
most other ways, Benjy's performance is not strictly consistent.
Occasionally he seems suddenly in his monologue to have acquired abilities which do not ordinarily belong to him. The
following excerpt is one of the few passages in which Benjy is
allowed the use of indirect discourse:

> Quentin climbed up the bank and tried to catch Versh,
> but Versh ran away and Quentin couldn't. When Quentin
> came back Versh stopped and hollered that he was going
> to tell. Caddy told him that if he wouldn't tell, they'd
> let him come back. So Versh said he wouldn't, and they
> let him. (p. 21)

It should be noted that by the time this passage occurs in
the text, the predominant idiosyncrasies of Benjy's "speech"
have already been established. Such flights merely mark the
absolute limits of his verbal capabilities.

A casual counting reveals that Faulkner allows Benjy a
working vocabulary of some 500 words. On the basis of usage
(a basis which admits some duplications, it is true), the
list includes slightly over 200 (210 by my count) different
nouns; 175 verbs or verbals (a verb has been tabulated but
once, no matter in how many different forms it occurs in
Benjy's "speech"); 61 adjectives (excluding verbals); 37

adverbs; 25 prepositions; and 13 conjunctions, coordinating
and subordinating. Besides, Benjy is allowed use of the personal pronoun in most of its first and third person forms and
a few indefinite pronouns. However surprising it may seem for
an idiot to "know" so many words and to "use" them accurately
enough, it is not the size so much as the nature of Benjy's
vocabulary which must be taken into account.

Benjy's nouns are the names of the people, places, and
things which exist in the restricted sphere he inhabits. Among
them are his familiar names for members of the Compson household and the animals on the place: Mother, Caddy, Quentin,
Uncle Maury, Dilsey, Luster, Queenie, Dan, Fancy. He distinguishes the prominent features of the natural world: sun, moon,
moonlight, stars, sky, wind, hill, trees, grass, ditch, branch.
He knows the Compson property: yard, fence, pasture, garden,
carriage house, pigpen, barn, drive. Inside the house he distinguishes the rooms--dining room, parlor, library, bed room,
kitchen, bathroom, cellar--and at times focuses his attention
upon particular items of household furnishings--chair, bed,
sideboard, rug, mirror, clock, sink, stove. He recognizes the
parts of the body--eyes, nose, mouth, chest, hands, arms,
shoulder, feet--though apparently he has no name for the private
parts. He singles out many of the objects which are related
to his daily routine: for dressing--clothes, trousers, shirt,
drawers, overalls, overcoat, overshoes, shoes, cap; for eating--
apron of high chair, bowl, spoon, glass; for watching the fire--
firedoor, fire light, blaze; for going to bed--nightie, bath-
robe, blanket, spread, pillow, covers.

It becomes apparent immediately that all of Benjy's nouns
are concrete. Each one names an object or condition which exists
in the real world and makes an appeal to one or more of the
five senses. Benjy's sensibilities are exceptionally acute;
but the power to abstract, to generalize, in short to think,
is denied him. He has no word for pleasure or pain, hope or
despair; no word for knowledge, belief, or desire.

One of the most revealing words in Benjy's vocabulary
is the noun *shapes*, or the phrase *bright shapes*, which occurs
a number of times in his monologue. The phrase is concrete
in that it prompts a visual image. Benjy is represented as
responding with this image indiscriminately to designate feelings and yearnings which he cannot differentiate and for which
therefore he can have no words. For instance, the term is used
to describe his reaction to riding in the carriage to Jefferson: "I could hear Queenie's feet and the bright shapes went
smooth and steady on both sides, the shadows of them flowing
across Queenie's back" (p. 11). Here apparently the shapes
Benjy sees are the result of the motion, of the landscape

sweeping past on either side. The context suggests that on this
occasion Benjy is experiencing a feeling of mild pleasure, of
contentment, of momentary happiness. At another time, when he
is sitting before the fire with Caddy, the phrase is used to
indicate a similar but more intense feeling: *"It's still rain-
ing, Caddy said. I hate rain. I hate everything. And then her
head came into my lap and she was crying, holding me, and I
began to cry. Then I looked at the fire again and the bright,
smooth shapes went again"* (p. 69). This time the image seems
to represent the warmth and security Caddy's affection in-
spires in him. Another experience which usually gives Benjy
a good feeling is going to sleep: "Then the dark began to go
in smooth, bright shapes, like it always does, even when Caddy
says that I have been asleep" (p. 92). The stimulus for the
bright shapes which he associates with sleep seems to derive,
not from motion or watching the fire or from any form of visual
excitement, but wholly from some prevailing inner satisfaction
or peace.

But the image *bright shapes* is used to describe still other
experiences which move him strongly. On the day of Caddy's
wedding, he, along with other members of the celebrating household, becomes drunk: "I was crying now, and something was
happening inside me.... It was still going around, and then
the shapes began.... They were going faster, almost fast
enough.... They went on, smooth and bright" (pp. 25-26). An
unrealized concern for what is happening to Caddy and the
strangeness and exhilaration of increasing intoxication prompt
the complex feelings which Benjy cannot differentiate. And
in his confused recollections of the disastrous attempt to
communicate with the school girls, the image serves him again:
"I was trying to say, and I caught her ... trying to say and
trying and the bright shapes began to stop and I tried to get
out.... But when I breathed in, I couldn't breathe out again
to cry, and I tried to keep from falling off the hill and I
fell off the hill into the bright, whirling shapes" (p. 64).
This incident is charged with complex emotions--lust, fear,
frustration--none of which Benjy can rightly name.

The image *bright shapes* is at once the mark and the measure of Benjy's verbal, and hence mental, limitations. It,
together with his uncontrollable moaning or bellowing, must
serve him in place of the myriad abstract nouns which intelligent men use freely to distinguish their feelings and their
thoughts.

Faulkner allows Benjy a surprising number of verbs, but
they, like his nouns, are strictly limited in kind. They
affirm his sensory awareness of objects or conditions which
exist and actions which occur within the range of his atten-

tion. Often the aptness, the specificity, of a verb verifies
the precision of Benjy's observations. For instance, besides
to *walk*, he is given the verbs to *waddle*, to *scuffle*, to
tiptoe, and to *stagger*. Besides to *say*, he is granted the use
of to *call*, to *tell*, to *holler*, to *scream*, and to *whisper*.
Among the verbals on his list are *curling*, *slanting*, *tilting*,
swinging, *jouncing*, *clutching*, *spinning*, *sloping*, *tumbling*,
whirling, *grunting*, *snuffing*, and *buzzing*. Such concrete and
specific verbs contribute much to the vividness which at times
distinguishes Benjy's monologue: "The carriage jolted and
crunched on the drive" (p. 10); "The calf was in the pig pen.
It nuzzled at the wire, bawling" (p. 33); "Dan came waddling
out from under the steps and chewed my ankle" (p. 56); "She
[Dilsey] wadded the drawers and scrubbed Caddy behind with
them" (p. 91).

But if Benjy, with Faulkner's help, is a good reporter
of actions and events which claim or have claimed his awareness, his competencies end just there. He has no power to make
assumptions or draw inferences from the data he collects.
This inability accounts for the fact that at times Benjy
mistakes object for agent. If he does not see a person act,
or if he cannot comprehend the means by which a person acts,
but merely sees or senses the resulting change after it has
been effected, he attributes agency to the object. For instance, at one time he is made to observe, "She brought my
bowl" (p. 29), but at another, "The bowl went away" (p. 30).
Turning on and off the lights at night is a baffling process
to Benjy. On one occasion it appears that he understands the
matter aright, for he is made to say, "So I hushed and Caddy
got up and we went into the kitchen and turned the light on ..."
(p. 58); but usually he notes merely the sudden change which
occurs: "The room went away" (p. 53) or "The room went black"
(p. 54). In the case of the disappearing flowers, Benjy does
not perceive that Luster is deliberately tormenting him:
"... and they went away. I began to cry.... The flowers came
back" (p. 66). The instance of Luster's using the long wire
to close the fire door of the kitchen stove is similar: "...
the fire went away. I began to cry.... The fire was there"
(p. 70). These incidents, which prove to an intelligent person
merely that the hand is quicker than the eye, reveal how
completely Benjy lacks the powers which would enable him to
think.

The tense of Benjy's verbs is another indication of his
mental limitations. All of the verb forms he is represented
as using are in the past tense: either the simple past (they
took; they *went*; we *stopped*), the past progressive (they
were coming; Luster *was hunting*), or a combination of the

auxiliary *could* followed by an infinitive (I *could see* them hitting). The auxiliary *could*, however, is not often used by Benjy in its proper meaning of *to be able to*, but instead in a loose sense to form with its infinitive an assertive force roughly equivalent to that of the simple past. Benjy's consciousness of the present is continually being invaded by his memories of the past, but he has no inklings of a future. He cannot predict or prophesy. He cannot anticipate.

The verb *to try*, like the phrase *bright shapes*, marks the limits of Benjy's verbal capabilities. *To try* is an abstract verb which can suggest particular images only when it is coupled with a concrete verb. Benjy is credited with saying "I tried to get up" (the wedding celebration, p. 24) and "She [Mrs. Patterson] was trying to climb the fence" (p. 15). In the short paragraph recounting his recollections of his assault upon the schoolgirls, he is represented as using the verb *to try* eight separate times, three of these in the poignant phrase *trying to say*. In this context the phrase seems to suggest a dim awareness of purpose and a wail of despair which come as near as ever Benjy could come to an understanding of the significance of his plight.

The other words in Benjy's vocabulary, his adjectives, adverbs, prepositions, and conjunctions, confirm the pattern already established. Allotted to him rather sparingly, his adjectives help to sharpen the sensory appeal of his monologue. He distinguishes the colors *red, white, brown, green, blue, black, yellow*, and *gray*, and notes other qualities described by such adjectives as *dark, bright, smooth, dry, wet, dusty, muddy, heavy*, and *empty*. Most of the common prepositions are made available to him, indicating that his sense of place, of direction, of the physical relationships which exist between himself and other people and things may be trusted much of the time. But occasionally an erratic use of a preposition betrays Benjy's deficiencies, as the following quotations illustrate: "It [the flag] flapped on the bright grass and the trees" (p. 2); "The glass broke on the table, and the water ran into the table" (p. 87). It is the severely limited inclusion of conjunctions in Benjy's section, however, which points up most clearly his mental deficiencies. Since forming generalizations, making deductions, and drawing conclusions are denied to him, conjunctions which indicate precise logical relationships between ideas must be excluded from his vocabulary.

The predominant grammatical pattern of Benjy's "speech" is the unadorned, skeletal simple sentence, made up of subject and verb ("Versh said"), or subject, verb, complement ("He put my overshoes on" or "The gate was cold"), or subject,

verb, modifier ("Uncle Maury went away" or "We came to the
branch"). Through indiscriminate use of the coordinating conjunction *and*, Benjy's clipped independent clauses are often
strung together in a series to form loose compound sentences:
"Then we quit eating and we looked at each other and we were
quiet, and then we heard it again and I began to cry" (p. 29).
This sentence reports in chronological sequence, without
evaluation or emphasis, the successive stages of Benjy's
response to a happening. He senses each observable change in
turn, but he cannot comprehend the whole.

The complex sentence in its more sophisticated forms represents a level of verbal ingenuity for which Benjy can have
little use. But Faulkner allows him to employ the type in
some of its most elementary forms. There are some 70 dependent
clauses in Benjy's "speech." Of these, 30 are clauses of
place, introduced by the subordinating conjunction *where*:
"They were coming toward where the flag was" (p. 1); "I leaned
my face over where the supper was" (p. 28); "I could see the
windows, where the trees were buzzing" (p. 92). Benjy's
temporal clauses are introduced by the conjunctions *when*
seventeen times, and *while* and *until* three times each: "The
moon shone on the water when we got there" (p. 42); "I watched
Roskus milk while T.P. was feeding Queenie and Prince" (p.
33); "Then the barn wasn't there and we had to wait until it
came back" (p. 24). There is one causal clause in Benjy's
"speech": "Fancy held her head over the door, because T.P.
hadn't fed her yet" (pp. 33-34). In addition, there are
several noun clauses in the few passages of indirect discourse
attributed to Benjy, and on several occasions *like* is used
as a subordinating conjunction. It is significant that such
conjunctions as *though*, *since*, *unless*, *as if*, *so that*, and
because (with the one exception) and such conjunctive adverbs
as *moreover*, *nevertheless*, *however*, *otherwise*, *therefore*,
consequently, and *accordingly* do not appear in Benjy's
"speech."[4]

These considerations of the limited vocabulary and rudimentary grammatical patterns Faulkner allowed himself in
fashioning Benjy's "speech" show clearly the extraordinary
kind of person Benjy is. His senses are active and keen, but
he has no power to form conscious judgments about his own
person, his plight, or the fortunes of the people around
him. His responses are purely instinctive, never rational.
The perfume offended Benjy's sense of smell and wrought a
strangeness in Caddy's presence which bewildered him. His
reactions at the time indicate no moral judgment on his
part, however it might seem to a casual reader. And his violent
behavior at the recognition of Caddy's fallen state is but a

sympathetic response to Caddy's own distress and humiliation:
"Her eyes flew at me, and away. I began to cry" (p. 84). Benjy
has no moral consciousness. It is his inviolable innocence,
his imperviousness, which frequently makes him seem to pass
judgment on the actions of others.

One must admire the ingenuity and consistency with which
Faulkner has defined Benjy's peculiarities through his "speech."
But even more notable is the fact that he has succeeded at
times, despite the self-imposed language limitations, in
putting into Benjy's mouth words which rise to eloquence--to
poetry. Perhaps it is not too much to claim that the contradictory attributes assigned to Benjy--his acute sensibility
on the one hand and his unreason on the other--acting in conjunction with each other are of themselves conducive of a
poetic quality. Vivid images and actions glow within Benjy's
consciousness. His absolute ignorance, or rather his complete
innocence, compels him to view things in extraordinary ways.
The following passage offers a good illustration: "The ditch
came up out of the buzzing grass. The bones rounded out of
the black vines" (p. 42). From the context a reader knows
that these are Benjy's impressions one night as he approaches
the ditch where Nancy, one of the Compson animals, had died
and decomposed. Always faithful to the reports of his senses,
Benjy ascribes agency to the object: the ditch *came up*, the
bones *rounded out*. Unaware of the loud busyness of unseen
insects like cicadas and crickets, he attributes the buzzing
to the grass and trees. For a reader the effect of these lines
is a moment of intense awareness, a gratifying sense of immediacy.

Faulkner makes good use of synesthesia, the substitution
or confusion of one sense for another, in Benjy's monologue.
Whether the unusual acuteness of Benjy's senses or his verbal
deficiencies account for such transference, the result is
effective:

> *She smelled like trees. In the corner it was dark, but
> I could see the window. I squatted there, holding the
> slipper. I couldn't see it, but my hands saw it, and I
> could hear it getting night, and my hands saw the slip-
> per, but I couldn't see myself, but my hands could see
> the slipper, and I squatted there, hearing it getting
> dark.* (pp. 88-89)

The first and last paragraphs of the monologue represent
Benjy's "speech" at its best, displaying its characteristic
limitations and its power:

> Through the fence, between the curling flower spaces,
> I could see them hitting. They were coming toward where

the flag was and I went along the fence. Luster was
hunting in the grass by the flower tree. They took the
flag out, and they were hitting. Then they put the flag
back and they went to the table, and he hit and the
other hit. Then they went on, and I went along the
fence. Luster came away from the flower tree and we
went along the fence and they stopped and we stopped and
I looked through the fence while Luster was hunting in
the grass. (p. 1)

The first sentence, with its initial adverbial phrases and
its framing image "curling flower spaces," is one of the most
artful sentences put into Benjy's mouth: it is a most apt and
inviting introduction to his monologue and to Faulkner's novel.
The second sentence with its dependent clause and the third
and fourth sentences are undistinguished. Not until the fifth
sentence do Benjy's speech eccentricities begin to emerge.
But by the end of the paragraph the verbal evidences of his
peculiarities, the distinguishing characteristics of his style,
have been demonstrated. The care, the indefatigableness with
which he will report sense impressions is illustrated in
the expanding sequence of loosely coordinated clauses. The
absence of antecedents for the pronouns *they*, *he*, and *other*
and the omission of direct objects for the transitive verbs
hitting and *hunting* (in short, the absence of any awareness
on his part of purpose in the golfers or in Luster) declare
Benjy's mental defect.

The concluding paragraph in the monologue is in Benjy's
most eloquent strain:

Father went to the door and looked at us again.
Then the dark came back, and he stood black in the door,
and then the door turned black again. Caddy held me
and I could hear us all, and the darkness, and something
I could smell. And then I could see the windows, where
the trees were buzzing. Then the dark began to go in
smooth, bright shapes, like it always does, even when
Caddy says that I have been asleep. (p. 92)

Fittingly, these lines repeat, regroup, some of the more
striking images which have appeared throughout the monologue:
the darkening doorway, the protecting Caddy, the sounds and
the smells of the night, the buzzing trees. The final reference
in the last sentence to "bright shapes" and "sleep" produces
the effect of a refrain, a benediction.

NOTES

1. F.L. Gwynn and J.L. Blotner, eds., *Faulkner in the University* (First Vintage Edition, 1965), p. 95.

2. *The Sound and the Fury* (Modern Library College Edition, 1929, 1946), p. 342. All references are to this edition and are given parenthetically.

3. The method of indicating direct quotations within the italicized portions of the Benjy section is different. Quotation marks are not employed, and commas, not periods, are used to set off directive clauses like "Caddy said." Question marks and exclamation points are still omitted.

4. Benjy is allowed to use the coordinating conjunction *but* on occasion and the adverbial conjunction *so* two or three times.

THROUGH THE POET'S EYE:
A VIEW OF QUENTIN COMPSON

François L. Pitavy

With the writing of his third novel, *Sartoris*, Faulkner
had discovered that his "own little postage stamp of native
soil was worth writing about" (*LG*, p. 255)--that it would be
the *subject* of his creation. But with his fourth novel, *The
Sound and the Fury*, he "learned to read and quit reading":
"in a series of delayed repercussions like summer thunder, I
discovered the Flauberts and Dostoievskys and Conrads whose
books I had read ten years ago."[1] No longer reading them for
mere enjoyment, but partaking creatively in the experience of
those "masters,"[2] he knew that writing was not so much the
telling of experience as experience itself--that it was not
for "fun" (*LG*, p. 255), but the very *object* of fiction. With
The Sound and the Fury, Faulkner was revealed to himself as
poet, that is, as creator.
A unique writing experience in his life, this novel always
occupied a privileged place in his mind and, above all, in his
heart:

> That's the one that ... I consider the best, not--well,
> best is the wrong word--that's the one that I love the
> most. (*FU*, p. 77)

*This is a much revised and enlarged version of an article
originally published in* Sud, *14-15 (May 1975), 62-82 (used
with permission).* The edition of The Sound and the Fury *cited
here is the first edition (New York: Jonathan Cape and Harrison
Smith, 1929), or the current Random House or Vintage editions,
which are photographic reproductions of the first printing.
Page references will also be given to* Lion in the Garden: Interviews with William Faulkner, 1926-1962, *ed. James B. Meriwether and Michael Millgate (New York: Random House, 1968), and*
Faulkner in the University: Class Conferences at the University
of Virginia 1957-1958 *(Charlottesville: University of Virginia
Press, 1959), abbreviated as* LG *and* FU *after the quotations.*

my personal feeling would be a tenderness for the one
which caused me the most anguish, just as the mother
might feel for the child, and the one that caused me
the most anguish and is to me the finest failure is *The
Sound and the Fury*. That's the one that I feel most
tender toward. (*LG*, p. 146)

Of all his novels, this is the only one toward which Faulkner
claimed he felt any tenderness: the child of his heart and
his flesh (he had "written [his] guts into" it[3]), born in
pain, but also in jubilation, and thus held in special affection. For agony and ecstasy presided simultaneously over the
writing of the novel and the encounter with an *oeuvre*, recognized here with absolute certainty. With *The Sound and the
Fury*, Faulkner took his literary vows, so to speak, or, to use
Wordsworth's expression in *The Prelude*, he became "a dedicated
spirit."

The *originality* of *The Sound and the Fury* seems due to the
conjunction, in the novel's genesis, of circumstance and
desire--a conjunction apparent in the first 1933 introduction,
all the more revealing on account of its almost intimate tone
and its seeming lack of posturing:

one day it suddenly seemed as if a door had clapped
silently and forever to between me and all publishers'
addresses and booklists and I said to myself, Now I can
write. Now I can just write. Whereupon I, who had three
brothers and no sisters and was destined to lose my
first daughter in infancy, began to write about a little
girl. ("Intr. I," pp. 158-59)

This absence of all external demands intruding upon the
creative process, this recognition of the possibility of pure
creation--itself its own object--must have unleashed Faulkner's
"demons,"[4] must have helped the sense of void or lack emerge
into awareness and language, as appears in the next paragraph
of the same introduction, so personal that indeed Faulkner
may have wanted to revise it, or not to have it published:

I did not realise then that I was trying to manufacture
the sister which I did not have and the daughter which
I was to lose, though the former might have been apparent
from the fact that Caddy had three brothers almost before
I wrote her name on paper.... the entire story seemed
to explode on the paper before me. ("Intr. I," p. 159)

The family scheme of *The Sound and the Fury* is viewed
here as a (literary) compensation for the (real) absence of
a sister. But the explanation is too deliberate to be satis-
factory. More profoundly, the sister is a metaphor for the

object of desire, as can be seen in the transfer near the end
of the introduction, which makes her a narcissistic and libidinal object:[5]

> There is a story somewhere about an old Roman who kept
> at his bedside a Tyrrhenian vase which he loved and the
> rim of which he wore slowly away with kissing it. I had
> made myself a vase. ("Intr. I," p. 161)

The sister-vase--work of art and fetish--is here revealed as
the creation of a desire suddenly recognized and liberated
by the circumstances of writing (the absence of constraints),
urging Faulkner to write precisely because he had emancipated
himself from the necessity of doing it. That is why he wrote
The Sound and the Fury in a sort of state of grace heretofore
unknown, and which he would never experience again:

> ... in *The Sound and the Fury* I had already put perhaps
> the only thing in literature which would ever move me
> very much: Caddy climbing the pear tree to look in the
> window at her grandmother's funeral while Quentin and
> Jason and Benjy and the negroes looked up at the muddy
> seat of her drawers. ("Intr. II," p. 710)

Faulkner repeatedly asserted that such was the image
originating and informing the novel, written day after day
with a sense of jubilation in discovering the secrets of the
unblemished page, but also with the anguish of experiencing
the impossibility of recapturing his dream, since its inscrip-
tion on the page could be nothing more than a pale or clumsy
reflection of that image. Hence the four sections of the novel,
then the 1945 "Appendix": the five successive attempts to tell
the story of that little girl and to retain her image, first
through the eyes of the three brothers, then through those
of the anonymous narrator who, in the "Appendix," is even
further removed from that object of impossible desire.

Faulkner is then the *poet* of Caddy--his "heart's darling"
(*FU*, p. 6). However, even though the fable of the vase seems
to make her into a purely narcissistic object, the unforeseen
and necessary writing of the text was rendered possible by the
writer's distancing himself from that object--which is achieved
both in the individual visions of the narrators and in their
succession one after the other. Discounting the symbolical
implications in using the idiot brother as the first narrator
and his loaded significance for the story, one sees that this
innocent vision provides at once the most transparent and the
most obscure narrative viewpoint, as the story is clearly
reflected but its meaning obscured in the reliable but
shattered mirror of idiocy. Conversely, Jason, the "sanest"

of the three brothers, yet the most outrageously insane, whose inverted desire has become hatred, affords the greatest distancing in the first-person narrative.

Of the three Compson brothers, Quentin is undeniably the one whose viewpoint is the most complex to define and the most interesting to study. Indeed, one would be wrong to reduce his role to that of a mere narrator. His hypersensitivity confers upon his vision of the world a lucidity, even though desperate, and a profundity absent in the other narrators. Like Darl Bundren in *As I Lay Dying*, he has more to say because he sees and understands or feels more, and also because he appears as an image of the artist (not, however, the alter ego or the spokesman of his creator, interchangeable with him[6]), a projection of the *poet*'s demiurgic power. That Quentin accomplishes nothing, besides his suicide, matters little, except to enable Faulkner, through what is also a parody of the artist, to distance himself from his "double" and thus to be better able to recognize and objectify his dream.

There is no doubt that, to Faulkner, Quentin was a privileged narrator. By the time he wrote *The Sound and the Fury*, Faulkner had already made him the narrator of two short stories, "That Evening Sun" and "A Justice," the first versions of which were most likely written shortly before the composition of *The Sound and the Fury*, even though the short stories were not published until 1931.[7] Both draw part of their effectiveness from the fact that Quentin does not understand all that he is recounting, since he is still a young boy: nine in "That Evening Sun," twelve in "A Justice." But in the narrative *frame*, Quentin is in both cases a man who looks back toward his past (he is twenty-four years old in the first paragraph of "That Evening Sun") in order to recall precise memories, Nancy's imminent death, or the origins and birth of Sam Fathers, as the Indian, Herman Basket, recounted them to Sam himself, who in turn relayed the story to the young Quentin. Thus Quentin's memories or narratives come to us from beyond death, that of Nancy, implicit but certain, or that of the meta-narrator, Sam Fathers.

With *The Sound and the Fury*, Quentin has become not only a narrator who reflects on his past as from a point beyond death--now his own[8]--but also a double, or rather a figure of the artist, as are such noted predecessors as Stephen Dedalus or J. Alfred Prufrock, undeniably his ancestors, or even Nick Adams. Admittedly, one could find some analogies between the "life" of Quentin Compson and that of William Faulkner,[9] but they would not account for the mystery of creation and the distance between the novelist and his narrator (no matter how privileged he may be), whom he made an admirable, and pitiful, figure of the poet.

It is straightaway noticeable that Quentin is invested
with certain traits generally associated with the *vulgar*
image of the poet: he is a rather feeble and clumsy young
man who, incapable of using a knife or firearm, eminently
symbols of war and virility, drops them or faints when he
must even try to use them; a hypersensitive type, he is gifted
with an almost visionary imagination enabling him to relive
past scenes in their primal intensity; finally, intent upon
morbid self-analysis, he ends up giving his psychological,
or physiological, problems a metaphysical dimension. Be that
as it may, these few, more or less stereotyped characteristics
are at best superficial, not indispensable: they scarcely
suffice to qualify this young man as poet.

Quentin is also the one who cannot bring himself to wor-
ship the false gods of the profiteering, corrupt, hypocritical
society in which he lives. Hence his violent rejection of
Herbert Head, the cheater who got himself expelled from
Harvard (an incident which he passed off as a bit of bad
luck), the unscrupulous and contemptuous man, ready to use
hypocritical flattery, even blackmail, to buy the silence
or complicity of Quentin, who then cannot bear the thought
that his sister could marry "that blackguard." Above all,
Quentin sees Herbert as an opportunist, whose conduct is
never guided by the least lasting ideal:

> listen I've been out in the world now for ten years
> things dont matter so much then you'll find that out
> let's you and I get together on this thing sons of old
> Harvard and all ... a young man gets these ideas and
> I'm all for them does him good while he's in school
> forms his character good for tradition the school but
> when he gets out into the world he'll have to get his
> the best way he can because he'll find that everybody
> else is doing the same thing (p. 135)

For Herbert, the *moment* of an act is only "temporary"--pre-
cisely the word that will bring Quentin to his death (it
reappears four times in his ultimate "conversation" with his
father). Thus Caddy's future husband is the mere double of
her first lover, Dalton Ames, whose "philosophy" is in no
way different, as he explains calmly to Quentin who has just
given him an ultimatum to leave the town: "listen no good
taking it so hard its not your fault kid it would have been
some other fellow" (p. 199).

Unlike worldly-wise people, unlike Jason ("the first sane
Compson since before Culloden," Faulkner writes ironically
in the 1945 "Appendix"), who respects and loves only money
and respectability (in this sense, Quentin's monologue is an

anticipated and ironical commentary upon his brother's),
Quentin is an idealist who will not accept temporariness and
thus recantation, who will dismiss everything that cannot
serve him as a principle of conduct, everything that is not
the immutable image of what he wants to believe. Therefore
Caddy represents for him much more than the object of his
sexual obsessions: she crystallizes his dreams of beauty and
truth, she is the image of the ideal vision that the poet
pursues. This explains her function in the economy of the
novel: she must remain an unattainable *object* of beauty, and
thus cannot be the *subject* of discourse--a legitimate narrator,
on a par with her brothers. One understands better now the
sense of ecstasy that presided at the writing of this book,
and the fact that Caddy always remained a moving image of
beauty for her creator: "To me she was the beautiful one, she
was my heart's darling. That's what I wrote the book about"
(*FU*, p. 6). An interesting remark, as Caddy is *not* beautiful;
that is, morally beautiful: despite her redeeming love for
Benjy, she is a bossy and unruly child, a promiscuous adolescent, a young woman repudiated by her deceived husband, aban-
doning her daughter or, so it seems, allowing her to be taken
away rather easily. (The "Appendix," showing her as the mistress
of a Nazi general on the French Riviera, hardly presents a
more flattering portrait.) Thus, for Quentin, Caddy's beauty
appears on a level other than that of her fictive existence.

In *Go Down, Moses*, during a lengthy discussion with his
cousin Ike, McCaslin Edmonds wonders why Ike did not fire at
the fabulous, long-hunted bear when he finally had the oppor-
tunity. Then, without even waiting for an answer, Cass attempts
to explain to young Ike the significance of his gesture, or
of his lack of gesture, by reading to him the "Ode on a Grecian
Urn":

> *'Listen,' he said. He read the five stanzas aloud and*
> *closed the book on his finger and looked up. 'All right,'*
> *he said. 'Listen,' and read again, but only one stanza*
> *this time and closed the book and laid it on the table.*
> *'She cannot fade, though thou hast not thy bliss,'*
> *McCaslin said: 'Forever wilt thou love, and she be fair.'*
> *   'He's talking about a girl,' he said.*
> *   'He had to talk about something,' McCaslin said.*
> *Then he said, 'He was talking about truth. Truth is one.*
> *It doesn't change. It covers all things which touch the*
> *heart--honor and pride and pity and justice and courage*
> *and love. Do you see now?'*[10]

Just as he is about to attain the goal of his quest--truth,
that is, "all things which touch the heart"--Ike stands still

and chooses not to kill the bear; in other words, not to
obliterate this vision of beauty, in order to retain it in
his memory, intact, forever alive. Quentin, too, is that
immobilized lover of Keats's poem, who can never have his
bliss: hence his (imaginary) confession of incest, which would
eternally isolate the two lovers in the pure flame of hell,
but which would leave Caddy untouched and untouchable, forever
safe from a degradation that Quentin knows all too well is
inevitable. This desperate ruse of idealism is the means by
which the young man attempts to conserve a vision of beauty
and truth that is his reason for living. Lacking this reason,
the unique recourse is death, which paradoxically precludes
the slow dying of the ideal by accomplishing it brutally: incapable of killing his sister to preserve her, it is himself
whom Quentin kills. In Cass's "explication" of the "Ode," the
girl becomes the signifier of a discourse on truth. Similarly,
never ceasing to brood on the virginity of a girl (who is
assuredly the focus of his affective universe), Quentin asserts
his desire for an absolute, of which the young girl Caddy is
the signifier. Like the Grecian urn, the symbol of ideal perfection, and like "the yet unmarred sheet beneath [the writer's]
hand," Caddy must remain forever "inviolate and unfailing"
("Intr. I," p. 709).

Quentin blinds himself then, refusing to see the inevita-
bility of Caddy's destruction or the soiling of his ideal.
That is precisely why, not being one of the group of children
who watch Caddy in the pear tree she had climbed up, he does
not see the soiled seat of his sister's drawers: when, later,
Dilsey inquires about Quentin's absence, Caddy rightly answers
that he is "mad" at her (p. 55). That evening, at bedtime,
Quentin turns toward the wall so as not to see his "dirty"
sister, nor to watch her undress. Here is signified his refusal to *see* reality, which, however, he cannot and does not
ignore: "Caddy do you remember how Dilsey fussed at you because your drawers were muddy" (p. 189). The distance between
the reality of a world he denies and must nevertheless inhabit,
and the ideal which is his reason for living, is the tear by
which he lets out his being—and his life: "all men are just
accumulations dolls stuffed with sawdust ... flowing from what
wound in what side" (p. 218). Unlike Caddy, the direct victim
of the disintegration of the Compson family, Quentin is a
victim in the second degree: what destroys him is the certainty
of Caddy's destruction.

During the last day of his life, Quentin's gaze focuses
obsessively on two series of signs, by which he unconsciously

welcomes and justifies the death he has already entered:
shadows, and images of eternity, that is, on the one hand,
what he refuses or cannot bear, and on the other, what he is
yearning for and what, rendering life intolerable, is his
reason for dying.

Shadows are above all symbols of time: from the beginning
of Quentin's monologue, this sign catches his attention, re-
minding him of his temporality and of the temporariness of
any human design:

> When the shadow of the sash appeared on the curtains
> it was between seven and eight oclock and then *I was in
> time again* (p. 93; italics mine)

As he cannot accept returning into time after sleep, that
little death, which freed him from it, Quentin seeks to obliterate all signs of it: he rips out the hands of his watch
(but its ticking, at once minute and loud, never stops tormenting him), he will not let the jeweller tell him the time,
nor will he look at public clocks, or listen to the noontime
whistle, and he tries constantly to abolish the present by
allowing himself to be possessed by his dreams; above all,
he seeks continually in his fantasies to obliterate his shadow,
at once the representation of fleeting time and the Jungian
image of the "lower" part of his consciousness, that part of
himself which he refuses to acknowledge, but which he knows
is lying in wait for him and will eventually catch up with
him: "Niggers say a drowned man's shadow was watching for him
in the water all the time" (p. 111). Thus, during that June
Second, 1910, he never ceases to try to get rid of his shadow,
attempting to give it the slip or to kill it, by stepping on
it, or crushing its bones, or walking on its belly:[11] the
recurrent corporal metaphors aptly signify that shadows are
indeed Quentin's black double, his *negative*.

As the time set for his death comes closer, Quentin is
caught up by memories of moments of insomnia when the entire
universe seemed to belong to shadows, that is, to all that
contradicts stability, permanence, the signs of eternity
which he wants to see in this world--precisely to all that
negates his ideal, and thereby his identity:

> I seemed to be lying neither asleep nor awake looking
> down a long corridor of *grey halflight* where all stable
> things had become *shadowy paradoxical* all I had done
> *shadows* all I had felt suffered taking visible form
> *antic and perverse* mocking without relevance *inherent
> themselves with the denial of the significance* they
> should have affirmed thinking I was I was not who was
> not was not who. (p. 211; italics mine)

No longer able to assert himself as "I," Quentin cannot even decline the terms of his identity, which slips from his hold and then is told negatively and in the third person: the disintegration of the syntax here expresses that of the consciousness.

The inverted reflection of Benjy's monologue that in a sense precedes the break of day, Quentin's monologue seems to come after its fall: the most significant memories that invade his consciousness and gradually take it into death are twilight[12] or nocturnal scenes, such as the game of love and death with Caddy at the edge of the creek, then the encounter with Dalton Ames to whom Caddy has just given herself (the lovers are then perceived as two melting shadows), the confrontation with Caddy in her room the evening before her wedding, or, during the preceding summer in the obscurity loud with insects, the conversation with Mr. Compson on virginity, women, and evil.

Shadows are then symbols of the temporary, of man's finitude. But that is precisely what the *poet* in Quentin refuses desperately, when the voice of his father (his double, the interlocutor of his consciousness) assures him that passion is not eternal, that suffering and despair cannot retain that original exquisiteness which alone would justify them:

> and i temporary and he you cannot bear to think
> that someday it will no longer hurt you like this ...
> it is hard believing to think that a love or a sorrow
> is a bond purchased without design and which matures
> willynilly and is recalled without warning to be re-
> placed by whatever issue the gods happen to be floating
> at the time ... and i temporary and he was the saddest
> word of all there is nothing else in the world its not
> despair until time its not even time until it was
> The last note sounded. (pp. 220-22)

The bell tolls for Quentin because he is prisoner and victim not only of his private contradictions, but also of the artist's dilemma, torn between his temporal state and his desire for eternity. Indeed, these are the two irreconcilable poles of his final discourse.

The fascination with eternity is the other major force polarizing Quentin's vision and determining his mental images. Permanence or motionless balance, sexual innocence (which in some way precedes time) or damnation (which comes after it), are, in Quentin's view, the opposite of change, of irremediable time, and of sexuality (that is, submission to time)--the

opposite of temporariness, to use again the word that compre-
hends all his obsessions.

To Quentin, the seagull represents a major figure of
eternity, suspended in the sky, a stranger to the fleeting
world far below. When he himself does not notice the seagull's
motionless flight, it is significant that in his consciousness
the thought of time frequently evokes (as a sanctuary of a
sort) the image of its contrary, the seagull:

> I could smell water, and in a break in the wall I saw
> a glint of water and two masts, and a gull motionless
> in midair, like on an invisible wire between the masts
> (p. 110)

> The hands [of the clock] were extended, slightly off the
> horizontal at a faint angle, like a gull tilting into
> the wind. (p. 105)[13]

Quentin is condemned at once by time and by the despairing
image of its opposite. The seagull's wings are a figure of
the transcendence beyond time, without ceasing, however, to
recall it. Liberation from time is no more than a dream: the
gull remains captive, as though held on an invisible wire; and
man has not been made to play the harp with angels:

> Father said a man is the sum of his misfortunes. One
> day you'd think misfortune would get tired, but then
> time is your misfortune Father said. A gull on an in-
> visible wire attached through space dragged. You carry
> the symbol of your frustration into eternity. Then the
> wings are bigger Father said only who can play a harp.
> (p. 129)

If Quentin soon associates Gerald Bland with the seagull,
it is because, in his eyes, both partake of the same permanence
and balance, and remain well above the puny, fluctuating
world:

> I could hear my watch and the train dying away, as though
> it were running through another month or another summer
> somewhere, rushing away under the poised gull and all
> things rushing. Except Gerald. He would be sort of grand
> too, pulling in lonely state across the noon, rowing
> himself right out of noon, up the long bright air like
> an apotheosis, mounting into a drowsing infinity where
> only he and the gull, the one terrifically motionless,
> the other in a steady and measured pull and recover that
> partook of inertia itself, the world punily beneath
> their shadows on the sun. (p. 149)

The two poles ordering Quentin's imaginary world appear clearly in this text where a cosmogony is outlined which is a figure of his divided consciousness: below is the realm of time, that is, of universal flux, of loudness (Quentin thinks at one time that he wants to isolate Caddy from this loud world), and of shadow; above is the eternal and infinite domain to which the suspended seagull already belongs and where Gerald rises in a movement so smooth as to transcend time. Such ascension is an "apotheosis": like the gull, Gerald appears free of his shadow in the lower world, unlike Quentin whose own shadow ties him down and prevents any ascension toward timelessness. In this oneiric abode, the light casts no shadow, it is a never-setting noonday sun, never declining toward obscurity; the long rays of the sun are the paths of the gods, or of Christ: "Like Father said down the long and lonely light-rays you might see Jesus walking, like" (p. 94).

Deified, eternal, Gerald Bland becomes a solar figure, like that other holder of virile power, Dalton Ames, whom Quentin makes into a *fiery* creature, noticing his brown complexion and his khaki shirt, and associating him with asbestos and bronze (pp. 113, 130, 197), thereby conferring upon him a permanence to which—a creature of shadow and of feminine water—he remains desperately a stranger. Gerald is thus on God's side, or rather, in a significant twist, it is God who is on Gerald's side: "God is not only a gentleman and a sport; He is a Kentuckian too" (p. 112). Rowing down the Charles River, Gerald thus finds himself in the company of the gods, "still pulling upstream majestical in the face of god gods. Better. Gods.... The wet oars winking him along in bright winks and female palms. Adulant" (pp. 137-38). God though he may be, he is no less the heart-breaker—the Caddy-killer. That is why Quentin provokes him and fights with him, all the while imagining that he is facing his real rival, Dalton Ames, who then cannot be made into a godlike figure.

Another image of eternity in Quentin's bestiary is the lone trout which swims up from the depths of the river to lip "a fly beneath the surface with that sort of gigantic delicacy of an elephant picking up a peanut" (p. 144), and which, like the old bear (an "ancestor," too), has remained for twenty-five years indifferent to all attempts made to catch it. Immobile, as though suspended in the current, it is in its element the counterpart of the gull in the air, "wavering delicately to the motion of the water above which the May flies slanted and poised" (p. 144). Like the seagull, it represents in its suspension a perfect, and perfectly inaccessible, modality of existence, an absolute and oxymoronic being conjoining time and eternity, motion and motionlessness—

for Faulkner, the very definition of art. Thus the trout can
elicit only admiration and despair: Quentin recommends the
three boys not to try to catch it, to leave its domain inviolate: "Only dont catch that old fellow down there. He
deserves to be let alone" (p. 148).

Certain memories that surface again in Quentin's consciousness are understandable only as they, too, evince his
fascination with eternity. He readily recognizes in Blacks
a timeless patience, an immobile serenity--what Faulkner,
playing on the two senses of the word, calls "endurance."
These are precisely the qualities Quentin lacks, and which
he associates with Blacks every time he comes to think of
them. One such revealing memory (which would otherwise seem
insignificant) involves Louis Hatcher (pp. 141-42). This old
man is so well accorded to nature and time that he avoids
all useless gestures and accomplishes those he deems necessary
only *in due time*: so he does not clean his lantern and will
not clean it, he says, until the next flood comes along,
since he had done that on the very night of the previous flood
and had found himself better off for it (the flood had raged
further North in Pennsylvania that time and anyway had not
threatened him). This is not simply magic, but the conduct
of a man who has *all his time*, and thereby transcends the
fretful agitation of the common run of people. Similarly,
old Louis Hatcher's voice seemed to Quentin to lose its
singularity and to become the sound of October nights themselves during possum hunts, "as though his voice were a part
of darkness and silence, coiling out of it, coiling into it
again. WhoOoooo. WhoOoooo" (p. 142).

The memory of the Negro seen one December morning in
Virginia, waiting for a train to move away from a road cross-
ing, sitting his mule so perfectly still that he seemed to
be a part of the countryside and contemporaneous with it,
points up Quentin's same desire for eternity:

> How long he had been there I didn't know, but he sat
> straddle of the mule, his head wrapped in a piece of
> blanket, as if they had been built there with the fence
> and the road, or with the hill, carved out of the hill
> itself.... (p. 106)

The nostalgia that he experiences then is not merely for the
South where he was born, but mainly for a permanence impervious to time, which will be his only in the pure flame of
hell or in death.

All of the numerous images of eternity in the novel mani-
fest the same yearning, which is profoundly the poet's insane
dream of transcending time. Quentin's impossible desire to

arrest time (also Sutpen's "innocent" dream) is indeed that
of every artist, as Faulkner himself put it in the 1956 *Paris
Review* interview:

> The aim of every artist is to arrest motion, which is
> life, by artificial means and hold it fixed so that 100
> years later when a stranger looks at it, it moves again
> since it is life. Since man is mortal, the only immor-
> tality possible for him is to leave something behind him
> that is immortal since it will always move. This is the
> artist's way of scribbling "Kilroy was here" on the wall
> of the final and irrevocable oblivion through which he
> must someday pass. (*LG*, p. 253)

Is this not, too, the dream of the poet contemplating the
urn in Keats's "Ode"? Doesn't that "leaf-fring'd legend,"
immobilized by art, continue to haunt the shape of the urn,
which then forever restores to life that "mad pursuit" of
"men or gods" and "maidens loth" to the eyes of the "stranger"
who looks at it "100 years later"? The reference to Keats is
not fortuitous. Faulkner invariably cited him in interviews
and discussions when questioned about his reading (in his
writing, a Keatsian echo can even be heard in certain composite
epithets condensing an entire sentence): to him, Keats was
the poet *par excellence*, who could reconcile the imaginary
and the sensory, or rather affirm the primacy of the former
over the latter, without thereby excluding the sensory from
the poetic creation. Is this not precisely what the poet says
to the urn:

> Heard melodies are sweet, but those unheard
>   Are sweeter; therefore, ye soft pipes, play on;
> Not to the sensual ear, but, more endear'd,
>   Pipe to the spirit ditties of no tone.[14]

Time's flight is arrested at a chosen moment, a point of perfection and beauty that the poet eternalizes in art. Thus
beauty becomes eternal (it is then synonymous with truth):
the lover forever pursues his beloved, whose beauty never
fades, while love can never grow stale with its consummation:

> She cannot fade, though thou hast not thy bliss,
>   For ever wilt thou love, and she be fair!
> . . . .
> More happy love! more happy, happy love!
>   For ever warm and still to be enjoy'd,
>   For ever panting, and for every young;
> All breathing human passion far above,
>   That leaves a heart high-sorrowful and cloy'd,
>   A burning forehead, and a parching tongue.[15]

The first three stanzas of the "Ode" could only lead Faulkner
to see Keats as the paradigmatic poet, accomplishing the
dream of every artist. Arresting motion, or life, is also
Quentin's major obsession: he never ceases to project his
desire for eternity into his vision of the world; and he would
like to conserve as an object of beauty a Caddy forever pure
of all sexuality, who could no more elude him than he could
satisfy his desire with her, in the manner of the lover and
the beloved in Keats's "Ode."

Quentin, however, is a poet only in the broadest sense of
the word. His only creation is the discourse by which he
represses his incestuous desire while gratifying it in a
poetic universe that he seeks desperately to substitute for
an intolerable reality. But he will reconcile the two worlds
only by physically "healing out to sea," entering "the caverns
and the grottoes of the sea" (p. 111).

Like God, the first poet, who named beings into existence,
the poet Quentin (re)creates his universe by *saying* it. Should
his sexuality contradict his desire for eternity, it is
immediately denied in a fantasy of castration, for which
Quentin himself gives the explanation:

> Versh told me about a man mutilated himself. He went
> into the woods and did it with a razor, sitting in a
> ditch. A broken razor flinging them backward over his
> shoulder the same motion complete the jerked skein of
> blood backward not looping. But that's not it. It's
> not not having them. It's never to have had them then
> I could say O That That's Chinese I dont know Chinese.
> (p. 143)

He believes that he must *say* his imaginary world for it to
be realized. In order to abolish sexuality, that is, temporality, he must deny its existence: language here is a tool
for decreation.

It is also a tool for creation (which comes to the same).
Incest does not exist otherwise than by and in the confession
to the father:

> *I have committed incest I said Father it was I it was*
> *not Dalton Ames* (pp. 97-98)

> *I'll tell you how it was I'll tell Father then itll*
> *have to be because you love Father then we'll have to*
> *go away amid the pointing and the horror the clean*
> *flame I'll make you say we did* (p. 185)

Here again, it is clear that for Quentin *being* exists only through *saying*. That he chose to say *incest* in order to arrest time is significant: it is in every society the transgression *par excellence*, the original sin, of which all others are only avatars. By accusing himself of the "unpardonable sin" (to take up Hawthorne's phrase), Quentin substitutes himself for God, and becomes the creator of his own eternity, or of his own hell.[16]

The character of the father may then appear as the most remarkable creation of the son's narrative. The absence of any typographical clues, of quotation marks, and, early in Quentin's monologue, of all punctuation at once signals the interiorization of the father's interventions in the son's consciousness: sententious maxims or disillusioned words that give verbal form--poetic existence--to the signs that hold Quentin's attention on that June Second, 1910--as, for instance, his watch or the books borrowed from the library (pp. 93, 99). Even more significant are the debates that take place in the son's consciousness, where the arguments that condemn him or that draw him deeper into despair take on the father's voice. Here, the authority, sanctioned by what Lacan calls the Name-of-the-Father (the Law), and the seemingly sententious irrefutability may be the alibis that Quentin unconsciously seeks, and creates, in order to make of his suicide--an act of *passion*--the logical and necessary culmina-tion of his situation, as appears, for example, in the "dialogues" on women and virginity (pp. 96, 143).

That is why the confession of incest is purely imaginary.[17] That, in the fictional space, conversations between father and son actually took place certainly ought not to be questioned, otherwise Quentin would not associate them with the *"rasping darkness of summer and August the street lamps"* (p. 119). Why, too, would he have invented his father's last piece of advice: to spend a month in Maine before his year at Harvard, as a change is as good as a rest (p. 221)? And one can attribute to Mr. Compson alone the Southerner's love for rhetoric or the vocabulary of a man well read in the classics.[18] But during the ultimate "conversation," the re-marks or objections of the father are clearly those of the son himself: the dialogue is with his own conscience, where the father--completely interiorized--has become one of the contending voices, bringing Quentin indirectly to recognize that his language is not demiurgical:

> and he you wanted to sublimate a piece of natural human
> folly into a horror and then exorcise it with truth
> and i it was to isolate her out of the loud world so
> that it would have to flee us of necessity and then the

> sound of it would be as though it had never been and
> he did you try to make her do it and i i was afraid to
> i was afraid she might and then it wouldnt have done
> any good but if i could tell you we did it would have
> been so and then the others wouldnt be so and then the
> world would roar away (p. 220)

Thus Quentin appears to be the creator of his father (but
unlike Stephen Dedalus, he does not even want to become his
own father: indeed, the father's voice is never abolished
here). Does he not admit it to himself, during an apparently
imaginary conversation with Caddy, in what is probably the
most obscure passage of his entire narrative:

> *Say it to Father will you I will am my fathers Progeni-*
> *tive I invented him created I him Say it to him it will*
> *not be for he will say I was not and then you and I*
> *since philoprogenitive* (p. 152)[19]

Faulkner seems to have Quentin say that by their admission
of incest, Caddy and he become their father's creators and
that their love for their father is the sign that they "invented" him jointly. Here Quentin is not unlike the three
boys met shortly before, who were already "selling" the twenty-
five-dollar fishing rod that they would not fail to get by
catching the trout which had defied sportsmen for twenty-
five years: "They all talked at once, their voices insistent
and contradictory and impatient, making of unreality a possibility, then a probability, then an incontrovertible fact,
as people will when their desires become words" (p. 145)

Quentin would like his words to create a universe in the
image of his adolescent and narcissistic idealism, a universe
where desire would express itself only in the play of language.
Far from being creative, then, his discourse ends by being
only a more and more fragile protection against a reality
which already engulfs him. In the long passage quoted above
(from p. 220), it is remarkable that Quentin has substituted
the false pretenses of the conditional and the hypothetical
for his demiurgical demand. In the preceding "confessions"
of incest, he never resorted to that despairing "if i could
tell you." He now seems to acknowledge (in the name of the
father, since a direct admission would be hardly tolerable)
the impossibility of sublimating the fault or error into an
eternal horror, since he exorcises it with truth: Quentin
desacralizes horror by confronting it with reality. He thereby
denies language its creative power and returns it to the
realm of the compensatory dreams, of *fiction*, that is, of
untruth. To acknowledge his incapacity to *say* the world is
already to yield to death.

The tragedy of Quentin boils down to believing that language can be substituted for the real--that words can be the substance of existence. Caddy has no need to verbalize her love for Dalton Ames in order to experience it: the beating of her heart is sufficient. And Benjy has no more need of Caddy's words to be secure in her love.

In *As I Lay Dying*, Addie Bundren acknowledges this divorce between words and "doing":

> I would think how words go straight up in a thin line, quick and harmless, and how terribly doing goes along the earth, clinging to it, so that after a while the two lines are too far apart for the same person to straddle from one to the other; and that sin and love and fear are just sounds that people who never sinned nor loved nor feared have for what they never had and cannot have until they forget the words.[20]

More lucid or more courageous than Quentin, Addie knows that words are screens for desires, whose realization they prevent. Language, then, serves more to obfuscate reality than to express it.

A failed poet though he may be (as Faulkner claimed he himself was), Quentin ultimately still expresses the demi-urgical urge of every artist, to whom despair is the gauge of the dream of perfection (again, to use Faulkner's own words). Such despair is also expressed in the last two stanzas of the "Ode on a Grecian Urn." (It is remarkable that in his allusions or citations, Faulkner limited himself to the first three stanzas, as if to conjure the despair.) After his contemplation of timeless visions and his celebration of the immortality of passion, the poet in Keats's "Ode" rediscovers time, knowing that the characters in the procession were obliged to leave a former place--that the "peaceful citadel" has been "emptied" of its folk, that the "little town by river or sea shore" is now "silent," "desolate," dead: the urn, teasing him "out of thought," is just "cold pastoral." Art is not thereby condemned, however: man should accept not to substitute it for reality, not to make it an absolute. This lesson in relativism, contained in the famous response of the urn at the end of the poem (possibly evading the issue), is what Quentin's *absolutism* rejects. If Keats accepts "the pious frauds of art," as he claims in one of his letters,[21] Quentin refuses compromission, the acceptance of his limitations. But for man, who is not destined to play the harp, angelism means death--a condition which Pascal has admirably recognized.

With *The Sound and the Fury*, Faulkner realized his most
remarkable portrait of the artist: a *negative* image, however.
For while Quentin possesses the poet's vision, he is also,
more mercilessly than other poet figures in any of Faulkner's
works, the poet *unmasked*: by making him a tragicomic figure,
the impotent--indeed insincere--defender of his sister's honor,
by pointing out in him the devious ways of desire, and above
all by exposing his narcissism and the radical infirmity of
his vision and of his language, Faulkner distanced himself
as much as possible from the character who remained eminently
his double. Thus, he could cease representing the artist as
faun or Pierrot, as warrior or wounded hero: he could make
him a *poet*. Such *reflection* demanded, on the part of the
author, a total investment, made possible by distancing and
exposing his alter ego. In writing his most intimate work,
he was obliged to detach himself from it in order to succeed:
hence Quentin had to be a failed poet, and *The Sound and the
Fury* the most splendid failure of its author.

At once exemplary and failed, admirable and pitiful,
Quentin has kept figuring the poet in Faulkner's imagination.
In *Absalom, Absalom!*, he is the only one of the narrators
capable of inventing, jointly with Shreve, the truth about
Sutpen. And he can already be recognized in one of Faulkner's
first short stories, "Carcassonne": by the force of his
visionary imagination alone, the anonymous poet transcends
time and tide and becomes the creator of his own apotheosis,
*"galloping up the hill and right off into the high heaven
of the world,"* on a too symbolical horse with *"a mane like
tangled fire."*[22] Most likely written as early as 1926, placed
significantly at the end of *These 13* and later of the 1950
Collected Stories, "Carcassonne" represents in Faulkner's
fiction the first true signature of the poet. Two years later,
with Caddy and Quentin, Faulkner would commit himself to his
most radical reflection on creation: hence the experience of
writing *The Sound and the Fury* had to be at once agony and
ecstasy.

NOTES

1. "William Faulkner: An Introduction for *The Sound and
the Fury*," ed. James B. Meriwether, *Southern Review*, N.S. 8
(October 1972), 705-10; p. 708. Faulkner wrote this introduction in the summer of 1933, for a limited edition of the
novel by Random House, which was never published. Another
version of this introduction, a somewhat more intimate text,
probably written previously, was published as "An Introduction

to *The Sound and the Fury*" in *Mississippi Quarterly*, 26 (Summer 1973), 410-15, and reprinted in *A Faulkner Miscellany*, ed. James B. Meriwether (Jackson: University Press of Mississippi, 1974), pp. 156-61 (the edition cited here). Page references to "Intr. II" and "Intr. I" will be in parentheses after the quotations.

2. *LG*, p. 112. See Michael Millgate, "Faulkner's Masters," *Tulane Studies in English*, 23 (1978), 143-45.

3. "Introduction" to the Modern Library edition of *Sanctuary* (1932), in *Essays, Speeches and Public Letters*, ed. James P. Meriwether (New York: Random House, 1965), p. 176.

4. See *LG*, p. 239, and *FU*, pp. 19, 194.

5. "The kissed vase is clearly a libidinal object or, more precisely, a fetish, that is, an object standing *instead* of something else, the mark and mask of an absence" (André Bleikasten, *The Most Splendid Failure: Faulkner's The Sound and the Fury* [Bloomington and London: Indiana University Press, 1976], p. 146).

6. This is where Sartre is mistaken, in his celebrated essay on *The Sound and the Fury*.

7. Joseph Blotner, *Faulkner: A Biography*, vol. 1 (New York: Random House, 1974), pp. 565-66. "That Evening Sun" was published in *American Mercury*, 22 (March 1932), then revised for *These 13*, and "A Justice" was part of *These 13*, published in September 1931. In these two stories, the Compson family includes only the three oldest children. That Benjy does not yet appear may be a sign of their preceding the composition of *The Sound and the Fury*. In the absence of any evidence as to dates, Blotner offers only conjectures (see the long note to p. 566, p. *82*).

8. That the character Quentin Compson appears in these two short stories, in *The Sound and the Fury*, in *Absalom, Absalom!*, and as the narrator in "Fool About a Horse" and "Lion" (he disappeared from these two stories when Faulkner reworked them for inclusion in *The Hamlet* and *Go Down, Moses*) in no way signifies that it is necessary to know the several avatars of the character to define and understand him, nor that one should conceive of all these texts as interrelated and therefore link, for instance, Quentin's view of, and identification with, Henry Sutpen with his obsessions regarding incest in *The Sound and the Fury*. In none of these works is there any mention of a "fact" indispensable to the understanding of another. It is also noticeable that in *Absalom, Absalom!* the Compson family is made up exclusively

of Quentin and his father (no mention is made here of a sister), and that in the two stories discussed above Quentin is about twenty-four, whereas he dies at twenty in *The Sound and the Fury*. This partly invalidates Estella Schoenberg's study of Quentin's avatars, which, among other things, aims at proving that not only is *Absalom, Absalom!* better understood through *The Sound and the Fury*, but also that the reverse is true--thus implying the necessity of a retroactive reading of the 1936 novel: "Quentin's working out the story of Sutpen's children ... is Faulkner's means of retelling Quentin's story and explaining Quentin's suicide" (*Old Tales and Talking: Quentin Compson in William Faulkner's Absalom, Absalom! and Related Works* [Jackson: University of Mississippi Press, 1977], p. 4). Such a thesis cannot be accepted, so true it is that Faulkner's different works are autonomous, despite the obvious "factual" links between them (the existence of Yoknapatawpha does not imply the "saga thesis"-- that tired critical battlehorse), each text being a new *experience* in the author's reflection upon creation. Shoenberg believes that the following sentence (the epigraph to her study), from a first version of the second chapter of *Absalom, Absalom!*, brings grist to her mill: "*That was the summer before Quentin died: that summer of wisteria everywhere.*" It seems on the contrary that by suppressing it Faulkner signified the autonomy of the two novels in which Quentin is a narrator. The fact remains, nonetheless, that this hypersensitive young man is a privileged narrator in Faulkner's fiction, the most remarkable "double," remarkably distanced, of the novelist.

    9. See Jackson J. Benson, "Quentin Compson: Self-Portrait of a Young Artist's Emotions," *Twentieth Century Literature*, 17 (July 1971), 143-59 (mostly the first part of the article).

    10. *Go Down, Moses* (New York: Random House, 1942), pp. 296-97.

    11. "Trampling my shadow's bones into the concrete" (p. 118); "I walked upon the belly of my shadow" (p. 119). See also pp. 114, 138, 149. In the second section of the novel, "shadow" is, after "water," the most frequently used noun (fifty-three times). On the shadow motif in the novel, see Kathryn Gibbs Gibbons, "Quentin's Shadow," *Literature and Psychology*, 12 (Winter 1962), 16-24; Louise Dauner, "Quentin and the Walking Shadow: The Dilemma of Nature and Culture," *Arizona Quarterly*, 21 (Summer 1965), 159-71; and Bleikasten, pp. 124-25.

    12. The original title of the novel (or of the first section) was "Twilight."

13. In the manuscript of the novel, this sentence is followed by "I chose that hour," corrected into "I took that one": in this former version, apparently, the hands of the clock told Quentin the time of his death--which points to the ambiguity of the seagull image.

14. John Keats, "Ode on a Grecian Urn," stanza 1.

15. "Ode on a Grecian Urn," stanzas 2 and 3.

16. Cf. Faulkner's comments on Quentin in the "Appendix": "Who loved not the idea of the incest which he would not commit, but some presbyterian concept of its eternal punishment." See another similar comment by Faulkner in Cleanth Brooks, *William Faulkner: The Yoknapatawpha Country* (New Haven and London: Yale University Press, 1963), pp. 444-45.

17. Faulkner confirmed this in 1958 (*FU*, pp. 262-63).

18. Mr. Compson's speech in the first paragraph of Quentin's monologue evinces these characteristics. Particularly noticeable are the Latin word "mausoleum," used metaphorically here, and the phrase "reducto absurdum," in which Mr. Compson (or Faulkner?) is in fact guilty of a barbarism and a solecism.

19. The rare and learned word "philoprogenitive" seems "translated" in another conversation (or is it the same?) between Quentin and Caddy on the same subject: *"I'll tell Father then itll have to be because you love Father"* (p. 185). It is likely that the word was brought to Faulkner's attention by T.S. Eliot's poem "Mr Eliot's Sunday Morning Service," opening with this unusual line: "Polyphiloprogenitive." The influence of T.S. Eliot can be sensed in several suggestions of a "waste land" in Sections II and IV of *The Sound and the Fury*; and the caverns and grottoes of the sea in which Quentin already sees his bones "healing out" recall the ending of "The Love Song of J. Alfred Prufrock," or Section IV of *The Waste Land*, "Death by Water." Eliot's influence will be explicitly acknowledged in *Pylon*.

20. *As I Lay Dying* (New York: Cape and Smith, 1930), pp. 165-66.

21. *The Letters of John Keats*, ed. H.E. Rollins (Cambridge, Mass.: Harvard University Press, 1958), II, 80. The expression is quoted by Jean-Claude Sallé in "The Pious Frauds of Art: A Reading of the 'Ode on a Grecian Urn,'" *Studies in Romanticism*, 11 (Spring 1972), 79-93. In my reading of Keats's "Ode," I am indebted to this article and to discussions with its author.

22. *Collected Stories* (New York: Random House, 1950), p. 895.

THE "LOUD WORLD" OF
QUENTIN COMPSON

Stephen M. Ross

When Quentin Compson, in *The Sound and the Fury*, tells
his father he has committed incest, he tries to make the act
"real" by framing it in words. He substitutes the word for
the deed so that he can, Mr. Compson explains, "exorcise it
with truth."[1] Unable to affect Caddy's loss of innocence
one way or the other, Quentin wants to transform the literal
fact into the only medium he is capable of manipulating, for
through the safe abstractions of language he can reshape the
world so as to make himself a causative agent in it, erasing
Caddy's actual lovers, asserting his role as the sole control-
ler of her "innocence" and her "honor." But of course he fails,
because the word and the act are always separate for Quentin.[2]
He can no more restore Caddy's virginity than he could actually
commit incest.

Quentin's failure to conjure the dead sound "incest" into
becoming a living act demonstrates Faulkner's consistent
warning (most thoroughly discussed by Olga Vickery[3]) that
words inevitably fall short of experience, that language
can at best echo experience and even then is likely to distort
the essential nature of any person's existence. As Vickery
puts it, truth in Faulkner's world lies in "the inseparability
of the word and the act," an inseparability difficult and
perhaps impossible to achieve.[4] Eric Larsen, in extending
Vickery's analysis, insists that language to Faulkner can
be a medium for discovering truth only when it is broken
through, only when the nonverbal ground of experience underlying language is reached.[5]

But Quentin's monologue is a more complex portrayal of a
particular kind of linguistic experience, a kind common in
Faulkner's works, than has anywhere been discussed. Beyond

From Studies in the Novel, *7 (Summer 1975), 245-57. Reprinted
by permission.*

being a demonstration that a word cannot become its referent,
beyond Quentin's hopeless lie to his father, is a life that
is "linguistic" to its very core, partaking of the inherent
frustrations and limitations which the medium of language en-
forces. Both in the manner through which he reveals Quentin's
consciousness to us, and in the substance of Quentin's memories
and actions, Faulkner builds his character's experience out
of dramatized language so that all phenomena take on the
symbolic significance of "word."

The particular kind of linguistic experience I am referring
to here is talking. Few novelists have made such varied use
of the human voice as has Faulkner; the sense of felt life he
creates always carries with it the sound of man's "puny in-
exhaustible voice, still talking."[6] Ranging from the verbosity
of the reporter in *Pylon* to the colloquial dialogue of poor
white farmers, from idle gossip in Jefferson to intense debates
about the meaning of history, talk is more than simply another
human activity to be recorded in Faulkner's world. Beyond its
mere occurrence talking (and its receptive counterpart, listening) become a crucial mode of confronting existence, an exem-
plum of man's unique but limited creative powers. Many of
Faulkner's central figures experience portions of their lives
through the voices of others, and they in turn try to formulate
verbal equivalents to their experience. Bayard Sartoris (and
his twin, John) were imbued with their romantic lust for danger
partly by hearing stories like those Aunt Jenny tells of Jeb
Stuart. Gail Hightower lives with phantoms first evoked by
the tales his Negro cook told him as a boy. Quentin Compson,
in *Absalom, Absalom!*, listens to Rosa Coldfield, to his father,
to Shreve, and even to himself rehearse versions of Sutpen's
rise and fall, until he can "hear" the story without having
to listen. Scenes of storytelling and listening, like the
brilliantly rendered opening of *Absalom, Absalom!* when Quentin
sits in Rosa's tomblike house listening to the ghost that
haunts her voice, serve often as critical moments of discovery and recapitulation. Ike McCaslin, in probably the most
famous such scene, tries to comprehend the moral dilemma of
all Southern history in his long debate with Cass in Part Four
of "The Bear"--even the ledgers Ike reads "sound" like a
dialogue from out of the past.

Faulkner frequently reveals his characters by having
someone in the story talk about them: in a sense Faulkner
dramatizes the effort he wants his readers to extend in contemplating his people by having us share the fascination of
some talker or listener. Byron Bunch, for example, learns of
Hightower's strange career in Jefferson from the anecdotes
the townspeople tell him.[7] We hear of Lena's travels with

Byron when the furniture dealer tells the story to his wife
(to put her in the mood for lovemaking). "Community narrators"
in such short stories as "A Rose for Emily," "Hair," or "Cen-
taur in Brass" talk to us and to characters within the story
about their fellow citizens. It is in conversations that men
like Gavin Stevens in *Light in August* and in *Intruder in the
Dust* and like the reporter in *Pylon* offer their analyses of
people they seek to understand. Though words are, for Faulkner,
insufficient to touch genuine experience, though they are
too often a "forlorn echo ... high in the air,"[8] they become
nonetheless a crucial version of experience, as again and
again Faulkner sets his people in motion by having them talk.

In this way, too, Faulkner dramatizes language itself.
In talking, language becomes experiential, and thus more than
simply a device for depicting event or revealing character.
Talking and listening are, after all, acts, something one
can do to affect his life. But because they are acts which
embrace language, they include the ironies of a medium once
removed from actuality. Linguistic experience, as Vickery
rightly insists, is a special kind in Faulkner, and it is
his continual use of conversation and storytelling which
brings that experience within the boundaries of his fictional
world. Usually, for example, when Faulkner employs a character-
narrator, he has him relate his tale to someone else *in* the
story, making that act of narration itself a dramatic event.
In this way the ambiguities of language become part of the
world we must contemplate because language is literally acted
out before us. Faulkner conceived of his fiction as articulated
drama, as tales "to be repeated and retold."[9] Malcolm Cowley
reports that when he asked Faulkner if he ever felt possessed
by a demon in his inkwell (the way Hawthorne did), Faulkner
responded that "'I listen to the voices, and when I put down
what the voices say, it's right.'"[10] In Quentin's monologue
Faulkner infuses the voices into every tortured convolution
of his character's thought and experience.

Faulkner's experiments with stream of consciousness in
The Sound and the Fury reflect his conception of fiction as
told story. He achieves the striking resonance in Quentin's
monologue by blending two techniques common in fiction--
straightforward first-person narration and associative stream
of consciousness.[11] Quentin's voice, we must remember, is
literally the only one we hear, for he is both the sole
narrator of events and the sole articulator of his own consciousness. He talks in the same sense that any first-person
narrator does, telling a story in a fashion that creates
the dramatic illusion of controlled speech. Much of his monologue, therefore, takes the form of highly conventional narra-

tive prose. From this talking Faulkner derives thought by
altering Quentin's storytelling so as to move it away from
objective narration toward more spontaneous associative
patterns, modulating the form of Quentin's talking so he can
move us in and out of the young man's agonized inner consciousness. The following passage typifies Quentin's "modulated narration":

> When it closed I crossed to the other side and leaned
> on the rail above the boathouses. The float was empty
> and the doors were closed. The crew just pulled in the
> late afternoon now, resting up before. The shadow of
> the bridge, the tiers of railing, my shadow leaning
> flat upon the water, so easily had I tricked it that
> would not quit me. At least fifty feet it was, and if
> I only had something to blot it into the water, holding
> it until it was drowned, the shadow of the package
> like two shoes wrapped up lying on the water. Niggers
> say a drowned man's shadow was watching for him in the
> water all the time. It twinkled and glinted, like
> breathing, the float slow like breathing too, and
> debris half submerged, healing out to the sea and the
> caverns and the grottoes of the sea. The displacement
> of water is equal to the something of something. Reducto
> absurdum of all human experience, and two six-pound
> flat-irons weigh more than one tailor's goose. What a
> sinful waste Dilsey would say. Benjy knew it when
> Damuddy died. He cried. *He smell hit. He smell hit.*
> (pp. 110-11)

Quentin's narrating here becomes steadily more disjointed:
the fantasy about tricking his shadow intrudes into the opening, controlled sentences, destroying their cohesion. A
Negro folk saying, an allusion to Coleridge's "Kubla Khan,"
a half-remembered version of Archimedes' principle--these
break into Quentin's irreproachably objective account of his
last day as he drifts into subjective rumination on the past,
so that by the end of the passage he merely quotes words
spoken far back in his Mississippi childhood. He is absorbed
into the past and seems actually to hear the voices he
quotes.

In a manner symbolically like the way any speaker varies
the tone, the intensity, or the pace of his speaking, only
far more extensively, Faulkner modulates Quentin's talking
to reflect the boy's erratic emotional meanderings through
time and event. He signals variations in Quentin's voice with
changes in form--in style, punctuation, paragraphing, printed
type, etc. Though Faulkner is deliberately inconsistent in

using such variations, he is consistent in varying the degree
of control Quentin has over any given statement or description.
When Quentin has complete control over his words, he talks as
an objective narrator does: he moves the action along chronologically, speaking in brief, lucid sentences; he fills in
the background of people we meet, such as Gerald Bland or
the Deacon; and he carefully identifies speakers when he
quotes them—this last sign of control is especially important
since so many of Quentin's memories are of spoken words. Faulkner indicates Quentin's control by writing prose in normal
form; when Quentin speaks in this manner, he is not merely
thinking out loud; he is telling a story, moving us through
a day's events, and thus he is accomplishing a potentially
public act of verbalization. Such talking becomes psychologically revealing of his private self because Quentin cannot
maintain his mastery over objective narrative apparatus.
Sometimes he seems able to choose what he will tell us, while
at other times the words form in his mind whether he wants
them to or not. Whenever he begins to lose control, whenever
his talking moves away from public articulation toward private
thought, his storytelling becomes distorted in form.

Standard narrative apparatus is not reserved for the day
at Harvard, but for any moment in the present or past that
Quentin seems able to face directly and control through his
talking. He can deliberately remember and report, in proper
form, some incidents from the past, as he does the anecdote
about Louis Hatcher (pp. 141-42). The day in school, however,
when he counts the remaining minutes on his fingers (p. 108),
is a bit more painful to recall, so the form of this episode
is slightly unconventional—the separate speeches are not
separately paragraphed. The more painful it is for Quentin
to remember an event, the more unconventional the narrative
form becomes, until he lets words tumble uninhibited through
his mind with only slight regard for punctuation, paragraphing, speaker identification—for the signs of controlled
narration. In those episodes which have affected him the
most severely—episodes which are all verbal confrontations
of some sort—the words of others echo from the depths of his
memory, beyond the reach of his narrative control. Normally
a storyteller, whether the author or a character, identifies
speakers to avoid confusion; when Quentin omits such identification it means he is involuntarily entangled in memory,
reliving instead of reporting the speech of others, no longer
able to serve as helpful narrator.

With this technique of modulated narration Faulkner
creates a remarkably flexible voice for Quentin. In discussing
the Quentin section Carey Wall identifies three voices: an

oral voice, which is properly punctuated and usually coherent;
stream of consciousness, which is elliptical and usually
unpunctuated; and the voice of Quentin's unconscious, printed
in italics.[12] Though this is a helpful schema, I do not think
we can make such clear distinctions between oral, stream of
consciousness, and unconscious voices, since they flow and
blend into one another. Indeed it would be difficult to account
for all the variations in voice without listing every altera-
tion, not merely in punctuation or typeface, but in syntax,
in speaker identification, in imagery. Italics, for example,
are not used exclusively for Quentin's deepest absorption in
thought, nor even for his most uncontrolled narration: he can
quote words, even his father's, in a reasonably careful fashion
"*Father said it used to be a gentleman was known by his books;
nowadays he is known by the ones he has not returned*" (p. 99).
And other passages, like the argument between his father and
mother, which seems out of conscious control, are printed
partly in italics (p. 118) and partly in roman type (p. 126).

The revisions which Faulkner made in the manuscript of
the Quentin section are informative here, for they suggest
that he did begin with Quentin's conscious talking and then
work toward modulations in voice and form as he moved deeper
into Quentin's story. He apparently began writing the section
as a standard first-person account, not as stream-of-consciousness monologue. From page numbers that have been crossed out
in the manuscript it appears that the conversation between
Caddy and Quentin at the branch (pp. 186-202 in the published
novel) originally opened the section.[13] In the manuscript
this entire episode is written in normal form with quotation
marks, internal punctuation, and speaker identification:

> "Is Benjy still crying?" she said without moving.
> "I don't know," I said. "He's gone to bed, I guess."
> "Poor Benjy," she said.
> I sat down on the bank. The grass was a little
> damp. I could feel that my shoes were damp.
> "Get out of that water," I said. "Are you crazy?"
> "All right," she said. But she didn't move. Her
> face was a white blur. Her hair framed it out of the
> sand.
> "Get out now," I said.[14]

In the typescript and final published versions, after Faulkner
had decided to distort the form of Quentin's talking and push
his narration closer to stream of consciousness, he rewrote
the dialogue to make it part of Quentin's uncontrolled memory:

> is Benjy still crying
> I dont know yes I dont know

> poor Benjy
> I sat down on the bank the grass was damp a little
> then I found my shoes were wet
>   get out of that water are you crazy
>   but she didnt move her face was a white blur framed
> out of the blur of the sand by her hair
>   get out now (p. 186)

Faulkner also enhanced the dramatic immediacy of this scene
by eliminating many of Quentin's conscious thoughts and leaving
only bare dialogue and frantic, run-on description. As originally
written this episode was far more under Quentin's narrative
control than it is in the final version. In the manuscript,
for example, appears the following passage which Faulkner considerably shortened (the lines I have bracketed are lined out
in the manuscript):

> "Yes," I said. "Yes. Lots of times. With lots of
> girls." Then I was crying. Her hand came out and touched
> my head. I moved my head but her hand came again, and
> then I was crying against her wet blouse and she was
> holding my head in her arms. Her blouse was still damp,
> but she was hard and warm under it, and she held me
> hard. Then she was lying on her back, looking up at the
> sky, and I bending over her. I could see her eyes looking
> past my head.
>   [I had a little knife.] Then I took my knife and
> opened it. [I thought about the knife Dilsey sliced
> meat with, and about Dilsey putting Benjy to bed, and
> about the night Damuddy died, when we all slept in the
> same room and the muddy bottom of Caddy's drawers in
> the pear tree.] I held the point against Caddy's throat.
> "Do you remember the day Damuddy died, when you sat
> down in the water in your underclothes?" I whispered.
>   "Yes," Caddy whispered. I held the point of the
> knife against her throat.[15]

The published version reads:

> yes yes lots of times with lots of girls
> then I was crying her hand touched me again and I
> was crying against her damp blouse then she lying on
> her back looking past my head into the sky I could see
> a rim of white under her irises I opened my knife
>   do you remember the day damuddy died when you sat
> down in the water in your drawers
>   yes
> I held the point of the knife at her throat. (p. 188)

By assigning all narrative duties to Quentin, Faulkner succeeds
in making fine and subtle adjustments in his revelation of
Quentin's consciousness without ever leaving the confines of
his character's mind. The variations in style, in prose rhythms,
in form and typography, come to represent the swirls of emotion
in Quentin's soul; the shape of Quentin's talking becomes a
linguistic equivalent of his consciousness. In this sense even
the most objective accounts Quentin gives us are part of his
thought and are in themselves self-revealing, for the carefully articulated sentences are restrained in the same willful,
clenched-teeth fashion that his actions on that last day are;
even his controlled talking, like his excessive neatness,
becomes a prelude to his suicide.

  The passage I quoted earlier, when Quentin stands on the
bridge watching his shadow in the water, is typical in content
as well as technique. The major portion of Quentin's memories
are either quotations or paraphrases of spoken words. In the
quoted passage, besides alluding to Coleridge, Quentin thinks
of what "Niggers say," he repeats his father's definition of
time as the "reducto absurdum of all human experience," he
thinks of what Dilsey would say about his suicide, and at his
deepest immersion in the past he simply quotes the spoken
words *"He smell hit."* All of Quentin's major experiences, as
remembered on this last day, take the form of verbal confrontations: arguments between his mother and father, arguments
with Caddy, with Herbert Head, with Dalton Ames, with his
father. So much do voices dominate Quentin's consciousness
that his mind seems like a room jammed with chattering people
none of whom makes any sense to him. He recalls a chorus of
voices, a chorus made up of his sister's despairing indifference to Quentin's cherished ideals of "Love" and "Honor,"
"I've got to marry somebody" (p. 143); a chorus that includes
his mother's *"voice weeping steadily and softly beyond the
twilit door"* (p. 117), his father's voice cynically proclaiming that women *"have an affinity for evil"* (p. 119), and
always in the background Benjy's *"voice above the gabble"*
(p. 130).
  It is ironically appropriate that we learn about Quentin,
and about the family, by listening to his voice, for most of
his life Quentin has listened passively to the voices swirl-
ing around him. Always being told things, he could never really
do anything, never affect events by his own acts either because there was nothing to do or because his conception of
action was so hopelessly romantic. Quentin's experience has
been an abstraction of real life the way words are abstractions of real things.

On his final day alive the words of others return to haunt his imagination. Quentin mentally objectifies his past as voices, reweaving the texture of his family's life out of their spoken words; people assume the shapes of their disembodied voices, distinguished by what they say or how they talk, not by what they do or how they look. Vocal imagery and references to voices and to talking occur throughout the monologue. The three boys Quentin meets on the bridge "all talked at once, their voices insistent and contradictory and impatient, making of unreality a possibility, then a probability, then an incontrovertible fact, as people will when their desires become words" (p. 145). Among Quentin's fondest memories of Negroes is that of Louis Hatcher, whose hunting call could be heard for miles: "When he called the dogs in he sounded just like the horn he carried slung on his shoulder and never used, but clearer, mellower, as though his voice were a part of darkness and silence, coiling out of it, coiling into it again. WhoOoooo. WhoOoooo. WhoOoooooooooooooooo" (p. 142). He thinks of death "as a man something like Grandfather a friend of his" and he hears the "murmur of their voices from beyond the cedars they were always talking and Grandfather was always right" (pp. 218, 219). At Caddy's wedding Quentin expresses his hatred for Herbert Head and for all the relatives and guests by imagining someone saying over and over *"Quentin has shot Herbert he shot his voice through the floor of Caddy's room"*; *"Quentin has shot all of their voices through the floor of Caddy's room"* (pp. 130, 138). Benjy's bellowing seems a palpable thing to him: *"his voice hammering back and forth as though its own momentum would not let it stop as though there were no place for it in silence bellowing"* (p. 154). Even his broken leg, which had to be painfully rebroken and reset, speaks to him: *"told me the bone would have to be broken again and inside me it began to say Ah Ah Ah and I began to sweat"* (p. 140).

Among the many symbolic patterns in which Faulkner embodies Quentin's agony—patterns like Quentin's concern with time, the imagery of water, and of fire—the vocal imagery and the quantity of remembered dialogue most clearly define the quality of Quentin's relationships with other people. Like a listener, Quentin allows others' words to formulate his life for him, passively absorbing experiences that he should actively engage in. The sexual confusion and nausea which underlie much of his suffering have been enhanced by his tendency to transmute experience into a verbal form that he can listen to safely. Except for his preadolescent sex-play with the "cow-faced" Natalie—a scene itself rendered primarily as a dialogue—Quentin has apparently had

no direct sexual experience. He has discovered sex, like so
much else, from what others have told him. His romantic notions
of honor and chastity can be traced to his mother's constant
harping on respectability, while his contradictory obsession
with physical sexuality was abetted by his father's words. Mr.
Compson's imagery reinforces the disgust and fascination
Quentin expresses as he thinks about Caddy and her lovers:
"Because women so delicate so mysterious Father said. Delicate
equilibrium of periodical filth between two moons balanced.
Moons he said full and yellow as harvest moons her hips thighs"
(p. 159).

Besides actually spying on Caddy, Quentin tries to get
her to tell him about her lovemaking, for maybe he can understand sex if it is put into words. He demands to know if she
loved her partners, being unable to imagine how she could have
intercourse if she did not love them, but at the same time
being unable to believe she could love a "cad," a "blackguard,"
or a "town squirt." He wants Caddy to admit her sin out loud,
to put it into words so he can deal with it:

> ... *Why must you marry somebody Caddy*
> *Do you want me to say it do you think that if I*
> *say it it wont be* (p. 151)

Even his major effort at protecting his sister's fragile honor
deteriorates into purely verbal confrontation, since all he
can do is fling melodramatic lines at Dalton Ames--"I'll give
you until sundown to leave town" (p. 198). Nor do words have
any more effect on Caddy, as she seems to ignore his attempts
to threaten her with incest and murder. For the same reason
he cannot cope with Caddy's surrogate at Harvard, the little
Italian girl he calls "little sister," since she too refuses
to respond to his words. Quentin is helpless when words will
not suffice, and for him they almost never do. Perhaps in
reaction to guilt he feels over his incestuous desire for
Caddy, Quentin is so horrified at his own sexuality that he
dreams of being devoid of it altogether. One remarkable
passage, beginning as so many of Quentin's memories do with
something he has heard, sums up his own sexual fears and
symbolizes the abstracted, secondhand, even linguistic nature
of his feelings about sex:

> Versh told me about a man mutilated himself. He went
> into the woods and did it with a razor, sitting in a
> ditch. A broken razor flinging them backward over his
> shoulder the same motion complete the jerked skein of
> blood backward not looping. But that's not it. It's
> not not having them. It's never to have had them then

> I could say O That That's Chinese I dont know Chinese.
> And Father said it's because you are a virgin ... and
> I said That's just words and he said So is virginity
> and I said you dont know. You cant know and he said
> Yes. On the instant when we come to realise that tragedy
> is second-hand. (p. 143)

Sex is indeed Chinese to Quentin--words he can hear but never
quite understand.

The most frequent references to what another has said are
to Mr. Compson: "Father said" runs like an obsessive refrain
through Quentin's thoughts.[16] Nowhere is Quentin's role as
listener more evident or more damaging than in his relationship with his father. Mr. Compson appears in his son's memory
as only a voice, never being described in any other way, by
an action, a gesture, or by physical appearance. In his own
thinking Quentin compulsively reiterates his father's cynical
comments on sex, time, women, on life itself. In some ways
Quentin's most traumatic memory, condensing into one painful
episode all his impotent gestures at forcing truth into his
own artificial mold, is the long debate he has with his father
shortly after Caddy's wedding.[17] He wants to persuade his
father (and himself) that things are not as they seem, that
he has been Caddy's lover all along and that he intends to
kill himself; he seeks to turn his own fantastic wishes into
"incontrovertible fact, as people will when their desires
become words." But partly because he cannot convince his father
of anything, only his suicide will become "incontrovertible."

Instead of persuading his father that his intentions are
genuine, Quentin is again forced to listen as Mr. Compson
analyzes him, erecting a wall of words impossible to break
through. In this confrontation Quentin desperately seeks to
discover a personally relevant explanation for what has
happened to Caddy and himself. Instead he finds Mr. Compson's
clever skepticism. Employing words as they can be so easily--
to avoid reality by abstracting it into general formulas--
Mr. Compson offers no true gesture of affection for his son.
His tragic mistake is that when confronted by his son's confession of deeply felt urges, Mr. Compson turns it into an
occasion for verbal gymnastics. Like an orator he insists
on broadening Quentin's personal anguish into a problem for
an entire audience, a mere instance of a "general truth the
sequence of natural events and their causes which shadows
every mans brow" (p. 220). His voice, in its effect on Quentin,
is that of a debater ticking off his winning points one by
one; when he thinks he has finally discovered the crux of
Quentin's problem, he sounds almost triumphant: "you cannot
bear to think that someday it will no longer hurt you like

this now were getting at it" (p. 220). Not a callous man,
Mr. Compson is only weak, seeking refuge in drink and unas-
sailable cynicism. He rightly sees that Quentin has "wanted
to sublimate a piece of natural human folly into a horror
and then exorcise it with truth" (p. 220), but the accuracy
of his analysis only heightens his failure. Intellectual perception and its clever articulation do not meet Quentin's
emotional needs, and when Quentin continues to insist on the
reality of his feelings, Mr. Compson can only suggest a hopelessly trivial--and ironic--reason why his son should stay
alive: "you will remember that for you to go to harvard has
been your mothers dream since you were born and no compson
has ever disappointed a lady" (p. 221).

We cannot assume, of course, that had Mr. Compson responded
differently to Quentin all would have been well; Quentin is
troubled by more than his father's words. But rather than clarifying matters, Mr. Compson only forces Quentin to play his
passive, listening role in another agonizing verbal confrontation to be recalled and relived. His father's becomes just
another voice to be drowned out by death--as his mother is
nothing more than a voice whining behind a door, Mr. Compson
is a voice proclaiming the futility of human existence.

Quentin's tragedy, which we hear in *his* voice, is that he
can never shut out the myriad voices whirling through his mind.
He cannot shut them out because they are really all he has.
He substitutes word for act because for him the word *is* the
act. Only by killing himself does he act wordlessly, seeking
silence in death, a soundless void away from his loud world
of voices: "it was to isolate her out of the loud world so
that it would have to flee us of necessity and then the sound
of it would be as though it had never been ... if i could tell
you we did it would have been so and then the others wouldnt
be so and then the world would roar away" (p. 220).

NOTES

1. *The Sound and the Fury*, p. 220. All references to *The
Sound and the Fury* are to the Random House edition reproduced
photographically from a copy of the first printing.

2. Eric Larsen makes this point in "The Barrier of Language: The Irony of Language in Faulkner," *Modern Fiction
Studies*, 13 (Spring 1967), 21.

3. *The Novels of William Faulkner*, rev. ed. (Baton Rouge:
Louisiana State University Press, 1964), pp. 266-81.

4. Ibid., p. 273.

5. Larsen, p. 28.

6. Faulkner's Nobel Prize Acceptance Speech, rpt. in *Essays, Speeches and Public Letters*, ed. James B. Meriwether (New York: Random House, 1965), p. 120.

7. Originally the story of Hightower's life in Jefferson (in Chapter 3 of *Light in August*) was literally told by someone in the town: remnants of the original, quoted colloquial anecdote are still in the manuscript (at the University of Virginia) along with the changes Faulkner made to render the story omnisciently.

8. The words are Addie Bundren's in *As I Lay Dying*, 1964 Random House edition, p. 167.

9. William Faulkner, Interview with Simon Claxton, rpt. *Lion in the Garden: Interviews with William Faulkner, 1926-1962*, ed. James B. Meriwether and Michael Millgate (New York: Random House, 1968), p. 277.

10. *The Faulkner-Cowley File: Letters and Memoirs, 1944-1962* (New York: Viking, 1966), p. 114.

11. Peter Swiggart, in *The Art of Faulkner's Novels* (Austin: University of Texas Press, 1962), pp. 61-74, and Carey Wall in *"The Sound and the Fury*: The Emotional Center," *Midwest Quarterly*, 11 (July 1970), 371-87, have discussed the standard narrative elements in the three Compson monologues.

12. Wall, pp. 377-78.

13. Quentin's section begins on page 34 of the manuscript. The six pages of the Caddy-Quentin conversation were originally numbered 34-40, but Faulkner crossed out these numbers and substituted, first, 43-49, then 44-50, and finally 70-76, the episode's final position in the story. The manuscript of *The Sound and the Fury* is deposited at the University of Virginia.

14. MS, p. 70. I am grateful to Mrs. Jill Faulkner Summers and to the University of Virginia for permission to quote from the manuscript.

15. Ibid., p. 71.

16. Nearly all the references to "Father said" were added to the monologue upon revision; as he made Quentin's narration less controlled, Faulkner also increased the importance given Mr. Compson's words in Quentin's memory. For example, Mr. Compson's statements about virginity, which immediately follow Quentin's reference to sex as "Chinese" (quoted above), were

added after the manuscript version was written. In the manuscript Mr. Compson speaks mainly in one scene, the debate
with Quentin; in the final version Faulkner scattered Mr.
Compson's words throughout the monologue, so that they per-
vade Quentin's thoughts. One other minor change, in the
debate itself, suggests Faulkner's care in pushing crucial
conversations deeper into Quentin's subconscious: the manuscript includes the word "said" with the speaker identification (and i said ... and he said). By leaving out "said"
Faulkner took away one more signal of Quentin's narrative
control.

17. Faulkner once stated that Quentin never actually
told his father he had committed incest, that he only wished
to make such a dramatic gesture (see *Faulkner in the University*, ed. Frederick L. Gwynn and Joseph L. Blotner [New
York: Vintage Books, 1965], p. 262). But whether Quentin
is remembering or imagining the debate with his father, the
psychological effect Mr. Compson's words have on him remains
the same.

THE RECOLLECTION AND THE BLOOD:
JASON'S ROLE IN *THE SOUND AND THE FURY*

Duncan Aswell

   The Sound and the Fury has attracted widespread critical
attention largely because of the technical brilliance and
difficulty of the Benjy and Quentin sections and the moving
Easter service that Dilsey attends near the end of the novel.
Considerably less emphasis has been placed upon the depiction
of Jason, one of Faulkner's most vivid, convincing, and humor-
ous portraits. Jason's monologue serves as an ironic commentary on the major themes of the novel, extending their significance in ways Jason is largely unaware of. His conception
of himself as a man of the world allows him to assert his
total unlikeness to Benjy and Quentin, neither of whom is
able to cope with the world at all. Yet Faulkner shows Jason
to be not only incompetent in practical, worldly affairs,
but driven by the same compulsions and forced to act out the
same obsessions as his unfortunate brothers.[1]
   The Reverend Shegog articulates a central theme of the
novel when he addresses his "breddren en sistuhn" in the
audience on the subject of "the recollection and the blood
of the Lamb." The preacher speaks to all mankind as his
brethren, and to an extent the search of the Compsons for
some significant truth or meaning in life is the dilemma
faced by every human being. But the preacher's emphasis on
"the recollection and the blood" is specially relevant to
the three Compson brothers in their relationships to their
sister, Caddy. Jason can no more free himself from the burden
of remembering and dwelling upon Caddy and compulsively re-
enacting his childhood relationship to her than Benjy and
Quentin can, and in so doing he bears witness to that blood
tie with all the Compsons that he continually attempts to
ignore or to use for his own benefit. His mother, his niece,
Dilsey, and his own thoughts continually remind him through-

From Mississippi Quarterly, *21 (Summer 1968), 211-18. Reprinted by permission.*

out the day of the duties and responsibilities owed to "flesh
and blood." In an ironic way, his actions bear eloquent testimony to his own statement that "blood is blood and you
cant get around it" (Modern Library edition, p. 260).

The heritage of blood shows preeminently in the way Jason
conducts his business and practical affairs. He considers
himself a resolutely self-reliant and independent fellow, convinced that the only way to get ahead in the world is to
trust no man and to take heed of nobody's feelings. He sees
human life as subject to no absolute and eternal powers but
only to the endless permutations of chance and change. In a
universe governed by *luck*, each man is worth as much as his
hands and brains can get for him. This doctrine is a debased
version of his father's philosophy, as it is recalled by
Quentin just before his monologue ends and Jason's begins.
Mr. Compson mocks Quentin's concern with infinitude, with
apotheosis, and urges him to keep his mind on "the sequence
of natural events and their causes which shadows every mans
brow" (p. 195). Every human act, every gesture, every feeling
can be characterized by the single adjective "temporary,"
and life to Quentin's father is a game of chance presided
over by the "dark diceman" (pp. 196-97). Faulkner elaborates
Mr. Compson's fatalism at this point in the novel not only
to suggest the compelling force behind Quentin's suicide, but
to provide an ironic framework for Jason's behavior. Jason
unwittingly lives his life according to the system of values
believed in by his father, for whom he holds nothing but
contempt.[2]

Yet Jason would not be a Compson if he did not turn his
code of behavior into an inflexible and unmanageable rule.
He converts a philosophy of extreme relativism into absolutism, makes temporality eternal. In a hilarious passage at
the height of his maniacal determination to catch his "flee-
ing niece, he imagines himself speeding past "the rear guards
of Circumstance" and "dragging Omnipotence down from His
throne, if necessary" (p. 322). This is apotheosis, of a
kind, the ultimate triumph of the private-enterprise system.
Yet the rear guards of Circumstance are, cruelly, not far behind. A moment later, when Jason discovers he has forgotten
to carry a camphor-soaked handkerchief on his journey toward
the Almighty, he sees himself "mocked by his own triumphing."
This, indeed, is the keynote of Jason's whole day, being
beaten by his own cleverness, or, as Job puts it, "You fools
a man whut so smart he cant even keep up wid hisself ... Mr.
Jason Compson" (p. 267). Jason consistently fails to reach
his specific, pragmatic goals because of his devotion to
unrealities and abstractions.[3] His business sense is seriously

impaired by his reliance on personal whims and prejudices for
the sake of demonstrating his independence. A nice example
is his refusal to bet on the Yankees, the team that won not
only the American League pennant in 1928 but the World Series
in four straight games. Jason's argument against them is
characteristic: "You think a team can be that lucky forever?"
(p. 269). Even in the face of logic and sense, he insists on
reducing all experience to temporary status, as if he were
his father.

While Jason considers all human events to be subject to
endless change, he views the human personality itself as
unalterably fixed and frozen. This conviction provides Jason
with one constant factor in a world of variables; having observed an individual's behavior, one can predict his actions
in the future. The fine irony of Jason's monologue is that
he can articulate such a belief about everyone he knows,
without realizing the ways in which he is fated to obey the
very same law. He is frequently incorrect in his predictions
about other people, but he manifests his own inescapable obsessions in every move he makes. His ignorance of himself
is most clearly and amusingly revealed at the very moments
when he expresses his sharp awareness that his behavior is
ludicrous. He is so completely concerned with the way his
actions appear to other people that he never considers the
impulses that drive him from within. When he first catches
sight of Quentin with the showman, he says of his following
them: "Me, without any hat, in the middle of the afternoon,
having to chase up and down back alleys because of my mother's
good name. Like I say you cant do anything with a woman like
that, if she's got it in her. If it's in her blood, you cant
do anything with her.... And there I was, without any hat,
looking like I was crazy too" (p. 250). The point, of course,
is that he is *acting* as if he were crazy, not just appearing
to be so. He has the madness in his blood, no less than
Quentin, and all of his clever awareness of his own and other
people's follies and incapacities is no help to him in check-
ing his irrationality. "Like I say blood always tells. If
you've got blood like that in you, you'll do anything. [!]
I says whatever claim you believe she has on you has already
been discharged; I says from now on you have only yourself
to blame because you know what any sensible person would do"
(p. 256). Jason's pronouns are delightfully ambiguous, suggesting the confusion in his mind between his own and other
people's actions, but the "you" in the last sentence can
certainly refer to himself. He cannot possibly be considered
a "sensible person," and his lack of sense is especially
pointed in his inability to learn from his own experience.

Jason's static and unyielding character as well as his
similarity to his brothers is emphasized by the structure of
his monologue. He announces his conviction about the human
personality in his very first statement, "Once a bitch always
a bitch, what I say" (p. 198), and then returns to it at the
very end of his narrative: "Like I say once a bitch always
a bitch" (p. 280).[4] Over and over again during the day he
introduces his remarks with the nagging refrain "Like I say,"
and the tag suggests how incapable Jason is of freeing himself
from his own formulas and simplifications. Yet the one su-
premely important subject that he cannot keep away from is
the promiscuity of Caddy and her daughter. He begins and ends
with it; his mind revolves endlessly around and around this
one track. His monologue, like Benjy's and Quentin's, moves
in a circle, but Jason's has the smallest radius. Benjy circles
back through time to his earliest memory of Caddy's kindness,
concluding with the pleasure of being put to bed by her as
a tiny child. The progression is backwards, but the circle
has passed through a great variety of images and impressions,
all of which Benjy still actually possesses as part of his
tangible enjoyment of the present instant. Quentin traces a
smaller, spatial circle, returning at the end to his starting-
point in his Harvard room. His aimless, compulsive wandering
and the scrupulous attention to petty detail on which his
monologue closes mock his desire for a confrontation with
eternity, a way out of the circle. But the scope of his
journeying seems enormous compared to the infinitesimal
area covered by Jason, for all his frantic scrambling around
the Mississippi countryside.[5]

Jason resembles Quentin not only in his obsessive concern
with his relative's promiscuity, but in his extravagant view
of the seriousness of the crimes he must punish and the lengths
to which he must go to avenge himself. Quentin visualizes an
eternity of suffering with Caddy as an answer to the meaninglessness and impermanence to which he and she are doomed.
Jason's pursuit of his niece is a ludicrous parody of Quentin's
teleological concern. He asserts an indifference to her fate
at one moment: "... I says far as I'm concerned, let her go
to hell as fast as she pleases and the sooner the better"
(p. 256), yet he qualifies this almost immediately when he
addresses his niece in his mind: "These damn little slick
haired squirts, thinking they are raising so much hell, I'll
show them something about hell I says, and you too. I'll make
him think that damn red tie is the latch string to hell ..."
(pp. 258-59). Like his brother, Jason will not be happy until
he can assure himself that he has tracked his prey to her
final, eternal restingplace. Such a concern with ultimates

and absolutes obscures for both brothers the extent of their
actual and literal complicity in the corruption for which
they seek revenge. Just as Quentin is shown smearing mud over
Caddy's body in a symbolic prefiguration of her sexual impurity
(p. 156), so Jason is accused by his niece of making her act
the way she does (pp. 276-77). Jason is not wholly responsible
for his niece's misconduct, nor did Quentin alone stain his
sister's honor, but the brothers' extravagant and unnatural
preoccupations--Jason's with respectability, Quentin's with
virginity--place intolerable demands upon the young lives
they should be protecting.

Jason's devotion to much the same kind of unreal, hopeless, and abstract upholding of "honor" as Quentin believes
in is appropriately concluded in a burlesque scene that might
have come straight out of Quentin's day. Jason's preposterous
tangle with the old man in a pullman car in Mottson is a
clear reminder of Quentin's quixotic attack upon Gerald Bland.
In both cases the recollection of dishonor leads to blood
at the hands of someone wholly unconnected with the family.
Quentin had been unable to distinguish the past from the
present, his memories from literal fact, while Jason manifests his delusion by assuming that his private affairs are
a subject of universal interest and ridicule. When he arrives
at the railroad siding in Mottson, he expresses his fear that
"the whole world would know that he, Jason Compson, had been
robbed by Quentin, his niece, a bitch" (p. 324). He provokes
the old man to attack him by assuming that his fantasy has
already come true; he calls the old man a liar for not revealing the whereabouts of people whose names have not even
been mentioned. The similarity of this incident to Quentin's
irrational behavior is pointed up when Jason's rescuer asks
him, "What were you trying to do? Commit suicide? ... You
her--brother?" (p. 327). Jason's perpetual worries about
bleeding from the blow of a hatchet also recall Quentin's
miserable performance as a fighter. Jason wasn't even struck
by the old man; he simply hit his head on a rail when he fell.
Quentin, likewise, wasn't hit by Dalton Ames, but "had just
passed out like a girl" (p. 181). Shreve embarrassedly reports
that Quentin *may* have struck Gerald Bland when no one was
looking, but there is no question about the blood streaming
from Quentin's nose (p. 183). The two brothers are equally
pathetic and inept defenders of the Compson name.

Having been reduced in foolishness and in public humiliation to the level of Quentin, Jason is now ready to experience even further degradation. As he sits completely immobilized in his car waiting for some Negro to drive him home,
he assumes the posture of the impotent Benjy on his afternoon

rides with T.P. Faulkner concludes the scene in Mottson with
a picture of Jason being driven home, his mind empty of all
but the thought that relief for his headache awaits him in
Jefferson:

> They drove on, along the streets where people were
> turning peacefully into houses and Sunday dinners, and
> on out of town. He thought that. He wasn't thinking
> of home, where Ben and Luster were eating cold dinner
> at the kitchen table. Something--the absence of disaster,
> threat, in any constant evil--permitted him to forget
> Jefferson as any place which he had ever seen before,
> where his life must resume itself. (p. 329)

The blood is quieted, the recollections still; for the moment
there is nothing for Jason to do but to surrender himself to
physical sensations in the manner of Ben. With this sight of
Jason utterly helpless and unable to think about his responsibilities, the novel swings back to Benjy and completes another
circle, returning to the situation of the opening pages. Ben
and Luster are again at the fence, watching the golfers in
the pasture. Despite Jason's and Quentin's absence, the life
of the Compsons has resumed itself, in all its pointless
repetitiveness.

Jason's descent through a series of ludicrous misadventures from cocksure man-of-the-world to a state of abject
dependency is the most brilliant touch in this masterful
portrait. While he likes to think of himself as an uncompro-
mising dispenser of favors and punishments, he is actually
as helpless to make any significant or lasting impression
upon those around him as is Quentin to perform a permanently
meaningful act. Jason might like to think that he is a ruthless villain, but he is incapable of hurting anyone but himself. Because he cannot escape the heritage of his past,
his life is quite as pathetic and miserable as Benjy's or
Quentin's. His final act, the rescuing of Benjy at the monument, is as meaningless a gesture as any of his others.[6] It is
not motivated by kindness or generosity, but by the same
compulsive concern for public propriety that has always driven
him. The reader's sense of justice is nicely satisfied by
seeing the worldly brother come to the aid of one who is unable to cope with the world, yet there is no consciousness
within the novel to record and profit from the irony. The
characters themselves are largely ignorant of the patterns
and correspondences that tie them together. Their recollections and their blood relationships are no source of joy and
strength to them, not aids toward knowledge and growth. The
movement of the novel is endlessly circular. The ending

represents a kind of triumph for Benjy; but the triumph of mindlessness in a work about the tortures and travail of the human mind is a Pyrrhic victory indeed.

NOTES

1. Jason's similarity to his brothers has been suggested by recent critics, but it has been demonstrated only in limited and theoretical ways. Lawrence E. Bowling, for example ("Faulkner and the Theme of Innocence," *Kenyon Review*, 20 [Summer 1958], 466-87), examines innocence as a characteristic of all three Compson brothers. He shows Jason to be innocent in a different sense from Benjy and Quentin because "he remains ignorant of basic human principles" (p. 475). Cleanth Brooks (*William Faulkner: The Yoknapatawpha Country* [New Haven: Yale University Press, 1963]) compares attitudes toward the future in the three brothers. He says, "Jason is so committed to preparation for the future that he is almost as enslaved as are his brothers" (p. 330). Brooks also emphasizes, however, Jason's difference from his brothers. He contrasts Quentin's commitment to "the code of honor" with Jason's repudiation of that code (p. 337). John W. Hunt (*William Faulkner: Art in Theological Tension* [Syracuse: Syracuse University Press, 1965]) is concerned with what he calls "the locus and status of meaning" for each of the characters, and he contrasts Jason's "purely personal" meaning and "pragmatic value" system with a meaning that, for Quentin, is "a general one, informing all of life" (p. 69). Quentin's and Jason's value systems are contrasted even more sharply by Lawrance Thompson ("Mirror Analogues in *The Sound and the Fury*," *William Faulkner: Three Decades of Criticism*, ed. Frederick J. Hoffman and Olga Vickery [New York and Burlingame: Harcourt, Brace & World, 1960], pp. 211-25): "Jason's sadistic scale of values is more nearly analogous to the values of Iago than to those of the almost Hamlet-like Quentin" (pp. 224-25). Irving Howe (*William Faulkner* [New York: Vintage Books, 1952, 2nd ed.]) draws sharp contrasts among the three brothers: "Benjy is the past recaptured; Quentin ... cannot hold the past with the purity Benjy can; Jason violently breaks from the past ..." (p. 161). Jason might like to think he breaks violently from the past; I hope to show that he is as trapped by it as are Benjy and Quentin.

2. Wendell V. Harris ("Faulkner's *The Sound and the Fury*," *Explicator*, 21 [March 1963], Item 54) has traced the influence of Mr. Compson on each of his children, but he limits Jason's debt to his father to "bitterness" and Jason's "petulantly cynical tone."

3. Contrast the traditional view of Jason as altogether incapable of abstract formulations, as a thoroughgoing pragmatist. See, for example, William R. Mueller ("The Theme of Suffering: William Faulkner's *The Sound and the Fury*," *The Prophetic Voice in Modern Fiction* [New York: Association Press, 1959]): "Jason was almost as incapable as Benjy of conceptual thought and was consequently poles apart from Quentin in this respect" (p. 117). Compare Lawrence E. Bowling ("Faulkner and the Theme of Isolation," *Georgia Review*, 18 [Spring 1964], 50-66): "Unlike Quentin, who judges human actions by an abstract ideal, Jason considers an act right or wrong solely on the basis of whether it results in his gain or loss of material goods" (p. 59).

4. Bowling ("Theme of Isolation") calls "bitch" the key word for Jason because it represents "Jason's naturalistic philosophy of life: he considers the whole human race no better than a pack of dogs, and he does everything he can to "free" himself from any connection with them" (p. 59).

5. The sense the novel provides of activity severely limited and circumscribed is described in terms of the characters' personal isolation by Bowling ("Theme of Isolation") and by William A. Freedman ("The Technique of Isolation in *The Sound and the Fury*," *Mississippi Quarterly*, 15 [Winter 1961-1962], 21-26). Freedman says: "Jason is forever asserting his own independence, his ability to 'stand on his own two feet.' Yet this is but a hyper-reaction to a strong sense of his own imprisonment" (p. 25).

6. John V. Hagopian ("Nihilism in Faulkner's *The Sound and the Fury*," *Modern Fiction Studies*, 13 [Spring 1967], 45-55) has accurately analyzed the effect of the closing pages. He concludes: "At the end Benjy is, of course, unaware of the futility of his more primitive kind of order in the face of existential nothingness; but the chaos he experiences and responds to with moanings and howlings, and the false order that ironically soothes him, dramatically frame the entire novel in the same way that Mr. Compson's sophisticated commentary frames the Quentin section. It is therefore Mr. Compson, and not Dilsey, whose values finally prevail."

THE RHETORIC OF COMMUNION:
VOICE IN *THE SOUND AND THE FURY*

Margaret Blanchard

"The human voice has a disarming quality (we
are not single, we are one)."--*The Waves*

Who is the narrator in the fourth section of *The Sound
and the Fury*? Most of us, stunned perhaps by encountering
what seems like conventional narration after charting our
course through the tortuous monologues of the first three
sections, take the fourth speaker for granted. Others, while
recognizing a presence, have unintentionally demonstrated the
inadequacy of existing critical terms to describe it: *omniscient*, *objective*, *semi-omniscient*, *third person objective*,
omniscient third person, *objective omniscient*, and so on.[1]
  Apparently most of us feel sufficiently reassured by the
speaker to relax in his presence. But why is he there? Is he
there to tell us the Truth, to gather the pieces together
and fill in the gaps of some coherent statement about the
universe or the South or the Compsons? If so, one feels it
was a failure (as Faulkner himself claimed). The fourth section
provides no summing-up, no final interpretation, no further
insight into the apparent center of the book, Caddy, no
essential truth we can hold in our heads as we walk away from
the novel.
  Even if one agrees with Hagopian's skillful analysis of
the last section as providing us finally with a nihilistic
comment on life,[2] one must admit that this interpretation
derives from the structure and not from the presence or voice
of that section. This presence asserts itself so powerfully
in the first sentence that, after the fragmented and distorted
viewpoints of the preceding sections, one is tempted to
assume it is omniscient:

From American Literature, 41 (January 1970), 555-65. *Copy-
right 1970, Duke University Press. Reprinted by permission.*

> The day dawned bleak and chill, a moving wall of
> grey light out of the northeast which, instead of dis-
> solving into moisture, seemed to disintegrate into
> minute and venomous particles, like dust that, when
> Dilsey opened the door of the cabin and emerged, needled
> laterally into her flesh, precipitating not so much a
> moisture as a substance partaking of the quality of
> thin, not quite congealed oil. (p. 330)[3]

A closer examination, however, reveals that the speaker is
neither "omniscient" (all-knowing) nor "objective" (without
bias or without involvement) but, rather, an extremely acute
and articulate observer. There is nothing in the passage above
which is not perceptible to any such spectator; at no point
do we know how Dilsey really feels or what is going to happen
to her.

"Omniscient" as a description of the authorial stance,
whether he is above or behind or beneath his fiction, is much
too vague because it is too absolute, allowing too few distinctions. "Objective" as a measure of the writer's involvement
with his material is supervague; perhaps one can say that
scientific language is objective, but when it comes to ascer-
taining the subjectivity of poetic language, one needs more
precision. If "omniscient" and "objective" have any meaning
at all in criticism, they designate degrees of privilege[4]
granted to the persona. And if these terms are used to measure
privilege, then they are at opposite poles on the scale,
which is: (1) ostensibly complete limitation: dramatic or
"objective"; (2) limited to the inside view of one character;
(3) limited to multiperson inside views; (4) omniscient but
fallible; (5) "omniscient" (knowing what) and "infallible"
(knowing why). The fourth section of *The Sound and the Fury*
cannot therefore be *both* omniscient and objective, as several
critics maintain.

A close examination of the section reveals that the
privilege of the narrator is almost completely limited. In
fact, until page 390 he is never allowed inside a character's
head. There are only three places where it might seem he has
penetrated to a character's viewpoint, but actually these
are conclusions woven into the conjectural narrative fabric
of a highly conscious spectator. Thus when the narrator states
that although Mrs. Compson could not see clearly, she *"knew
that [Dilsey] had lowered her face a little"* (p. 339), or
that Luster was using "the mallet with which [Dilsey] had
been making beaten biscuit *for more than thirty years*," or
that Dilsey "thought Mrs. Compson was asleep," he is only
stating what would be obvious to a spectator who saw the
whole scene and heard the dialogue within it: "Dilsey said

nothing. She made no further move." (Thus Mrs. Compson knew.)
"'You're not the one who has to bear it,' Mrs. Compson said."
(Thus we know she knew.) We know Dilsey thought Mrs. Compson
was asleep because she "was about to close the door when the
other spoke" (p. 373). These are the only instances, in the
first part of the section, of the slightest privilege.

What might seem like foreshadowing as foreknowledge, the
description of Luster's hand on the chair "as if he were
picking an inaudible tune" before we discover him in the cellar
with the saw, is really just another example of acute perception. The typical stance of the narrator is shown in his
description of Quentin's room: "It was not a girl's room. It
was not anybody's room" (p. 352). He describes it as if he
were seeing it for the first time and yet as one who has been
exposed to the family long enough to guess at its import:
"that dead and stereotyped transience of rooms in assignation
houses."

Only once between pages 330 and 380 does the narrator
attempt to explain an action:

> Mrs Compson said nothing. Like so many cold, weak
> people, when faced at last by the incontrovertible
> disaster she exhumed from somewhere a sort of fortitude,
> strength. In her case it was an unshakable conviction
> regarding the yet unplumbed event. "Well," she said
> presently, "Did you find it?" (p. 373)

One doesn't need much exposure to Mrs. Compson to be able
to arrive at this somewhat grudging ("from somewhere a sort
of") acknowledgment.

The only view through which the narrator's voice is
allowed to filter is Jason's, and this occurs only gradually.
The first few pages of Jason's pursuit of Quentin (pp. 376-
80) are restricted to the same dramatic description found
in the beginning of section four, the outsider's view heightened by the use of "a": a narrow street, a frame house, a
big man; and by hesitant phrases like "seeming to" and "appear."
On page 380 the narrator first tentatively enters Jason's mind:
"He looked at the sky, *thinking* about rain." At first the
privilege flows from observation of action and dialogue:
"'See if you can elect a man to office that can stop me,' he
said, thinking of himself entering the courthouse" (p. 381),
but gradually it penetrates deeper and deeper into his consciousness as he sees "himself mocked by his own triumphing"
(p. 383).

The perspective never becomes Jason's point of view
though--the contrast with section three is sharp. The voice
retains its own integrity, emerging from the filter to express

Jason's reactions in its own terms: "dragging Omnipotence
down from His throne" (p. 382), and "He could see the opposed
forces of his destiny and his will drawing swiftly together
now, toward a junction that would be irrevocable" (p. 384).
Very seldom are words given which can only be Jason's: "a
bitch of a girl." The distance between Jason and the narrator
is underlined by phrases repeating the third person: It seemed
to him; he imagined himself; he could see; Jason saw; he
believed; he felt himself; he wasn't thinking of.

On the other hand the persona never becomes "omniscient";
he knows nothing more than Jason's thoughts. He does not know
what will happen to Jason, any more than Jason does, or why,
and he has no control over what does. He never rises above
the second level of privilege: limited to the inside view of
one character. At best he can speculate about alternatives:
"It never occurred to [Jason] that they might not be there"
(p. 385). Such speculation, again, could flow from the perspective of a spectator who is considerably less hysterical
about the events he witnesses than are the participants. After
Jason's mad chase (pp. 376-92) the narrator returns to his
strictly limited perspective.

The restrictions of this perspective are stressed by the
conjectural quality of most of the narrative. Although some
of this is characteristic of Faulkner's style in general, the
extent of conjecture in this section calls special attention
to it. Almost every page contains at least one conjectural
phrase: as though, as if, appeared, seemed, it might have
been; or a phrase which stresses the limited knowledge of the
perceiver: something without particular tune, attitude that
of one who, insignificant looking, with something like con-
sternation.

A typical passage is the following:

> Luster returned, wearing a stiff new straw hat with
> a coloured band and carrying a cloth cap. The hat seemed
> to isolate Luster's skull, in the beholder's eye as a
> spotlight would, in all its individual planes and
> angles. So peculiarly individual was its shape that
> at first glance the hat appeared to be on the head of
> someone standing immediately behind Luster. (p. 360)

This tentativeness of the spectator is heightened by the constant use of analogy ("as a spotlight" above) as if to make
the reality witnessed more familiar to the speaker (like a
tug, like butterflies, like a man on a tight rope, like a
little boy, like marbles, like a big foolish dog, and so on)
and by the strings of adjectives, attempting, it seems, to
pin down that reality: "her face flaccid and querulous, in-

terminable, clairvoyant yet obtuse" (p. 349). The effect
stresses both the (illusion of) reality and the limitation
of the speaker: *This is so real I can't quite get a hold of
it*. As a result of his perspective, the narrator wisely sticks
to those more immediate forms of presentation, narrative,
description, and scene, with very little commentary and none
of the more abstract and privileged devices of summary or
analysis.

Along with these conjectural elements there is a certain
progression of insight by the speaker. Just as he gradually
enters Jason's mind, so he moves from being the spectator
as outsider to becoming an insider but still a spectator.
This movement is summarized neatly in the following passage:

> *A woman* was with [Luster]. "Here dey come," Dilsey
> said. They passed out the gate. "Now, den," she said.
> Ben ceased. Luster *and his mother* overtook them. *Frony*
> wore a dress of bright blue silk and a flowered hat.
> She was *a thin woman, with a flat, pleasant face.* (p.
> 361)

The narrator thus moves from seeing Frony as if for the first
time, recognizing her as Luster's mother, remembering her name,
then describing her, still as if having seen her for the first
time. One might wonder at this point if Faulkner is playing a
game with his reader. If the narrator is seeing her for the
first time, how does he know who she is? Perhaps the persona
is one who had never seen Frony but had heard enough about
her to recognize her when he saw her. Or perhaps the movement to recognition is strictly a visual one: initially the
woman is too far away from him to know who she is or to notice
details of dress and feature. Either way the perspective is
decidedly limited.

When critics speak of the narrator's "objectivity," I
think they are pointing to a question of his relationship
with the material, which involves the degree of temporal
and spatial *distance* between speaker and subject (from close
to remote) and the degree of *engagement*, personal risk,
identification, meshing of self with characters or action
(from involved to detached). It does not follow that if one
is close to the material, he is automatically involved or
that if he is remote, he is automatically detached--although
such relationships do seem the more expected.

The persona of the fourth section has no more temporal
distance from his subject than is afforded by the use of the
past tense. The detailed precision of his observations--"She
wore a dressing gown of quilted black satin, holding it close
under her chin. In the other hand she held a red rubber hot

water bottle" (pp. 332-33)--suggests that he is also close
spatially. The speaker, however, while not without his bias,
is relatively detached: he does not insist that we adopt his
interpretation; he does not seem to risk a personal rejection
in offering it.

Gathering all this evidence together, we emerge with a
description of the speaker's perspective as limited, having
no foreknowledge, no control over events, privileged access
into one mind only, and much recourse to conjecture, rewarded
at times with progressive insight and empathetic sharing of
a character's viewpoint, with a spectator's close but restricted
view of events, and his detachment. The person whose perspective fits this description is not a god paring his fingernails,
not Faulkner, not Dilsey, but *the reader* (which is the long
way round to Swiggart's intuition, stated but not substan-
tiated, that "the language of Dilsey's section suggests the
point of view of a reader"[5]) enduring enough to have finished
the first three sections and intelligent enough to have com-
prehended them.

This is not to say, however, that the narrator is the
reader, but only that the narrator--out of respect for the
reader perhaps--has adopted the reader's perspective. Because
perspective--the relationship between the speaker and his subject, involving questions of distance, engagement, privilege,
filter--can be distinguished from tone--the speaker's attitude
toward self, subject, and audience--we can say that while the
narrator's perspective is that of a reader, his tone is his
own.

That the speaker's perspective is the reader's explains
several aspects of the narration otherwise puzzling. Why are
we allowed access to Jason's mind only and not Dilsey's or
Mrs. Compson's? Because the reader, having already absorbed
Jason's perspective through his monologue, is able to project
himself into Jason's mind; he has not had the same experience
of the interior responses of other characters in the last
section (except Ben's and he no longer needs access to know
Ben's reactions) and thus must wait for them to reveal themselves (fortunately Dilsey's expression is so integrated
with her character that one need not get inside her to appreciate her).

At the same time the reader's experience of certain
characters has been so restricted to their own views of themselves that he can be startled when he sees them from the
outside. It would be like hearing someone on a record or
telephone or radio and then seeing him in person. Even if he
has been described by others, he will look, at least momen-
tarily, like a stranger. Descriptions by people who already

know him contain their own interpretations ("a damn oversize
mothball" [p. 232]). Thus when the reader first sees Ben,
he is baffled:

> ... a big man who appeared to have been shaped of some
> substance whose particles would not or did not cohere
> to one another or to the frame which supported it. His
> skin was dead looking and hairless; dropsical too, he
> moved with a shambling gait like a trained bear. His
> hair was pale and fine. It had been brushed smoothly
> down upon his brow like that of children in daguerrotypes.
> His eyes were clear, of the pale sweet blue of corn-
> flowers, his thick mouth hung open, drooling a little.
> (p. 342)

Somewhere in the midst of this observation the reader says
to himself, "Oh, it's Benjy ... of course." The scientific
description of Benjy at this point is not meant to be cold
and callous; it serves instead as a measure of the reader's
previous empathy with Benjy. The more he accepted the character's view of himself, the more he is apt to be startled by
his actual appearance. For all Jason's grossness, it is somewhat surprising to see him as the caricature of a bartender.

The reader's acquaintance with the first three sections
of the novel explains the limits of his knowledge. He remembers, for example, the white satin slipper Caddy gave to
Benjy: "It was yellow *now* and cracked and soiled" (p. 395).
He notices the "running shadow patches" which Benjy experienced
as going on "smooth and steady but a little slower" and which
Quentin trod all daylong until they disappeared into darkness.
He remembers how long Dilsey has been there (more than thirty
years) and Jason's "old premonitions" and Frony's name. Anything not in the first three sections he must guess about,
and since much in these sections is partial, elusive, and
contradictory, he is in a position of guessing most of the
time.

As several critics have noted, the first three sections
force the reader to participate in the novel, to become in
a way the narrator. Faulkner seems to formalize this role
in the final section by adopting as the fourth perspective
the reader's perspective. Almost as reward to the reader
willing to become writer, Faulkner grants recognition by
himself, the writer, becoming reader. Perhaps he was suggesting this in the Nagano interview: "I knew that it was not anywhere near finished and then I had to write another section
from the outside with an outsider, which was the writer, to
tell what had happened on that particular day."

The narrator's voice, while incorporating the perspective
of the reader, maintains through style its own attitudes;
thus it gains in rhetorical persuasiveness. The narrator honors
the reader by sharing his perspective and compliments him by
the controlled complexity of his sentence structure (see the
first full sentence on p. 331), the abstract precision of his
diction (*arpeggio, desiccation, burgeoning, retrograde, ob-
verse, reconnoitred, hiatus*), and the range and quality of
his figures and allusions: *like old silver or walls of Mexican
houses, machine-like, his wooden avatar, like a medieval
jailer's key ring, like a tug nudging at a clumsy tanker,
with the covertness of nocturnal animals, like an alto horn,
succubus like, like a crucifix, like an old nun praying,
organlike basso*.

While all this may be dismissed as typical of Faulkner's
style, it also functions (relative at least to other examples
of Faulkner's style where sentence structure is much more
involved and diction more inflated, or where the narrator
is less educated and more provincial) to reveal the narrator's
intelligence, sophistication, and freedom from provinciality
and from the obsessiveness exposed in the similes of Quentin
and Jason. And such a revelation reflects his respect for his
reader, his assumption that such qualities can be shared.

Thus the narrator, having already conditioned the reader's
perspective by the selection of detail in the first three
sections and by forcing him to participate in the narration,
establishes empathy in the fourth section by adopting his
perspective and complimenting him by the way he speaks to
him. Consequently the reader is much more ready to adopt,
in turn, the narrator's tone, no matter how demanding its
implications.

This tone manifests itself through such heightening of
diction as: *regal and moribund* color, *somnolent and impervious*
guts, *coordinating* the meal, *evincing an enigmatic profundity,
random and tentative* sun, *grave hopeless sound of all voiceless misery*; and by such mythic images as: Dilsey's *indomitable
skeleton ... rising like a ruin or a landmark*; the preacher
*a meagre figure, hunched over upon itself like that of one
long immured in striving with the implacable earth ... like
a worn small rock whelmed by the successive waves of his
voice ... that, succubus like, had fleshed its teeth in him*
(p. 367); *the horse's gait resembling a prolonged and suspended fall in a forward direction*; the *scarce-broken* meal;
the clock tick-tocking *solemn and profound ...* (like) *the
dry pulse of the decaying house itself*.

As Swiggart observes, the narrator is "anxious to establish
figures like Benjy and Dilsey as symbolic archetypes." If we

look again at the first paragraph of this section, we see
Dilsey almost immediately established as the archetype of
survival: standing against the bleak attack of dawn and dust,
she *endures*. I think Swiggart is wrong, however, when he
concludes that the "artificial rhetoric" is used for self-
mockery or "serio-comic" effect. However strained and therefore perhaps unintentionally comic the style may seem, the
effect is not comic, not even ironic (contrast it for example
with the appendix: "as a miniature replica of all the whole
vast globy earth may be poised on the nose of a trained seal,"
so Quentin's concept of Compson honor balanced on Caddy's
virginity).

The irony of this section is not verbal but dramatic,
such as Mrs. Compson's using the first person plural, "None
of *us* ever go in there except Sunday to clean it," and her
complaint, "When I've tried so hard to raise them Christians";
or situational, Jason's gasoline allergy and his contribution
at the end to reestablishing Benjy's order. Other ironic
effects such as the echo of Jason's eyes, the eyes of the
statue of the Confederate soldier, and Benjy's eyes as *empty*
are hardly comic. Even such descriptions as Jason's "invisible
life ravelled out about him like a worn out sock" has more
of pity in it than scorn.

I think that just as Shakespeare raised Macbeth's nihilistic
tale to a formulation positive because it is art, so Faulkner
is attempting to raise the dying fall of the Compson chronicle
to meaningful articulation by heightening its mythic under-
tones. (Therefore I disagree with Irving Howe, who thinks that
the narrative tone--dead, sterile, public--parallels the
collapse of the Compsons; I think the tone, neither dead nor
sterile, serves as a counterpoint to the plot.) As Florence
Leaver expresses it: "Making use of abstract terms around
which have clustered untold associations, he makes language
transcend itself by hypersuggestion.... By the rhetoric of
abstraction Faulkner repeatedly impregnates the simplest
acts with cosmic significance."[6]

When, for example, he speaks of Luster *invisible and
blind within and beyond his wooden avatar* (p. 340), the
speaker links such a prosaic subject as the pile of logs
Luster carries with a Hindu incarnation. That the splinters
from a shattered society and the meager fire they yield can
represent a god's coming down in bodily form to the earth
and that the minister of this rite is Luster may indeed seem
ironic, but not so far removed from the mythic implications
of other incarnations such as that of a brown carpenter who
died on a wooden cross.

Thus the narrator of the fourth section tells the tale which otherwise would not be told (except by the clock which tells time stutteringly with only one hand), neither by the mute but bellowing "idiot" Benjy; by the tattletale Jason, more concerned with the release of telling than with the substance of what is told ("his sense of injury and importance feeding upon its own sound"); by the all too articulate Quentin, obsessed with not telling and unable to communicate because he escapes into words which signify no reality; nor by the silent Dilsey. Except for her, "they all talked at once, their voices insistent and contradictory and impatient, making of unreality a possibility, then a probability, then an incontrovertible fact, as people will when their desires become words" (p. 145).

The Compson telling is indeed full of sound and fury signifying nothing, but the tale told about them is fully expressed and meaningful, just as is the tale of the preacher: "I tells you breddren, en I tells you sistuhn," which also echoes through the voices of its characters: "We gwine to kill you little Jesu (This sentence is a perfect example of how speaker's voice, character's point of view, and audience perspective can blend: the language and the tone--*little* Jesus--are the speaker's voice with the audience perspective but the characters'-- "we"--intention.) "Dey done kilt my Son!"; "Dey kilt Me dat ye shall live again" (p. 370).

Despite the nihilistic ending of the novel, we discover-- within a fictive world as artificial as the "painted back-drop" in which a road "like a cut ribbon" fails to reach the "painted church," the scene "as flat and without perspective as a painted cardboard set upon the ultimate edge of the flat earth" (p. 364)--a presence as compelling as that of the Negro preacher moving from virtuosity on the "cold, inflectionless wire of his voice" (p. 366) to articulation gathering up all the "tatters of sound" and giving voice to "all voiceless misery under the sun" (p. 395).

NOTES

1. Olga Vickery: *objective*; Peter Swiggart: *semi-omniscient*; Melvin Backman: *objective*; Walter J. Slatoff: *omniscient and objective*; William Van O'Connor: *objective and omniscient*; Hyatt H. Waggoner: *omniscient*; John W. Hunt: *the usual third person objective narration*; Harry M. Campbell: *omniscient, ironic objectivity*; Lawrence Edward Bowling: *regular omniscient rendering, strictly objective attitude*; John V. Hagopian: *objective and authorial*; Michael Millgate: *omniscient author*.

2. John V. Hagopian, "Nihilism in Faulkner's *The Sound and the Fury*," *Modern Fiction Studies*, 13 (Spring 1967), 45-55.

3. All quotations from the novel are from the Vintage paperback edition (New York, 1946). Page references will be included within parentheses in the text of the paper. All italics are mine; section four has no italicized passages.

4. See Wayne Booth, *The Rhetoric of Fiction* (Chicago, 1961), p. 160, for a more detailed study of this term.

5. Peter Swiggart, *The Art of Faulkner's Novels* (Austin, Texas, 1962).

6. "Faulkner: The Word as Principle and Power," *William Faulkner: Three Decades of Criticism* (New York, 1960), p. 201.

THE COMIC STRUCTURE OF
THE SOUND AND THE FURY

Fred Chappell

Only two things militate powerfully against our reading
The Sound and the Fury as a comic novel. These are the complexity and density of the background material, and the special
intensity of presentation. If we abstract ourselves for a
moment from these two strategies, if we somewhat ponder the
novel, it begins to take on a much different color from the
one it has as we read it page to page. I believe that this
personal abstraction away from the work is what Faulkner intends for the reader to experience, since he has arranged
the four sections in order of *decreasing* intensity, from the
almost unbearable immediacy of Benjy's perceptions to the
much cooler (though still not distant) third-person narrative
of the final part.... And there is too always the fact that
not even the shape of the book is clear to us until sometime
after we have put it away on the shelf.

Saith the Gospel of Matthew: *Take therefore no thought for
the morrow: for the morrow shall take thought for the things
of itself. Sufficient unto the day is the evil thereof.* This
is a maxim that the American Negro still--alas!--has to take
very much to heart, to live his life by. The Biblical injunc-
tion may be translated into this American bromide: "Just take
it one day at a time, that's all." Of the characters in *The
Sound and the Fury*, only Dilsey and a few other black characters are able to live up to this necessary imperative. All the
other characters are obsessed with the bright ungraspable phantoms they glimpse in the dead past or in the stillborn future.

Originally published in a French translation by Robert Louit,
"Structure comique de *Le Bruit et la fureur*," *Magazine Littér-
aire*, no. 133 (February 1978), 30-32. The present version in
English was made by the author, with corrections of errors.

From Mississippi Quarterly, *31 (Summer 1978), 381-86. Reprinted by permission.*

If we take--leaving aside for a moment June 2, 1910--the
order of events in present time on April 6-7-8, 1928, we see
the following design. April 6 introduces us to Jason; it is
entirely his day, a day filled with petty and scurrilous little
triumphs. He cheats Earl, his boss, out of a half-day's work,
browbeats his mother into more than her normal hysteria, cheats
his niece Quentin out of money twice, brutalizes her, insults
every person in sight, chagrins Luster by burning the show
tickets, and makes a nervewracking shambles of the evening
meal. He does all these things because it is his pleasure
to do them; he is a monster. But after all, he is a recogniz-
able monster; we find in him much of Scapin, much of Harpagon,
and a great deal of Shakespeare's Thersites. Jason is in many
respects the monomaniac villain of a stage farce. If *The Sound
and the Fury* were presented as a stage farce, we would see this
very familiar outline: Act I (April 6), Jason thwarts and
bamboozles all his acquaintances; he seems invincible; Act II
(April 7), forces of which he is ignorant, but which he has
at least partly set in motion himself (dramatic irony), are
moving against him; Act III (April 8), Jason falls; he is
robbed (legally, or at least without legal recourse), frustrated
and humiliated; and the lovers (though they are not noble
lovers) are united. The biter bit. Neatly done; in fact, it
is almost too symmetrical to be a classical farce.

The objection might be brought that Jason is not very
much on stage during Act II. And that is true, though we do--
through Dilsey and Quentin especially--feel the exacerbating
force of his presence. But *The Sound and the Fury* is after all
not a play, and April 7 is mostly concerned with others besides
Jason. Here are the springs of motion for the major events of
April 7, 1928: (1) Dilsey wants to prepare a suitable birthday celebration for Benjy; (2) Luster must have a quarter so
that he can attend the traveling musical show; (3) Quentin
wants to attract a beau in order to escape Jason's tyranny;
(4) Benjy is engaged in his unending search to recapture a
memory of the presence (and not of the absence) of his sister
Caddy.

Each of these desires comes to fruition. Dilsey manages
to bake the cake and to set thirty-three candles upon it. The
celebration in the kitchen is not entirely successful, however,
and Benjy has to be removed to the library. Luster does get
his quarter; Quentin gives it to him, and presumably it is a
part of the ten dollars given her the day before by Jason to
mollify her for being cheated--so that it is Jason who pays
Luster's way to the music. Quentin does attract someone,
passerthrough-with-the-red-tie, to take her away from Jason's
dominance; but actually it is Luster who attracts him by

hinting strongly that Quentin is sexually available (the empty prophylactic container). And because he has been removed to the library where a large open fire once burned and because he sees Quentin's escape down the pear tree, Benjy is able to seize two incontrovertible images of his sister's former presence: "Caddy's head was on Father's shoulder. Her hair was like fire, and little points of fire were in her eyes, and I went and Father lifted me up into the chair too, and Caddy held me. She smelled like trees." And finally: "Caddy held me and I could hear us all, and the darkness, and something I could smell. And then I could see the windows, where the trees were buzzing. Then the dark began to go in smooth, bright shapes, like it always does, even when Caddy says that I have been asleep."

This day, April 7, comes to a happy, even a blissful, conclusion for its principal questers.

June 2, 1910--the story of Quentin Compson's last day on earth--is set apart from the rest of the novel in any number of ways. Quentin's story is also a comic story, I think, but the comedy is darker and profounder here than in the rest of the book. But if we at once describe Quentin's character as *quixotic,* we shall have come immediately at Faulkner's intention. Quentin's destiny is tragic--as is the destiny of Cervantes' great figure--but his character is comic, like the Don's. The figure of a tragic destiny proceeding from a comic flaw always makes an audience uneasy; we laugh and cry at once, regretting that what must be so is indeed so. The gallant ridiculous man who has for no sensible reason set himself at odds with the universe draws our laughter but our sweetest sympathies also. (Buster Keaton knew this fact, and Chaplin.) Quentin's motives, like Quixote's, spring from literature, from a fairy-tale tradition about an ideal of honor which never really existed in this world. The concept of "honour" that Quentin imagines his forebears to have possessed, they never possessed; we know this well enough from the other stories that Faulkner wrote about them, and from his raffishly ironic treatment of them in the "Appendix." Quentin--against his father's very wise advice--has allowed himself to believe in, to be taken in by, a phony Southern tradition of former glory and high honor. Quentin's forefathers were men who simply did what at the time they felt they had to do; and the things they did were not always honorable, nor even always scrupulously honest.

Because we see the events of June 2, 1910, from inside Quentin's very intense consciousness (like Benjy, he is a lyric poet trapped and maimed by circumstance), and because we already know of his coming suicide, we are likely to lose

sight of his comic aspect. Still, Faulkner keeps pushing him
at us as a figure of ridicule. On his final day, this knight-
ly protector of Southern womanhood is arrested for kidnapping
a little girl (whom he calls "Sister") with intent to molest.
This whole scene is laid out as farce, with the uncomprehending outraged brother, the desultorily corrupt hamlet officials,
and the properly horrified twittery girls from Boston. If we
can manage to see him from outside, the obsessed perfervid
Quentin merely looks silly. (*Silly* is what his father calls
him.) Afterward, in the clearest analogue to episodes from
Cervantes, Quentin attacks Gerald Bland for being a womanizer
("Did you ever have a sister?") and is soundly drubbed for his
gallantry. The probable truth of the matter is that Bland is
not much a womanizer; all that notion is just loose trashy
talk he and his mother indulge in. We sympathize with Quentin
for hitting Bland, and sympathize with him all the more because he is whipped, but he is still ridiculous. He is so
ridiculous, in fact, that Shreve his roommate can only look
at him with bemused amazement.

These two comic episodes are more darkly ironic than most
of the other comic episodes in the novel, and they point up
a strain in Faulkner's work we often overlook. Faulkner likes
to employ—I suspect that he enjoys—the cruel physical
peasant joke that we find so plentiful in Cervantes, Rabelais,
Le Sage, and Smollett. The cruel peasant joke is what Faulkner
sees as the world's rough-and-ready rebuff to false idealism.

Faulkner's humor colors everything he writes, of course,
and *The Sound and the Fury* is full of characters we recognize
as comic at first sight: Luster, Roskus, T.P., Uncle Maury,
the horse Queenie (Faulkner's Rocinante), and even the tire-
somely predictable mother, Caroline, are more or less standard
comic figures. Some of the episodes are comic in the usual
way. Uncle Maury, for instance, has to attend father Jason's
funeral with a black eye because he had no better judgment
than to send a letter of assignation by an idiot. And some
episodes which we fully expect to be sad are presented comical-
ly. Caddy's wedding, for example, we expect to be gloomy since
it is the last time that Benjy shall ever see his sister. But
Faulkner presents it instead as slapstick: T.P., mistaking
the wedding champagne for sarsaparilla, gets both himself
and Benjy drunk; he then sets up a large box at the window
to watch the ceremony, but being drunk he tips the box over
backward, trapping Benjy underneath; and Caddy has to rush
out in her strange finery to rescue her brother. (Fully to
appreciate the joke, a reader must understand what great
store Southerners set by such ceremonies as weddings. Champagne
hauled into Jefferson, Mississippi, for God's sake.)

Henri Bergson's analysis of the comic character is especially relevant to a reading of *The Sound and the Fury* as
comedy. Bergson delineates the comic character as that which
acts mechanically, predictably, single-mindedly, no matter
what changes occur in the outer circumstances which surround
the character. All the Compsons gathered in this novel are
almost demonically single-minded. They are in fact so one-
purposed that they *never* change. They are the same as adults
as they were as children; in fact, Faulkner in presenting
them to us first as children invites us to predict their
adult characters. We have no trouble in doing so: Jason with
his hands in his pockets, and so forth. If comic characters
must follow settled routines, never deviating, then this
household is straitly comic, for its routine revolves about
the well-being of Benjy, and Benjy cannot tolerate any change
whatsoever in the strict order of his world. The final public
humiliation of Jason is brought about because Luster unknow-
ingly upsets the mechanical order of things, going the wrong
way round the statue.

The Compsons are trapped in their comic mechanical orders
because present time does not exist for them. Except perhaps
for Jason the father they have all given their allegiances
to an impossible past, as Quentin and Benjy have done, or to
an equally improbable future, as Jason the son has done. Of
the principal characters only Dilsey is able to live in
present time, to live one day at a time, to see sufficient
evil here and now without trying to discover more in past
or future. And Dilsey may be the one character in the novel
who is not comic, but an appreciably admirable person.

In describing *The Sound and the Fury* as a comic novel,
I do not *of course* mean to say that it is a happy novel. It
is not. I find its tone, its mood, wistful, regretful, ele-
giac, tender. But then I don't know that I can think of a
great comic novel which is happy. Not *Dead Souls*, not *Oblomov*,
not *The Magic Mountain* or *Bouvard and Pécuchet*, not, certainly not, *Don Quixote*.

FORM AND FULFILLMENT IN
THE SOUND AND THE FURY

Beverly Gross

The ending of any novel is the place where the success of
its form is most fully to be realized. Yet despite the extensive and elaborate criticism which has been directed to the
structural aspects of *The Sound and the Fury*, the ending remains a puzzlement--puzzling both in its implications and in
its position as the fulfillment of the novel's form.

It is a form that is of unusually compelling interest.
The novel's content cannot be even faintly understood until
the essentials of its form are grasped. This reverses the
normal practice of reading a novel: usually it is the content
that is in the forefront of our consciousness, and our interest
in form comes only after we have absorbed the essentials of
the content. Indeed, unless our reading habits are trained in
analytics, we do not pay much attention to the form. But *The
Sound and the Fury* is the kind of novel that simply cannot
be read unanalytically, for without a developing notion on the
reader's part of when and how the events detailed fit into
some continuum of time, some cycle of cause and effect, its
content would be incomprehensible. Consequently, the reader
finds himself asking why events are ordered in so disorderly
a fashion, and raising similar questions about why the novel
is the thing it is: why, for instance, no frame of reference
or formal exposition is anywhere expressed for him--why he
must piece one together for himself. For the form of this
novel calls marked attention to itself: the balanced juxtaposi-
tions of past and present action; the attempt to build a
structure out of successions of apparently random moments
from both past and present; the shifting of point of view and
the base of narrative present time from one section to the
next.

From Modern Language Quarterly, *29 (December 1968), 439-49.
Reprinted by permission.*

And because *The Sound and the Fury* is, for the most part,
a novel of consciousness, the reader is quickly made to see
that what will serve as the novel's organizing principle is
not a line of action. Yet the novel has additional complications which make its principles of organization even harder
to discern. Because past and present are often so complexly
interfused and because it is initially so difficult to pene-
trate the subjectivity of its narration, the novel creates
"'suspense in reverse'--instead of wondering what will happen
in the future, the reader wonders what has happened in the
past."[1] Not only must past be distinguished from present, but
the many threads of past action must be separated from each
other. The reader works inductively, forming a picture of the
continuum of the Compson past from the scattered fragments
which are given to him intermittently through each section:
mere images and sensations, bits and pieces of conversation
and event, sometimes even whole scenes and fully developed
sequences lasting many pages. But the present shifts too from
one section to the next, and with it, the whole frame of reference; the reader is successively made to start his painstaking investigations all over again. And each new section
further clarifies and enriches what has come before.

It is fairly easy to see retrospectively in what technical
senses the last section serves as a culmination to the other
three. For one thing, its action occurs farthest along in time.
It is the only section of the novel that deals exclusively
with the present, and it is a present time in advance of all
others. The novel makes other formal progressions: for instance, a notable development in the separate points of view
toward a greater and greater rationality and objective normalcy. We move from Benjy's confused sensations to Quentin's
twisted obsessiveness to Jason's "logical rational contained"[2]
literalness, and finally to the objective, omniscient third-
person narration of the last section. The character dominat-
ing but not narrating this last section is the Negro maid
Dilsey. Her good sense, generosity, dignity, and faith present
a contrast to the diseased Compsons: fractured personalities
like Benjy whose brain cannot comprehend his world, and
Quentin whose obsessions will not allow him to live in it,
and Jason whose all-encompassing nastiness makes him regard
the whole world as his natural enemy.

There is a progression from Benjy to Quentin to Jason:
we see the brothers becoming more and more responsible for
their destructive acts, more and more diseased, less and less
capable of love. We see the "Bascomb" in the family triumphing more and more over the "Compson." The sense of Compson
doom has been so fully projected, amplified, and intensified

that when in the last section the Compson point of view is
dropped, their doom is actually made that much more poignant
and final by the contrasting perspective afforded by Dilsey's
vision of salvation. Faulkner is using a kind of reversal
here, but it is not the action that is being reversed so much
as it is the emotional quality, the pathos, expressed through
the narration. With regard at least to the emotional pitch
toward which Faulkner is driving, no alternate arrangement
would have been so effective or meaningful.

These few remarks should give some idea of the many and
varied kinds of development provided by the structure of the
novel. The vision of the Compson doom grows from one section
to the next, not merely by addition, but by accretion. An
example of this accretion is the emergence of Benjy through
the novel. In his own section, we see Benjy as a tortured
subjectivity. In Quentin's section, Benjy's presence diminishes
sharply as he becomes a passive exponent of the Compson family
tragedy. In Jason's section, he is even less, for Jason sees
Benjy as a lumbering object, an obstacle in Jason's way, an
embarrassment, and a financial burden to his family which
is already burdened enough with its "kitchen full of niggers
to feed" (p. 247). But Jason's heartlessness makes us react
to Benjy with added pity: we realize the extent of Benjy's
neglect, the deprivation which had been only suggested in
Benjy's own section. Quentin and Mr. Compson are dead, and
Caddy is gone. The surviving members of the family—Jason,
Miss Quentin, and Mrs. Compson—despise him. Benjy is, in
the words of Irving Howe, "the past forsaken."[8]

In the final section, Benjy emerges as a special object
of compassion. The change in our view comes from the way in
which Dilsey and the narrator regard him: Dilsey treats Benjy
with loyalty and love, while the narrator further manipulates
our ideas and feelings about Benjy by presenting him in some
altogether new contexts and lights. Benjy's presence at the
Negro Easter service sets his suffering in the context of the
Christian sacrifice: "In the midst of the voices and the hands
Ben sat, rapt in his sweet blue gaze. Dilsey sat bolt upright
beside, crying rigidly and quietly in the annealment and the
blood of the remembered Lamb" (p. 313). For Benjy is, we are
told by Dilsey, "de Lawd's chile" (p. 333), a phrase that
suggests more than just Benjy's idiocy: it points up his
quintessential humanness in addition to providing a suggestive
identification with the Lamb of God, the Lord's child literally. Finally, the third-person omniscient narration of the
last section can do something which could not be done through
any of the three previous narrative consciousnesses: it can
discover and interpret significance. Benjy's suffering is

endowed with cosmic meaning: "Then Ben wailed again, hopeless and prolonged. It was nothing. Just sound. It might have been all time and injustice and sorrow become vocal for an instant by a conjunction of planets" (pp. 303-4). Our perceptions of and receptivity to the Compson world in general are made to undergo some radical shifts. Benjy's identity is only one part of this, but a very key part; for, as we can see by the novel's ending, the nature of Benjy's world is the image that furnishes Faulkner with an expressive conclusion to his presentation of the Compsons.

Three interrelated narrative threads are contained in the last section of the novel: the culmination to the line of present (1928) action with Jason's discovery that Miss Quentin has run away with his money; Dilsey's Easter morning; and Benjy's trip to town at the novel's end. The minute depiction of Sunday morning in the Compson house initiates the first two threads. We see Dilsey's patient and loving labor as she warms up the house and sets its life in motion. The breakfast scene culminates in Jason's discovery of Miss Quentin's flight with his hoard. Later, this thread is picked up again as we follow Jason on his trip to Mottson in his futile attempt to find Miss Quentin and the man with the red tie. The intervening action is the Negro Easter service. This completes the picture of the constituents of Dilsey's world: the kitchen, the Compson family, the church--all are her domain, her estate. She brings to all of them life and love, warmth and devotion. She stands as the abiding contrast to the sense of bleakness, pain, and egotistical withdrawal which characterizes what we have seen of the Compsons. Faulkner has been tracing the history of a family's deterioration; Dilsey represents the contrary state of endurance. The critics have pointed out how the Compson brothers in their narrations betray various kinds of inability to understand and accommodate themselves to time, with all that this implies both psychologically and symbolically. Dilsey alone knows how to live in time. She knows how to measure it--she knows, for instance, to add three hours to the number of chimes given off by the one-armed clock in the Compson kitchen. She responds to the Reverend Shegog's sermon with her own eternal vision. In short, Dilsey is perfectly in tune with both present reality and the promise of eternity.

The final thread--Benjy's trip to town--is the novel's concluding episode. It is a short scene and, purely in terms of the requirements of the action, an unnecessary coda. It requires close examination, for it is not really clear to most readers what Faulkner might be intending by it. To calm down Benjy, whom Luster has been tormenting into an unappeas-

able bellow, Dilsey gives Luster permission to drive the surrey
for Benjy's Sunday trip to the cemetery. Benjy's bellowing
subsides as he is prepared for his trip. Luster picks him a
broken narcissus which he splints with a twig. "Ben quit
whimpering. He sat in the middle of the seat, holding the re-
paired flower upright in his fist, his eyes serene and in-
effable" (p. 334). The serene gaze and the narcissus are used
repeatedly to depict Benjy in his tranquilized state. Benjy
is described "holding the flower in his fist, his gaze empty
and untroubled" (p. 335) when Luster makes the mistake of
swinging Queenie around the left side of the monument. Benjy's
equanimity is shattered and he bellows again. Jason, who has
just returned from his unnerving trip to Mottson, rushes across
the square, violently slashes the elephantine Queenie, strikes
Luster, and in so doing, again breaks the stalk of Benjy's
delicate narcissus. The surrey is swung around to the right
side of the monument, and Luster takes Benjy home. The final
sentence of the novel conveys an image of Benjy's world restored to tranquillity and order: "The broken flower drooped
over Ben's fist and his eyes were empty and blue and serene
again as cornice and façade flowed smoothly once more from
left to right; post and tree, window and doorway, and sign-
board, each in its ordered place" (p. 336).

This then is the novel's ending. In no way is it a dramatic
conclusion to the action; instead, it is a concentrated image
of intense disruption and disaster. Benjy's equanimity in the
last few pages has been twice violated and twice restored. Despite the fact that the novel closes on a note of tenuous order, the real climax of this episode and what abides most is
Benjy's anguished howling: "There was more than astonishment
in it, it was horror: shock; agony eyeless, tongueless; just
sound" (p. 335). Benjy's howl is a final reflection of the
disorder, the outrage, the meaninglessness to which the
Compsons are reduced. Thus the ending provides the novel's
most intense depiction of sound and fury.

The conclusion of the novel is thus a poetic rather than
a dramatic resolution of its forces. Dramatic resolution is
a novel's progress toward such ends as focus, equilibrium,
and clarity: a focusing of what had been divergent and disparate narrative elements; a final equilibrium of the tensions
and conflicts which had impelled and intensified the action;
and a clarification of such matters as the mysteries of character motivation, the connection among events and among characters, the outcome of challenging and distressing situations.
Dramatic resolution is a novel's synthesizing of its elements
to convert order out of disorder, equilibrium out of tensions,
meaning out of mystery. But Faulkner's novel is after some-

thing else, another kind of fulfillment. It is true that some
elements of the last section constitute an important culmination to much of the material that has come before, but not in
any traditional way and not, probably, in any totally "satis-
fying" way either. Some of the narrative threads and tensions
which are introduced through Benjy's observations on April 7
are further amplified in Jason's dealings on April 6, and
reach a focus and a climax on April 8; but it does not really
seem that Miss Quentin's escape with Jason's cache constitutes
much of a conclusion to the manifold experience this novel
deals with. Nor can we read the last section with the anticipation of any major climactic resolution to the multiple
strands of action--past and present--upon which the novel is
built.

The novel's structure is decisively against it: the fragmentation of the action and the refraction of the points of
view do not lend themselves to the expectation that this novel
is heading toward the fulfillment of a climax and a subsequent
resolution to its complications. The divisions of the novel
are individually unclimactic. The first three sections end
at arbitrary cutoff points: a time span is terminated, not an
action. Benjy's day concludes with his falling asleep, un-
comprehendingly recalling how Caddy used to put him to bed.
Jason's section closes with his self-satisfied ruminations
at the end of his day. Only in the Quentin section does the
final act constitute something of a dramatic climax to what
the hero has been doing and thinking about all day. The end
of his section shows Quentin concluding both his day and the
mesmeric preparations for his suicide. But Benjy's day and
Jason's day are supposed to be typical representations, ending, it seems, like all other days in their lives. Their
sections gain whatever sense of fulfillment they have by concluding with characteristic gestures which summarize and
epitomize the condition of both brothers.

The concluding episode of the last section has a cutoff
point that is even more arbitrary, for nothing, neither an
action nor a time span, is ended by the event. This makes the
episode stand even more starkly in need of explanation and
justification. In certain respects the ending of this section
is also a summary and an epitome--but of the whole book. The
ending epitomizes the emotional violence of the novel which
had depended throughout on certain patterned fluctuations:
the alternation between comicality and pathos; the explosive
shifts in dominant mood between serenity and rage, between
deliverance and pain, which mark the turmoil not only of
Benjy's experience, but the experience of all the Compsons.
Also reflected here is the tension between order and chaos

which implicitly relates the decline of the Compsons to a
larger moral plane. The novel becomes more objectified, more
outwardly social, more universalized in its focus from its beginnings. We see the freakish idiocy of Benjy suggestively becoming more and more an embodiment of the suffering of all mankind. This is especially pronounced during the Easter sermon,
where Benjy is repeatedly identified as the object of Christ's
sacrificial blood. We have seen Benjy's final howling invested
with universality as "the grave hopeless sound of all voiceless misery under the sun" (p. 332). For these reasons, Benjy's
outrage at the disorder he senses might be taken as a reflection of some externally real chaos in the world. In terms of
the moral sphere which the novel projects, it would seem to
be the destruction of a bygone world of heroism, morality,
tradition, and decency as the Compsons (Quentin, Caddy, Mr.
Compson) have given way to the Bascombs (Jason, Mrs. Compson),
and as even the Bascombs are now giving way to the usurping,
unidentified "Snopeses" (Miss Quentin, the man in the red
tie).

This explanation of "theme" is just one possible interpretation, which, if valid, would also suggest how difficult
it is to extract the meaning of this novel. The ending is
there to be interpreted: because of its position as the last
event of the novel, because it offers suggestiveness rather
than conclusiveness, this final episode demands that the
reader engage in some act of interpretation. Faulkner is
using the preeminent position of the novel's ending to provoke
the reader into a search for a meaning that is only remotely
suggested. The ending is meant to be immediately, and perhaps
even finally, disturbing. It disturbs by virtue of both its
meaning and its mood, so odd, so unfitting, so unfulfilling
a conclusion does it seem to be.

But disturbance can function structurally. The ending
to this novel contains one special justification for its
violation of form: Faulkner apparently felt the need to shatter
the equilibrium the novel has been working toward. The final
section of *The Sound and the Fury* has been offering up the
solution to the novel's present (1928) line of action: the
conflict between Jason and Miss Quentin. The triumph of justice implied by Jason's loss and humiliation has been giving
a certain comic and even melodramatic turn to the quality of
much of the third and fourth sections. Without this reminder
of unsettled pain, without this final glimpse of disorder,
the last half of the novel might otherwise be felt to be a
severe diminution of the emotional engagement of the first
two sections. The final episode by its sheer shock manages
to recall much of the subjective intensity expressed through

Benjy's and Quentin's consciousness earlier in the book. It
restores the novel all the more poignantly to its tragic beginnings.

In still another way, the ending recalls the novel's
beginnings. The last scene parallels many features of an
earlier ride to the cemetery reenacted in Benjy's consciousness near the beginning of the first section. In the earlier
episode Mrs. Compson is with Benjy on the drive to the cemetery to visit the graves of Quentin and Mr. Compson. Benjy
is holding a single flower from his mother's bouquet. T.P.
has just been granted permission to drive the surrey because
of Roskus' rheumatism (Luster at the end is given permission
to drive because T.P. is away). T.P., like Luster, takes
pleasure in whipping the old horse and voices the same command
that Luster voices at the end, "Hum up, Queenie." When they
get to town, Jason meets them in the square in sight of the
monument to the Confederate soldier. He enjoins his mother
to stop weeping by asking her, "Do you want to get that damn
loony to bawling in the middle of the square" (p. 31). And
the episode concludes as they continue to the cemetery with
Benjy's serene perception: "The shapes flowed on. The ones
on the other side began again, bright and fast and smooth,
like when Caddy says we are going to sleep" (p. 32). This
succession of images is repeated in the last sentence of the
Benjy section and the last section of the novel itself.

Faulkner's duplication of scenes plays upon both their
similarities and differences. The differences furnish irony
and a sense of decline in stability and decency as reflected
through Benjy's uncomprehending perception of the two events.
The dominant mood of the first scene is passive equanimity,
of the second, disruption and turmoil. A combined view of the
scene at the beginning with the one at the end gives us a
simultaneous sense of both historic continuity and timelessness. The Negroes furnish the sense of continuity, presented
as they are in their changing generations, with Luster being
to T.P. at the end what T.P. had been to Roskus at the beginning. But the circumstances of the two events are so uncannily
unchanged that they provide a sense of fateful recurrence.
Unchanged too are the three surviving Compsons: Benjy because
his intelligence is fixed, Mrs. Compson and Jason because
their characters are. Jason is retrospectively his same
pettish self. Mrs. Compson is still the nagging, self-pitying
neurasthenic who had even then been complaining, "It's a
judgment on me. But I'll be gone too, soon" (p. 31).

Without at least one rereading, it is unlikely that the
reader would connect the novel's ending with this earlier
event. But, once recognized, the affiliation between these

two episodes becomes an ordering force which gives still
another aspect of significance to the ending, providing as it
does an additional element of balance to the novel's design.
Most novels are ordered by their unity of action; this novel
quite obviously must depend on other principles. To discuss
the structure of *The Sound and the Fury* inevitably involves
us in talking less about the ordering of events than about
the ordering of its impact: what we seem to have is not a
structure of action so much as a structure of effect. Although
the ending fails to complete an action, it does complete our
vision of the degenerative process which the novel has been
depicting. It is a process which, however, is not played out
in time; for it is not the process itself which reaches its
conclusion in the novel, but our apprehension of that process.
The last event of *The Sound and the Fury* happens also to be
the last event in its temporal sequence. But it is preeminently
the novel's culmination and fruition because it furnishes the
most intense visualization of a moral universe gone awry.

Probably the best testimony to the narrative openness of
The Sound and the Fury is the Appendix which Faulkner later
added to the novel. At the request of Malcolm Cowley, who was
then engaged in editing *The Portable Faulkner*, Faulkner wrote
what was supposed to have been a kind of reader's guide to
the novel. The Appendix, however, is quite clearly less a
guide to the novel than it is a kind of supplement to it. It
has subsequently appeared as both a Preface and an Appendix
in various reprinted editions of *The Sound and the Fury*. It
is difficult to say whether the Appendix is more appropriately
appended before or after the novel since it goes both backward and forward beyond the novel's chronology. Its intent
was to put the Compsons within the framework of history by
setting the scope of the novel back several centuries to 1699
and by projecting the chronology ahead to the time the Appendix
itself was composed, 1945. In bringing the history of the
Compsons up to date, Faulkner was transforming his novel into
something like a growing, living chronicle.

But the most significant fact of the Appendix for our
interests here is that it could have been meaningfully provided in the first place. The addition of relevant material
to push back the boundaries of either the beginning or the
end of a traditional narrative structure would contradict the
idea of its unity and completeness, for, as Aristotle tells
us, the beginning of a unified plot is that which nothing
precedes, and the end is that which nothing follows. It is
hard to imagine any contribution to the plot of *Tom Jones*
if Fielding had widened the demarcations of time already
established in that novel, or a meaningful extension of the

action of *The Great Gatsby* if Fitzgerald had followed up the
marital life of the Buchanans or the midwestern life of Nick
Carraway. Most novels do not allow for further pursuit of
their matter without becoming irrelevant and malformed. *The
Sound and the Fury*, on the other hand, is a novel that, like
André Gide's *The Counterfeiters*, not only "might be continued,"
but in fact *was*. Indeed, we cannot even determine that the
Appendix finished off the possibilities for further relevant
projection of the novel's material. According to Cowley, "The
novel that Faulkner wrote about the Compsons had long ago
been given its final shape; but the pattern or body of legend
behind the novel ... was still developing."[4] The Appendix is
not necessary to *The Sound and the Fury*, nor is *Ulysses* really
necessary to the self-contained *Portrait of the Artist as a
Young Man*; but it is interesting that both these novels allow
so readily for further projections of themselves.

The *Sound and the Fury* demonstrates that there can be
significant narrative form that is not based primarily on
unity of action. The development of an action through a beginning, a middle, and an end is only one kind of organizing
principle in narration. It happens to be the most common and
traditional means of giving order to the narrative impulse.
Unity of action has been the organizing principle sought by
almost all novels of the eighteenth and nineteenth centuries.
The so-called plotless novels of the twentieth century have
been so designated because they lack this most apparent kind
of organization: a novel like *The Sound and the Fury* depends
for its structural cohesion on something having to do more
with its narrative purpose than with traditional principles
of unity, balance, and design. *The Sound and the Fury* illustrates something about the possibilities of narrative structure. It thoroughly refutes the cherished idea that form is
a predetermined configuration whose existence is anterior to
the narrative content which fills it. To an unusually great
extent, the narrative structure of Faulkner's novel seems to
have been forged out as a function of its narrative content
and purpose.

Despite an ending that is unresolved, the plot of *The
Sound and the Fury* can still be said to attain resolution--
a completeness in itself. Faulkner's Appendix does not make
the book any more complete or closed; it merely provides an
additional perspective--historic and prophetic--on the Compsons. *The Sound and the Fury* is itself fulfilled and completed
by its own ending, an ending that is a symbolic situation
with no immediate key to its symbolism, an ending that forces
the reader to look back upon the rest of the novel to find
such a key. "Completed" need not mean that the novel attains
dramatic closure, but merely that its larger impulsions reach

their fruition. "Fulfilled" need not mean that the currents of narrative action become finalized or that the currents of thought become crystallized, but merely that, through the ending, action and thought attain their potential heightening and illumination. The ending of *The Sound and the Fury* is a significant and suggestive reflection on the novel as a whole. It concludes not an action, but the enactment of a process; the novel ends not with an ending, but with an unforgettable epitome of itself.

NOTES

1. Perrin Lowrey, "Concepts of Time in *The Sound and the Fury*," in *English Institute Essays, 1952*, ed. Alan S. Downer (New York, 1954), p. 61.

2. William Faulkner, *The Sound and the Fury*, Modern Library ed. (New York, 1946), p. 16. References, all to this edition, will be cited parenthetically in the text.

3. *William Faulkner: A Critical Study*, 2nd ed. (New York, 1962), p. 159.

4. Introduction to *The Portable Faulkner* (New York, 1946), p. 9.

BIBLIOGRAPHY

In the following bibliography priority
has been given to books and articles published
since 1974. For earlier criticism, see my extensive annotated bibliography in *The Most
Splendid Failure: Faulkner's The Sound and
the Fury*, pp. 243-68.
Items preceded by asterisks are reprinted
in this collection.

Adams, Richard P. *Faulkner: Myth and Motion*. Princeton, N.J.:
    Princeton University Press, 1968, pp. 215-48. A well-in-
    formed and stimulating study of Faulkner's "mythic method"
    (parallels with Christ, the Grail Legend, the Persephone
    story).

Aiken, Conrad. "William Faulkner: The Novel as Form." *Atlantic
    Monthly*, 164 (November 1939), 650-54. Included in *A Re-
    viewer's ABC*. New York: Meridian Books, 1958, pp. 200-7.
    Rpt. in Hoffman, Frederick J., and Olga W. Vickery, eds.
    William Faulkner: Three Decades of Criticism. East Lansing:
    Michigan State University Press, 1960, pp. 135-42, and
    in Warren, Robert Penn, ed. *Faulkner: A Collection of
    Critical Essays*. Englewood Cliffs, N.J.: Prentice-Hall,
    1966, pp. 46-52. A brilliant and perceptive early essay
    on Faulkner's technique and art, with shrewd observations
    on *The Sound and the Fury*.

Aiken, David. "The 'Sojer Face' Defiance of Jason Compson."
    Thought, 52 (June 1977), 188-203. Argues for a deeper,
    fuller understanding of Jason, and interprets him as a
    modern hero of demonic defiance and self-assertion, as
    tragic in his ultimate despair as Macbeth or Milton's
    Satan.

*Aswell, Duncan. "The Recollection and the Blood: Jason's Role
    in *The Sound and the Fury*." *Mississippi Quarterly*, 21
    (Summer 1968), 211-18. An excellent essay, pointing out
    similarities between Jason and his brothers, and consider-
    ing his monologue as an ironic commentary on the novel's
    major themes.

Backmann, Melvin. *Faulkner: The Major Years. A Critical Study.*
Bloomington: Indiana University Press, 1966, pp. 13-40.
A useful general study, with discerning comments upon the
novel's symbolic motifs.

Baum, Catherine B. "'The Beautiful One': Caddy Compson as
Heroine of *The Sound and the Fury.*" *Modern Fiction Studies,*
13 (Spring 1967), 33-44. The first full discussion of
Caddy. Does justice to the complexity of the character,
but distorts its significance through unwarranted depen-
dence on the "Compson Appendix."

Benson, Jackson J. "Quentin Compson: Self-Portrait of a
Young Artist's Emotions." *Twentieth Century Literature,*
17 (July 1971), 143-59. Investigates the close relationship of Quentin to his creator. Sometimes questionable,
but stimulating.

*Blanchard, Margaret. "The Rhetoric of Communion: Voice in
The Sound and the Fury." *American Literature,* 41 (January
1970), 555-65. A fine analysis of the narrative perspective and tonality of the fourth section, suggesting that
the point of view adopted is in fact the reader's.

Bleikasten, André. *The Most Splendid Failure: Faulkner's The
Sound and the Fury.* Bloomington and London: Indiana University Press, 1976. XI + 275 pp. A book-length study,
attempting to analyze the novel from various critical
perspectives.

Blotner, Joseph. *Faulkner: A Biography,* vol. I. New York:
Random House, 1974, pp. 566-79, 588-90, 602-28, 636-39,
666-68, 810-13, 1196-98, et passim. Relates the novel to
the biographical context and provides extremely useful
information on the circumstances of its composition and
publication.

Bowling, Lawrence E. "Faulkner: Technique of *The Sound and
the Fury.*" *Kenyon Review,* 10 (Autumn 1948), 552-66. Rpt.
in Hoffman, Frederick J., and Olga W. Vickery, eds.
William Faulkner: Two Decades of Criticism. East Lansing:
Michigan State College Press, 1951, pp. 165-79. An early
discussion of Faulkner's narrative technique and a justification of its thematic appropriateness.

————. "Faulkner and the Theme of Innocence." *Kenyon Review,*
20 (Summer 1958), 466-87. Describes the novel as an exploration of the concept of innocence from the conflicting
views of puritanism and humanism.

————. "William Faulkner: The Importance of Love." *Dalhousie Review*, 43 (Winter 1963-64), 474-82. Sees the absence of love as the major cause of the family disintegration.

————. "Faulkner and the Theme of Isolation." *Georgia Review*, 18 (Spring 1964), 50-66. Focuses on symbols and imagery and emphasizes the theme of cultural crisis.

————. "Faulkner: The Theme of Pride in *The Sound and the Fury*." *Modern Fiction Studies*, 11 (Summer 1965), 129-39. Supplies a relevant analysis of the imagery of the novel's second section.

Brooks, Cleanth. "Primitivism in *The Sound and the Fury*." In Downer, Alan S., ed. *English Institute Essays, 1952*. New York: Columbia University Press, 1954, pp. 5-28. A vigorous refutation of the mistaken notion of Faulkner's primitivism.

————. "Man, Time, and Eternity." In *William Faulkner: The Yoknapatawpha Country*. New Haven, Conn., and London: Yale University Press, 1963, pp. 325-48. One of the best studies of *The Sound and the Fury*, though it is restricted to theme and character.

Broughton, Panthea Reid. *William Faulkner: The Abstract and the Actual*. Baton Rouge: Louisiana State University Press, 1974, pp. 27-28, 90-91, 92-93, 112-16, 116-17, 188-91. Argues that the Compsons fail to come to terms with life because of their rigid insistence on order.

Brown, Calvin S. "Dilsey: From Faulkner to Homer." In Zyla, W.T., and W.M. Aycock, eds. *William Faulkner: Prevailing Verities and World Literature--Proceedings of the Comparative Literature Symposium*, vol. 6. Lubbock: Texas Tech University, 1973, pp. 57-75. Contends that Dilsey should be seen as a servant figure, and not as a racial stereotype.

Brown, May Cameron. "The Language of Chaos: Quentin Compson in *The Sound and the Fury*." *American Literature*, 51 (January 1980), 544-53. Competent, but adds little to previous discussions of the subject.

Brylowski, Walter. "The Dark Vision." In *Faulkner's Olympian Laugh: Myth in the Novels*. Detroit, Mich.: Wayne State University Press, 1968, pp. 59-85. Discusses Faulkner's structural use of Christian myth, and contrasts Quentin's "mythic mode of thought" with Benjy's pre-mythic mode and Jason's rational-empirical mode. Provocative, but the application of Cassirer's concepts is at times procrustean.

*Cecil, L. Moffitt. "A Rhetoric for Benjy." *Southern Literary Journal*, 3 (Fall 1970), 32-46. A judicious study of the two levels of language in the first section: Benjy's own "speech" and the remembered speech of other characters in the novel.

*Chappell, Fred. "The Comic Structure of *The Sound and the Fury*." *Mississippi Quarterly*, 31 (Summer 1978), 381-86. A welcome corrective to conventionally "tragic" readings of *The Sound and the Fury*. Chappell calls our attention to the novel's comic characters and comic episodes, and relates Faulkner's cruel and tender humor to the great tradition of comic fiction initiated by Rabelais and Cervantes.

Cohn, Dorrit. *Transparent Minds: Narrative Modes for Presenting Consciousness in Fiction*. Princeton, N.J.: Princeton University Press, 1978, pp. 248-55, et passim. Clarifies Faulkner's use of stream-of-consciousness techniques by pointing out the specific features of his "memory monologues." Extremely relevant.

Coindreau, Maurice-Edgar. "Preface to *The Sound and the Fury*," trans. George M. Reeves. *Mississippi Quarterly*, 19 (Summer 1966), 107-15 (originally published in French in 1938). Included in *The Time of William Faulkner: A French View of Modern American Fiction*, ed. and trans. George M. Reeves. Columbia: University of South Carolina Press, 1971, pp. 41-50. A still suggestive introduction to the novel by Faulkner's most prominent French translator.

Collins, Carvel. "The Interior Monologues of *The Sound and the Fury*." In Downer, Alan S., ed. *English Institute Essays, 1952*. New York: Columbia University Press, 1954, pp. 29-56. First revised edition in Malin, Irving, ed. *Psychoanalysis and American Fiction*. New York: Dutton, 1965, pp. 223-42; second revised edition in Meriwether, James B., comp. *The Merrill Studies in The Sound and the Fury*. Columbus, Ohio: Charles E. Merrill, 1970, pp. 59-79. An influential essay, stressing Faulkner's debt to Shakespeare and to Joyce, and suggesting the possibility of an indebtedness to Freud's theory of psychic agencies.

————. "The Pairing of *The Sound and the Fury* and *As I Lay Dying*." *Princeton University Library Chronicle*, 18 (Spring 1957), 114-23. Focuses on thematic and structural parallels between the two novels, and defines their common subject as "the general effect of lack of love in a family."

————. "Miss Quentin's Paternity Again." *Texas Studies in Literature and Language*, 2 (Autumn 1960), 253-60. Demon-

strates conclusively that the identity of the girl's father
must remain a mystery.

Cowan, James C. "Dream-Work in the Quentin Section of *The Sound
and the Fury.*" *Literature and Psychology*, 24, no. 3 (1974),
91-98. A Freudian reading of some of Quentin's reveries.

Cowan, Michael H., ed. *Twentieth Century Interpretations of
The Sound and the Fury*. Englewood Cliffs, N.J.: Prentice-
Hall, Inc., 1968. The utility of this critical anthology
is impaired by the drastic condensation of the essays included. Cowan's introduction is well informed and competent.

Dauner, Louise. "Quentin and the Walking Shadow: The Dilemma
of Nature and Culture." *Arizona Quarterly*, 21 (Summer 1965),
159-71. A Jungian analysis of shadow imagery in the second
section, with emphasis on the theme of the double.

Davis, Boyd. "Caddy Compson's Eden." *Mississippi Quarterly*,
30 (Summer 1977), 381-94. A well-documented study of the
image of the enclosed garden in Faulkner's early writings
and in *The Sound and the Fury*.

Dickerson, Mary Jane. "'The Magician's Wand': Faulkner's Compson Appendix." *Mississippi Quarterly*, 28 (Summer 1975),
317-37. A careful and suggestive examination of the Appendix, exploring its thematic connections with the fiction
Faulkner wrote between 1929 and 1945, and tracing its influence on later writings.

Edel, Leon. "How to Read *The Sound and the Fury*?" In Burnshaw,
Stanley, ed. *Varieties of Literary Experience: Eighteen
Essays in World Literature*. New York: New York University
Press, 1962, pp. 241-57. Included in *The Modern Psycholog-
ical Novel*. New York: Grosset & Dunlap, 1964, pp. 162-76.
A fine general essay, emphasizing the originality of
Faulkner's fictional procedures and the necessity of "a
new way of reading."

Faber, M.D. "Faulkner's *The Sound and the Fury*: Object Rela-
tions and Narrative Structure." *American Imago*, 34 (Winter
1977), 327-50. Investigates Quentin's regressive and
ambivalent relationship to the mother figure. A strictly
Freudian reading.

Fasel, Ida. "A 'Conversation' between Faulkner and Eliot."
Mississippi Quarterly, 20 (Fall 1967), 195-206. Examines
the thematic, structural, and technical similarities between Faulkner's novel and *The Waste Land*.

Fletcher, Mary Dell. "Jason Compson: Contemporary Villain."
Louisiana Studies, 15 (Fall 1976), 253-61. Sees Jason as
"Faulkner's modern dehumanized man."

Freedman, William A. "The Technique of Isolation in *The Sound and the Fury.*" *Mississippi Quarterly*, 15 (Winter 1961-62), 21-26. Discusses symbols of confinement and isolation, and examines their function in the novel's thematic structure.

Geffen, Arthur. "Profane Time, Sacred Time, and Confederate Time in *The Sound and the Fury.*" *Studies in American Fiction*, 2 (Autumn 1974), 175-97. Examines the novel in the light of Mircea Eliade's concepts of sacred and profane time; suggests symbolic connections between critical events in the Compson story and significant dates in Confederate history.

Gibbons, Kathryn Gibbs. "Quentin's Shadow." *Literature and Psychology*, 12 (Winter 1962), 16-24. Another Jungian reading of the shadow symbol in the Quentin section.

Gordon, Lois. "Meaning and Myth in *The Sound and the Fury* and *The Waste Land.*" In French, Warren, ed. *The Twenties: Fiction, Poetry, Drama.* Deland, Fla.: Everett/Edwards, 1975, pp. 269-302. Relates the novel to Eliot's poem in terms of philosophical outlook and aesthetic design.

Grant, William E. "Benjy's Branch: Symbolic Method in Part I of *The Sound and the Fury.*" *Texas Studies in Literature and Language*, 13 (Winter 1972), 705-10. Comments on Christian symbolism in the first section and its relationship to the other sections, with special emphasis on the motif of ritual cleansing.

Gregory, Eileen. "Caddy Compson's World." In Meriwether, James B., comp. *The Merrill Studies in The Sound and the Fury.* Columbus, Ohio: Charles E. Merrill, 1970, pp. 89-101. A judicious rehabilitation of Caddy and so far the most discerning essay on this character to have appeared.

Gresset, Michel. "Psychological Aspects of Evil in *The Sound and the Fury.*" *Mississippi Quarterly*, 19 (Summer 1966), 143-53. Revised for inclusion in Meriwether, James B., comp. *The Merrill Studies in The Sound and the Fury.* Columbus, Ohio: Charles E. Merrill, 1970, pp. 114-24. Describes *The Sound and the Fury* as "a novel about an ordeal."

Griffin, Robert. "Ethical Point of View in *The Sound and the Fury.*" In Langford, Richard E., ed. *Essays in Modern American Literature.* Deland, Fla.: Stetson University Press, 1963, pp. 55-64. Argues that each section refers back to a distinct moral point of view.

Groden, Michael. "Criticism in New Composition: *Ulysses* and *The Sound and the Fury*." *Twentieth Century Literature*, 21 (October 1975), 265-77. A knowledgeable essay on Joyce's influence.

*Gross, Beverly. "Form and Fulfillment in *The Sound and the Fury*." *Modern Language Quarterly*, 29 (December 1968), 439-49. A very fine discussion of the novel's ending.

Guetti, James. *The Limits of Metaphor: A Study of Melville, Conrad and Faulkner*. Ithaca, N.Y.: Cornell University Press, 1967, pp. 148-53. A brilliant and stimulating study based on questionable assumptions.

Gunter, Richard. "Style and Language in *The Sound and the Fury*." *Mississippi Quarterly*, 12 (Summer 1969), 264-79. Included in Meriwether, James B., comp. *The Merrill Studies in The Sound and the Fury*. Columbus, Ohio: Charles E. Merrill, 1970, pp. 140-56. An appreciative review of Irena Kaluza's book (see below). Also personal comments upon Jason.

Hagopian, John V. "Nihilism in Faulkner's *The Sound and the Fury*." *Modern Fiction Studies*, 13 (Spring 1967), 45-55. Included in Meriwether, James B., comp. *The Merrill Studies in The Sound and the Fury*. Columbus, Ohio: Charles E. Merrill, 1970, pp. 102-13. A rigorous structural analysis of the last section. Its conclusions are debatable.

Hill, Douglas B. "Faulkner's Caddy." *Canadian Review of American Studies*, 7 (Spring 1976), 26-35. Offers perceptive comments upon Caddy's central position in the novel's narrative and thematic structure.

Howe, Irving. *William Faulkner: A Critical Study*. Second edition, revised and expanded (first edition, 1952). New York: Vintage Books, 1962, pp. 46-52, 157-74. A sympathetic reading, despite minor reservations about Faulkner's use of symbolism and his characterization of Quentin.

Humphrey, Robert. "Form and Function of Stream of Consciousness in William Faulkner's *The Sound and the Fury*." *University of Kansas City Review*, 19 (Autumn 1952), 34-40. Revised for *Stream of Consciousness in the Modern Novel*. Berkeley: University of California Press, 1954, pp. 17-21, 64-70, 104-11. Relates Faulkner to the development of stream-of-consciousness fiction, arguing that his originality lies in a successful combination of interior monologue and traditional plot.

Hunt, John W. "*The Sound and the Fury*: The Locus and Status of Meaning." In *William Faulkner: Art in Theological*

Tension. Syracuse, N.Y.: Syracuse University Press, 1965, pp. 35-99. A thoughtful and searching analysis, slightly warped by its theological assumptions.

Irwin, John T. *Doubling & Incest/Repetition & Revenge: A Speculative Reading of Faulkner*. Baltimore and London: The Johns Hopkins University Press, 1975, pp. 27-28, 52-53, 60-61, 124-25, 169-71, et passim. A highly stimulating Freudian reading, paying close attention to the interconnections between *The Sound and the Fury* and *Absalom, Absalom!*

Iser, Wolfgang. "Perception, Temporality, and Action as Modes of Subjectivity. William Faulkner: *The Sound and the Fury*." In *The Implied Reader: Patterns of Communication in Prose Fiction from Bunyan to Beckett*. Baltimore and London: The Johns Hopkins University Press, 1974, pp. 136-52. A rewarding phenomenological study of Benjy, Quentin, and Jason as reduced forms of the self.

Izsak, Emily K. "The Manuscript of *The Sound and the Fury*: The Revisions in the First Section." *Studies in Bibliography*, 20 (1967), 189-202. A useful scholarly study of Faulkner's revisions and additions in the first section.

Kaluza, Irena. *The Functioning of Sentence Structure in the Stream-of-Consciousness Technique of William Faulkner's "The Sound and the Fury": A Study in Linguistic Stylistics*. Krakow: Nakladem Uniwersytetu Jagiellonskiego, 1967. Reprinted by Folcroft Library Editions in 1970. A full and careful linguistic analysis of the first three sections. One of the few serious attempts to elucidate the novel's language and style.

Kartiganer, Donald M. "*The Sound and the Fury* and Faulkner's Quest for Form." *English Literary History*, 37 (December 1970), 613-39. Rightly emphasizes the close interdependence of moral concerns and aesthetic preoccupations in Faulkner's fiction.

————. *The Fragile Thread: The Meaning of Form in Faulkner's Novels*. Amherst: University of Massachusetts Press, 1979, pp. 3-22. Argues that *The Sound and the Fury* is a book "that struggles, with all the signs of its struggles showing, toward wholeness."

King, Richard H. "From Time to History: The Lacerated Consciousness of Quentin Compson." In *A Southern Renaissance: The Cultural Awakening of the American South, 1930-1955*. New York and Oxford: Oxford University Press, 1980, pp. 111-19. Places Faulkner's novel in the context of "the Southern family romance."

Kinney, Arthur F. *Faulkner's Narrative Poetics: Style as Vision.*
Amherst: University of Massachusetts Press, 1978, pp. 139-
61, et passim. Contends without valid reason that *The Sound
and the Fury* is "Benjy's book," yet on the whole his treatment of the novel is well balanced and sensible.

Longley, John L. "Faulkner Villains." In *The Tragic Mask: A
Study of Faulkner's Heroes.* Chapel Hill: University of
North Carolina Press, 1963, pp. 144-50. Offers keen in-
sights into Jason.

————. "'Who Never Had a Sister': A Reading of *The Sound and
the Fury.*" *Mosaic*, 7 (Fall 1973), 35-53. A general essay
focusing on the major characters.

Lowrey, Perrin H. "Concepts of Time in *The Sound and the Fury.*"
In Downer, Alan S., ed. *English Institute Essays, 1952.*
New York: Columbia University Press, 1954, pp. 57-82. A
seminal essay on Faulkner's uses of time.

McGann, Mary E. "*The Waste Land* and *The Sound and the Fury*:
To Apprehend the Human Process Moving in Time." *Southern
Literary Journal*, 9 (Fall 1976), 13-21. Another study of
the aesthetic and philosophical affinities between the
two works.

Mellard, James M. "Faulkner's Jason and the Tradition of Oral
Narrative." *Journal of Popular Culture*, 2 (Fall 1968),
195-210. Demonstrates convincingly that in Jason's speech
Faulkner has used the traditional procedures of oral narrative.

————. "Jason Compson: Humor, Hostility and the Rhetoric of
Aggression." *Southern Humanities Review*, 3 (Summer 1969),
259-67. Analyzes the respective functions of "humor,"
"wit," and "the comic" in Jason's "rhetoric of aggression,"
and the ways in which they serve the author's satiric
purpose.

————. "Caliban as Prospero: Benjy and *The Sound and the
Fury.*" *Novel*, 3 (Spring 1970), 233-48. Relates the first
section to the archetype of romance and to the tradition
of pastoral satire, and suggests parallels with *The
Tempest.*

————. "*The Sound and the Fury*: Quentin Compson and Faulkner's
'Tragedy of Passion.'" *Studies in the Novel*, 2 (Spring
1970), 61-75. Contends that the second section meets the
requirements of the "tragedy of passion" archetype as
defined in Northrop Frye's *Fools of Time.*

————. "Type and Archetype: Jason Compson as 'Satirist.'" *Genre*, 4 (June 1971), 173-88. Examines how the ambivalences of Jason's character can be related to the formal demands of satire.

————. *The Exploded Form: The Modernist Novel in America*. Urbana: University of Illinois Press, 1980, pp. 54-81. A discussion of the novel in generic terms.

Meriwether, James B. "Notes on the Textual History of *The Sound and the Fury*." *Papers of the Bibliographical Society of America*, 56 (Third Quarter 1962), 285-316. Republished in revised form as "The Textual History of *The Sound and the Fury*," in Meriwether, James B., comp. *The Merrill Studies in the The Sound and the Fury*. Columbus, Ohio: Charles E. Merrill, 1970, pp. 1-32. A scrupulous investigation of Faulkner's writing of the novel and of its publishing history. Corrects a number of mistakes and provides extremely useful information.

————, comp. *The Merrill Studies in The Sound and the Fury*. Columbus, Ohio: Charles E. Merrill, 1970. A valuable collection of essays.

Messerli, Douglas. "The Problem of Time in *The Sound and the Fury*: A Critical Reassessment and Reinterpretation." *Southern Literary Journal*, 6 (Spring 1974), 19-41. Takes issue with earlier analyses and attempts to reinterpret the problem of time in the light of Eugène Minkowski's "lived time" phenomenology.

Millgate, Jane. "Quentin Compson as Poor Player: Verbal and Social Clichés in *The Sound and the Fury*." *Revue des Langues Vivantes* (Bruxelles), 34 (1968), 40-49. A refreshing and intelligent essay on a neglected aspect of the novel.

Millgate, Michael. *The Achievement of William Faulkner*. New York: Random House, 1966, pp. 86-103. Still one of the best general studies of the novel. Derives additional value from its use of manuscript and typescript evidence.

————. "William Faulkner: The Problem of Point of View." In La France, Marston, ed. *Patterns of Commitment in American Literature*. Toronto: University of Toronto Press, 1967, pp. 181-92. Included in Meriwether, James B., comp. *The Merrill Studies in The Sound and the Fury*. Columbus, Ohio: Charles E. Merrill, 1970, pp. 125-39. Discusses Faulkner's handling of point of view and relates it interestingly to the narrative techniques of his later fiction.

Milliner, Gladys. "The Third Eve: Caddy Compson." *Midwest Quarterly*, 16 (September 1975), 268-75. Interprets Caddy as an Eve figure, seen differently by each of her three brothers.

Minter, David. *William Faulkner: His Life and Work*. Baltimore and London: The Johns Hopkins University Press, 1980, pp. 94-105, et passim. A well-informed and insightful account of the making of the novel, with comments on its autobiographical implications.

Morrison, Gail Moore. "'Time, Tide, and Twilight': *Mayday* and Faulkner's Quest Toward *The Sound and the Fury*." *Mississippi Quarterly*, 31 (Summer 1978), 337-57. A valuable source study, exploring the close relationships between *Mayday* and the later novel.

Murphy, Denis. "*The Sound and the Fury* and Dante's Inferno: Fire and Ice." *Markham Review*, 4 (October 1974), 71-78. Points to "structural and philosophical" similarities between Faulkner's novel and Dante's *Inferno*.

Peavy, Charles D. "Faulkner's Use of Folklore in *The Sound and the Fury*." *Journal of American Folklore*, 79 (July-September 1966), 437-47. Comments interestingly on Faulkner's use of popular beliefs and superstitions, and on the symbolic suggestions they add to his imagery.

————. "Jason Compson's Paranoid Pseudocommunity." *Hartford Studies in Literature*, 2 (1970), 151-56. An investigation of Jason's neurosis based on Norman Cameron's concept of "paranoid pseudocommunity."

————. "'If I Just Had a Mother': Faulkner's Quentin Compson." *Literature and Psychology*, 23, no. 3 (1973), 114-21. Psychoanalytical comments on Quentin's neurosis.

*Pitavy, François. "Quentin Compson, ou le regard du poète." *Sud* (Marseille), no. 14/15 (1975), 62-80. A sensitive study of Quentin as a failed poet.

Reed, Joseph W. *Faulkner's Narrative*. New Haven, Conn., and London: Yale University Press, 1973, pp. 74-83. Provides no methodical discussion of the novel as narrative, but offers provocative observations on the reader's response to the four sections of the book.

Rosenberg, Bruce A. "The Oral Quality of Reverend Shegog's Sermon in William Faulkner's *The Sound and the Fury*." *Literatur in Wissenschaft und Unterricht*, 2 (1969), 73-88. A very useful study of Faulkner's indebtedness to the tradition of the oral sermon.

*Ross, Stephen M. "The 'Loud World' of Quentin Compson."
    Studies in the Novel, 7 (Summer 1975), 245-57. A fine,
    original essay on the significance and function of "talk-
    ing" and "listening" in Quentin's section.

────────. "Jason Compson and Sut Lovingood: Southwestern Humor
    as Stream of Consciousness." *Studies in the Novel*, 8 (Fall
    1976), 278-90. Examines the similarities between the two
    characters and stresses Faulkner's indebtedness to the
    tradition of Southwestern humor.

Sartre, Jean-Paul. "A propos de 'Le Bruit et la fureur': La
    temporalité chez Faulkner." *La Nouvelle Revue Française*,
    52 (June 1939), 1057-61; 53 (July 1939), 147-51. Included
    in *Situations I*. Paris: Gallimard, 1947, pp. 70-81. Trans.
    by Martine Darmon, in Hoffman, Frederick J., and Olga W.
    Vickery, eds. *William Faulkner: Three Decades of Criticism*.
    East Lansing: Michigan State University Press, 1960, pp.
    225-32. Another translation is Annette Michelson's in
    Literary and Philosophical Essays. London: Rider and Co.,
    1955, pp. 79-87. The latter is reprinted in Warren, Robert
    Penn, ed. *Faulkner: A Collection of Critical Essays*.
    Englewood Cliffs, N.J.: Prentice-Hall, 1966, pp. 87-93.
    A seminal essay, the first to signal the importance of
    time in Faulkner's fiction.

Scott, Evelyn. *On William Faulkner's "The Sound and the Fury."*
    New York: Jonathan Cape and Harrison Smith, 1929. Partly
    reprinted in Cowan, Michael H., ed. *Twentieth Century
    Interpretations of The Sound and the Fury*. Englewood
    Cliffs, N.J.: Prentice-Hall, Inc., 1968, pp. 25-29. An
    enthusiastic essay by a fellow novelist who had read the
    galley proofs. Published as a pamphlet at the same time
    as the novel.

Slabey, Robert M. "The 'Romanticism' of *The Sound and the
    Fury*." *Mississippi Quarterly*, 16 (Summer 1963), 146-59.
    Points to romantic traits in Quentin's character.

Slater, Judith. "Quentin's Tunnel Vision: Modes of Perception
    and Their Stylistic Realization in *The Sound and the
    Fury*." *Literature and Psychology*, 27, 1 (1977), 4-15.
    An astute psychological study of the imagery of enclosure
    and escape in Quentin's monologue.

Slatoff, Walter J. *Quest for Failure: A Study of William
    Faulkner*. Ithaca, N.Y.: Cornell University Press, 1960,
    pp. 149-58, 254-55, et passim. Explains the novel's un-
    resolved ambiguities and suspended meanings in terms of
    Faulkner's supposed "quest for failure." Interesting, but
    thesis-ridden.

Spilka, Mark. "Quentin Compson's Universal Grief." *Contemporary Literature*, 11 (Autumn 1970), 451-69. Sees Quentin's drama as a tragic quest for timeless values.

Stewart, George R., and Joseph M. Backus. "'Each in Its Ordered Place': Structure and Narrative in Benjy's Section of *The Sound and the Fury*." *American Literature*, 29 (January 1958), 440-56. An elaborate attempt to unravel the chronology of the first section.

Stonum, Gary Lee. "The Search for a Narrative Method." In *Faulkner's Career: An Internal Literary History*. Ithaca, N.Y., and London: Cornell University Press, 1979, pp. 61-93. Considers *The Sound and the Fury* a transitional work, "poised between the visionary and the realistic."

Strandberg, Victor. "Faulkner's Poor Parson and the Technique of Inversion." *Sewanee Review*, 73 (Spring 1965), 181-90. An excellent essay, particularly illuminating on the Easter service episode in the closing section.

Swiggart, Peter. *The Art of Faulkner's Novels*. Austin: University of Texas Press, 1962, pp. 38-40, 61-70, 87-107. A comprehensive study, dealing with theme, narrative technique, and symbolic patterns. Still useful, especially for its close analysis of imagery.

————. "Moral and Temporal Order in *The Sound and the Fury*." *Sewanee Review*, 61 (Spring 1963), 221-37. Takes issue with Sartre's interpretation of time in *The Sound and the Fury*, but fails to supply a consistent interpretation of his own.

Terrier, Michel. "Structures and Meaning in Benjy's Monologue." *Langue* (Annales de l'Université Jean Moulin), II, Lyon: L'Hermes (1978), 101-12. Probes the paradoxes of Benjy's monologue: meaning in absurdity, order in chaos. A rewarding scrutiny.

Thompson, Lawrance R. "Mirror Analogues in *The Sound and the Fury*." In Downer, Alan S., ed. *English Institute Essays, 1952*. New York: Columbia University Press, 1954, pp. 83-106. Reprinted in Hoffman, Frederick J., and Olga W. Vickery, eds. *William Faulkner: Three Decades of Criticism*. East Lansing: Michigan State University Press, 1960, pp. 211-25, and in Warren, Robert Penn, ed. *Faulkner: A Collection of Critical Essays*. Englewood Cliffs, N.J.: Prentice-Hall, 1966, pp. 109-21. Argues persuasively that the mirror analogue can be extended to the novel's thematic structure.

————. *William Faulkner: An Introduction and Interpretation*.
New York: Barnes and Noble, 1963, pp. 29–52. A concise
general study, focusing on Faulkner's use of thematic
counterpoints.

Traschen, Isadore. "The Tragic Form of *The Sound and the Fury*."
Southern Review, 12 (Autumn 1976), 798–813. Contends that
The Sound and the Fury exemplifies the traditional tragic
form.

Ulich, Michaela. *Perspektive und Erzählstruktur in William
Faulkners Romanen*. Heidelberg: Carl Winter, 1972, pp. 23–
44. An original analysis of narrative perspective and
narrative structure.

Vahanian, Gabriel. "William Faulkner: Rendezvous with Existence." In *Wait Without Idols*. New York: George Braziller,
1964, pp. 93–116. A Christian reading of the novel, focusing on Dilsey and the Easter service.

Vickery, Olga W. "*The Sound and the Fury*: A Study in Perspective." *PMLA*, 69 (December 1954), 1017–37. Slightly revised
for *The Novels of William Faulkner: A Critical Interpretation*. Baton Rouge: Louisiana State University Press,
1959 and 1964, pp. 29–49. Though written in the early
fifties, Olga Vickery's compact and comprehensive study
of *The Sound and the Fury* has retained its critical relevance.

Volpe, Edmond L. *A Reader's Guide to William Faulkner*. New
York: Farrar, Straus, 1964, pp. 87–126, 363–77. A full
and worthwhile general study. Helpful chronologies and
guides to scene-shifts are appended.

Waggoner, Hyatt H. "'Form, Solidity, Color.'" In *William
Faulkner: From Jefferson to the World*. Lexington: University of Kentucky Press, 1959, pp. 34–61. Emphasizes
Christian elements, but refrains from imposing a Christian
interpretation on the novel.

Wall, Carey. "*The Sound and the Fury*: The Emotional Center."
Midwest Quarterly, 11 (Summer 1970), 371–87. A stimulating
essay on the Compsons' experience, defined in terms of
"spiritual pain."

Weber, Robert Wilhelm. *Die Aussage der Form: Zur Textur und
Struktur des Bewusstseinromans. Dargestellt an William
Faulkners "The Sound and the Fury."* Heidelberg: Carl
Winter, 1969. A painstaking book-length study of the
novel's structure and texture.

Weinstein, Arnold L. "Vision as Feeling: Bernanos and Faulkner." In *Vision and Response in Modern Fiction*. Ithaca,
N.Y., and London: Cornell University Press, 1974, pp. 91-
153, especially 111-35. Stresses the power and originality
of Faulkner's "affective technique," and attempts to define
the reader's emotional involvement in the novel.

Weinstein, Philipp M. "Caddy *Disparue*: Exploring an Episode
Common to Proust and Faulkner." *Comparative Literature
Studies*, 14 (March 1977), 38-52. An intriguing exploration
of the resemblances between the "sister" episode in the
Quentin section and the "petite fille bercée" episode in
La Fugitive.

Weisgerber, Jean. *Faulkner and Dostoevsky: Influence and Con-
fluence*. Athens: Ohio University Press, 1974, pp. 179-92.
Argues that "among the sources of *The Sound and the Fury*
we must reserve a high place for *Crime and Punishment* and
an honorable mention for *The Brothers Karamazov*."

Wilder, Amos N. "Faulkner and the Vestigial Moralities." In
Theology and Modern Literature. Cambridge, Mass.: Harvard
University Press, 1958, pp. 113-31. Included in Barth,
J. Robert, ed. *Religious Perspectives in Faulkner's Fiction: Yoknapatawpha and Beyond*. Notre Dame, Ind.: University of Notre Dame Press, 1972, pp. 91-102. Overempha-
sizes the significance of Dilsey and misreads the last
section as most theologically-oriented interpreters do.

Williams, David. *Faulkner's Women: The Myth and the Muse*.
Montreal and London: McGill-Queen's University Press,
1977, pp. 61-95, et passim. Examines the novel's female
characters in the light of Carl G. Jung's theory of archetypes.

Wittenberg, Judith Bryant. *Faulkner: The Transfiguration of
Biography*. Lincoln and London: University of Nebraska
Press, 1979, pp. 73-88, et passim. Suggests that *The
Sound and the Fury* was written "in a mood of anger and
despair," and that the drama of the Compsons echoes Faulk-
ner's own tensions and torments.